# Jewels of the Plains

## Wild Flowers of the Great Plains
## Grasslands and Hills

D0082015

The University of Minnesota Press
gratefully acknowledges the publication assistance
provided by Mr. and Mrs. Richard G. Gray, Sr.

# Jewels
# of
# the Plains

## Wild Flowers
## of the Great Plains
## Grasslands and Hills

### Claude A. Barr

**University of Minnesota Press**

**Minneapolis**

Copyright © 1983 by the University of Minnesota
All rights reserved.
Published by the University of Minnesota Press,
2037 University Avenue Southeast, Minneapolis MN 55414
Printed in the United States of America

**Library of Congress Cataloging in Publication Data**

Barr, Claude A.
Jewels of the plains.

Bibliography: p.
Includes index.
1. Wild flowers—Great Plains. 2. Wild flower
gardening—Great Plains. 3. Great Plains. I. Title.
QK135.B37 1983      582.13'0978      82-13691
ISBN 0-8166-1127-0


The University of Minnesota
is an equal-opportunity educator
and employer.

To my Mother, Anna L. (Bacon) Barr, in whose
unique vegetable garden a prominent niche was always
filled with flowering ornamentals.

# Foreword

*Jewels of the Plains* is a unique work. Its subtitle, *Wild Flowers of the Great Plains Grasslands and Hills*, does not begin to give a hint of the richness of its content.

This is no mere checklist or manual of showy wild flowers of that vast midland province of the United States. It is instead a delightfully readable account of one rare man's years of experience with the native Plains plants—in the field, in the herbarium, and in the garden.

Claude Barr, as the reader will discover, devoted a large portion of an otherwise very busy life as a rancher in South Dakota to learning everything there was to know about the specialized flora of his homeland. Then after many years of study and experimentation he sat down to write about these plants that had come to mean so much to him.

His writing reflects not only those years of intimate association with the plants themselves, but also the strong influence of his classical education. His cadenced prose, never too spare, never too ornate, give the reader a distinctive and colorful picture of each flower he describes in his alphabetical encyclopedia. In addition, for each entry, he provides the horticulturist reader with sound growing advice. And he does not hesitate to let his own preferences show through.

In fact, this is one of the charms of the book. For each species in each genus Claude Barr has managed, in words, to create a picture that brings the plant to life. Never does he fall into a dreary repetitious pattern so often characteristic of encyclopedic writing. Here there are personal anecdotes, sly digs, private sidelines, and even occasionally corny jokes.

This book does fit somewhat into a specialized tradition. One thinks of Lester Rowentree, Carl Purdy, Kathleen Marriage, Ira Gabrielson, Edgar T. Wherry—all devoted to the study of, and growing of, the native plants of their particular region. Yet none of them was more thorough, nor more perceptive, and certainly none more verbally enchanting than Claude Barr.

There should be a wide readership for this unique piece of work, especially among that increasing band who love and want to grow native American plants.

Where can we get for our gardens these Jewels of the Plains as plants or seeds now that Prairie Gem Ranch is no longer in business? We can only pray that some reader of this book will be inspired as Claude Barr was when young and that we can look forward to a new generation of explorers, experimenters, and gardeners to carry on a tradition so beautifully presented in these pages.

H. Lincoln Foster
Falls Village, Conn.

When asked about his philosophies, Claude says, "My life's ambition is a *full life* (I have it), a well-rounded life (I'm working toward it), and a life that has made the best of the opportunities at hand." Certainly Claude has fulfilled most of these ambitions and his greatest pleasures in life have come from his intimate personal associations with others from over the entire world who are interested in wild flower culture. A letter from Scotland, an unannounced visit by a scientist, and special biographical recognition by the Bailey Hortorium in the publication *Baileya* all serve to give Claude his *full life*. His varied experiences, which include everything from raising cattle to selling specialties, have given him a well-rounded life. To have achieved worldwide acquaintanceship and national recognition from a humble South Dakota homestead and a one-acre wild flower nursery on gumbo soil is proof enough that Claude has made the best of the opportunities at hand.

*Harry R. Woodward, presenting*
*the John Robertson Memorial Medal*
*of the South Dakota Horticultural Society*
*to Claude Barr in 1958*

# Preface

I do not have the fondest memories of Arkansas, where I was born near Bentonville on August 27, 1887. My family starved out of Arkansas, paying a farm purchase loan at ten percent interest and selling eggs as low as three cents a dozen. However, it was there I came to know the fragrance of many flowers and fruits, and the taste of wild grapes, persimmon, Mayapples, black and red haws, pawpaws— in fact, the taste of everything that was tasteable and of many things that were not. I was charmed by the yellow lady's-slipper, walking fern, deer-tongue, cowslip, buttercup, *Houstonia minima, Anemonella thalictroides*, and, on my very own, successfully transplanted some of them into the "spring yard" at the age of ten.

The earliest experience I can recall that would indicate I was interested in plants occurred when I was a very small boy. With my two older sisters I went over a hill in early spring to gather fresh green stuff—grass, as far as I remember—for Easter baskets. There I came upon a plant that grew in a neat gray carpet, close to the ground, with soft silky surfaced leaves in pleasant pattern, one of the pussy-toes. In contemplating it I derived a keen and unaccustomed pleasure.

From Arkansas, we moved to St. Louis. While in high school I was offered a very modest scholarship to Drake University in Des Moines, Iowa, for three years. Times were hard but it never occurred to me not to finish, and so in 1914 after some delays I received an A.B., with majors in English, Greek, and public speaking. I was then twenty-six years old.

While selling stereoscopes and views in eastern South Dakota during a vacation from college in 1909, I heard of land available for homesteading in the southwestern corner of the state. My parents were eager to leave the city of St. Louis, where we had been living for eleven years, and return to farming. Since I had learned to read land descriptions, I went with my father to help him file a claim. Deciding that a homestead would be a good property investment for myself, I filed also, taking time out from Drake in April 1910.

Thus my Prairie Gem Ranch began as a government homestead of 160 acres in the early years of the century. The limited acreage was the traditional allotment to an individual or a family, whether in the region of America's finest farmlands or in the Great Plains of progressively higher elevation, lower rainfall, and with often unusable, alkaline, ground water. Homesteaders of this southwest corner county of South Dakota, bordering the southern tip of the Black Hills, rated their land in terms of the familiar corn belt areas from which most of them had come. The deficiencies of the land were wholly unsuspected.

In 1910 there were only two fair rains in early June. In 1911 corn planted in May germinated in August. The few "old-timers" from an earlier immigration, occupying the better soils and valley locations, called it an abnormal year and told of years when the grass of the prairie "reached a horse's belly," and an unreasonable hope spread among the newcomers that the plowing under of the grass and more rain would bring better conditions. But the soil was tough—"gumbo" clay—different from anything we had ever known. Tractors broke down under the strain and plowshares bent. The year 1912 gave some promise; then came two more dry years. By 1915 the homesteaders, each one on 160 acres, had found conditions impossible. Prospects of better years were no longer considered; the gumbo had lost all attraction. Right and left, the discouraged ones were preparing to depart. My parents fared no better than others. On their dry upland they had made a start at a windbreak and small fruit plantings; but their vision of better years to come had grown dim. A further depressing factor was the impending abandonment by neighbors and friends. Now sixty years old and with funds much depleted, my parents were totally at a loss to picture another start elsewhere. Their letters to me bore an unmistakable message of despondency. Giving up an offer of a graduate scholarship at Harvard, I decided to return home and keep my parents company.

I brought with me my first wife, Kate Dean, whom I had married in December 1914. Kate had a little money; it lasted only about two years, but it enabled us to purchase a number of cattle, for which the soil is primarily suited. (By 1963, when I felt I was too advanced in years to continue running the ranch, I had 144 cattle and 1,485 acres of land.)

Although the climate and soil were demanding, there were certain unique benefits. From our doorstep we could see the Badlands and Black Hills in opposite directions. More important, I had many opportunities for acquainting myself with new plants. Since my father always chose to drive the team on our numerous trips to town, I was left free to observe to the fullest, details of scenery, vegetation, and other new facets of the country. In this way I saw for the first time such marvels of beauty as the great white evening primrose known as Gumbo Lily and the Sego Lily, or Mariposa. Off the wagon I would hop, to kneel and study the blossom closely, then run to catch up. Other finds that first spring were the prairie bluebell, a thrilling charmer, and some dwarf Penstemons in rosy lavender and glowing sky blue, new to me even as to family. As the days and years went by there were many, many more such experiences. Certain parts of the western prairies are treasure troves of floral delight.

Soon I learned that these native things would grow and prosper in the environment of my home, even now and again inviting themselves into the yard and garden, whereas the plants we tried to adapt from the moister climate we had known would often perish under such care as we knew how to give them.

After my first wife passed on, I married Jeannette, a native of Chadron, Nebraska. We worked closely with my parents on our two homesteads, even building a large barn together. It was entirely out of our way of thinking to consider failure. We planned to make this our home and we did; myself to the present, my parents into old age in the 1940s.

As for "making the best of it," I am the only one in the eastern end of Fall River County, a strip thiry-three miles long and twelve miles wide, living on an original homestead without tillable soil, without bottomland grasses, and without a natural source of water. I have earthen reservoirs and cisterns. I have 100 pines, 20 cedars, 24 apple trees (a luxury, not a financial asset), plums, cherries, grapes, Russian mulberries, and Russian olives, lilac, and other hedge plantings.

In the early days, we went to the Black Hills for little pines to start our groves. By chance and inclination, I brought back in a spadeful of soil a plant of the large-flowered, pink, creeping phlox and another of our South Dakota state flower, the Pasque, or "crocus" as it is commonly known. A young Black Hills pine was placed where its nighttime singing would be convenient to an open window. The shade at its foot contributed to the long life of the pasque flower, *Pulsatilla (Anemone) patens*. In an April of fine flowering, I snapped a photo that recorded seven wide and close-clustering blossoms on the plant. The act of preserving this delightful impression was to prove a significant step toward the writing of this book.

I submitted the black-and-white picture of the lovely pasque flower, with a short column of notes, to *House and Garden*, New York. The article was accepted and published in 1932, and I was paid $20 for it, which seemed like a munificent price. Following this opening into the new world of garden writing, I selected the subject of *Calochortus*, mariposa tulip or sego lily, two species of which are native to the Great Plains. About that time a picture of a California mariposa was featured on the cover of *Horticulture*, Boston. The flower had been photographed in the Connecticut garden of Mrs. C. I. De Bevoise, one of the founders of the American Rock Garden Society. Naturally, I was eager to make Mrs. De Bevoise's acquaintance. She gave me information on the many species of *Calochortus* to be found farther west, and I soon began to supply her rock garden and native plant nursery with attractive natives of the Plains, which she listed in her catalog. As a result of our friendship, I became a member of the Rock Garden Society in 1934.

In 1935 I sent out my first catalog, "Beautiful Native Plants of the High Plains, Badlands, and Black Hills," to be furnished directly to customers, and began a collecting and nursery business. It was a welcome sideline to cattle ranching in those very lean years of the early 1930s.

For some years Mrs. De Bevoise continued as my best customer, until I built up a mailing list by advertising. Her gratuitous tips on selecting plant materials and on conditioning, packing, and mailing plants were detailed and invaluable. Among the inspirational books she presented to me was Ira N. Gabrielson's *Western American Alpines*, based on his own nursery experience and wide exploration in the northwestern states. Dr. Gabrielson served as president of the

American Rock Garden Society in its early years and was to become director of the Federal Office of Fish and Wildlife. His book, which takes the reader into the mountains by word and picture and shows many plants in picturesque haunts, is to be regarded as a treasure by any lover of the rare and beautiful. I studied it with fascination — and with the frequently recurring awareness that a species described as an alpine could be matched in beauty by a sister species of the Great Plains. With this awareness came the further realization, at first provocative, then obsessive, that numbers of Great Plains plants of high merit had no counterparts at all among the Western alpines. There could be but one solution: there must be a companion volume covering the jewels of the Plains.

I began to work at once on this absorbing project. The plan required full acquaintance with the flora of the region. I acquired manuals and references listing recorded species; collected and pressed specimens and sent them to authorities for identification; avidly pursued such activities as searching for, observing, photographing, and listing associated plants in distinctive habitats; and made the acquaintance of local and distant botanists, gardeners, and suppliers of plants.

I soon discovered that the Great Plains region was still the Great American Desert to people of the East and of the farther West, including botanists. Species common here were often missing in the available reference works, or if listed often lacked distribution data, specimen collections in the herbaria of local institutions thus being disregarded. I found that the states and provinces invariably concentrated on local checklists. A common consequence was that identifications by printed descriptions often turned up varying names for the same plant, so that second or subsequent authorities had to be consulted. Here in the field I learned much botany by checking tentative or uncertain descriptions with the plants at hand. Each discrepancy provided a lesson in close observation. Even today no single technical work covering the Plains as a whole is to be found. Much is to be said for the chief early explorer of this region, P. A. Rydberg, who observed his species in many and varied localities and under seasonal variation. Rydberg probably knew firsthand more species of the Plains than any other botanist of his time or later. Yet his voluminous works also lack completeness.

Situated in about the middle of the region and at an elevation of 3,300 feet, Prairie Gem Ranch, with its naturally treeless upland exposure, its difficult soil, and its lack of water facilities, has proved a tough but successful testing ground through the years. I learned many things about plants by trial and error. My garden has served as a commercial nursery, as a propagating ground for superior types of plants, and as a trial home for unfamiliar species. Thus did I develop something of a botanical garden where probably more species typical of the Plains environment have been brought together than anywhere else. Growing and studying the plants was a pure delight for me, and the garden grew apace, spurred by the need to increase stocks year by year, by the ready response of the wild flowers to garden care, and by income from this spare-time nursery business.

During the early years of the 1930s—and the Great Depression and the Dust Bowl era—the Department of Agriculture repurchased various areas across the Plains that had proved submarginal for farming. It then issued permits to homesteaders who owned at least 1,600 acres—in contrast to the traditional homestead of 160—which entitled them to use the government land as pasturage for their cattle. Since we had been continually adding to our land holdings, Jeannette and I found we could qualify for the new supervised grazing plan. The setup enabled us to let our cattle range over a wider area. Permittees were directed to gather scattered remnants of fencing to enclose pasture boundaries, and the supervised summer pastures were soon in operation. The stocking rate for the six-month season was set at one cow and calf or one steer per *22½ acres*. In more favorable climates, a ratio of one cow per acre is the norm.

In the middle of the decade-long drought came the bountiful year 1935. All possible hay was put up, and some alfalfa seed matured into a cash crop. Then came 1936 with extreme temperatures and so little rain that all surface water supplies were exhausted. That July, we had to drive the cattle each day to distant wells. Sometimes water was hauled to the ranch. The pasture grasses, dried to brittleness before maturity, crumbled under the cattle's tread. When winter came, many of our cattle died from nutrient deficiencies. Before spring, we had purchased more hay. From a county agent's annual report: "All banks in the county are closed; all stocks of seed grain are exhausted; the Government is making loans for crop planting." Feed grain from government stocks was brought in and distributed gratis to ranchers during the worst of the crisis. Earthen dams were constructed in the grazing district pastures to provide adequate watering from runoff. The project furnished relief employment for those who could furnish a four-horse team to power a "fresno" road scraper. Meltwater from good snows early in 1937 filled many dams.

Income had long since determined our activities. Cattle and poultry products were the standbys: our weekly income was based on butterfat and eggs, and there were seasonal returns on marketable cattle. I took temporary jobs in the township office and did occasional roadwork.

By the late 1940s the government grazing plan had been in operation ten years. Pastures had reponded remarkably well to lighter stocking and to the gentle, soaking rains that marked the later years of the decade. Cattle growth and market conditions were rewarding. About this time a fortunate rise in cattle prices cleared me of all my financial obligations—including college debts.

Although the ranch was now operating at full capacity, the layout, or "spread," was much too small to support year-round help. Many tasks could be performed without hired help. For example, cattle branding was done cooperatively, much veterinary work single-handedly or with exchange labor. But providing a winter feed supply for our cattle remained a problem. We had never bought a tractor for the ranch, following the good advice of friendly neighbors: "You can't pay for your tractor with what you can raise on that upland gumbo." Hence we had to hire machines and help for haying—alfalfa, crested wheat grass, native grasses, sweet clover—and for harvesting fodder cane. We also hired Sioux Indians to help in the nursery-garden in the growing season and to care for the trees. (Even the thirty-foot pines are still under cultivation.) As I devoted more time to the plant and seed business, I dropped various other activities, but made hardly any headway with the writing of this book.

However, change was in the making. With the passage of years, care of the cattle, pasture riding to check for holes in fences, and the share of fence upkeep were obviously becoming burdensome; and I came to realize that the digging and shipping of plants could be never-ending. Still, the plant business increased and it was an indispensable part of our living.

In 1957 I sold the milk stock to gain time for "the book." I spent this time growing and shipping plants to every state in the union and every province in Canada, to seven European countries, to Japan, Australia, and New Zealand. I sold the beef cattle in 1963—and still had little time for writing. In 1965 I devoted every available minute to the plant business. By the time that stressful year ended, it had become clear that *Jewels of the Plains* would never get written unless I gave up much of the plant and seed work. So I made the decision to continue only with seeds—this to keep in touch with the world—and to concentrate on my writing.

My determination to finish *Jewels of the Plains* helped sustain me through a difficult period. In June 1962, Jeannette died, after years of invalidism. She was seventy at the time; I was seventy-five.

Accustomed to bearing the burden of the work but feeling very much alone, I calculated the cost of continuing to run the ranch. Reluctantly, I decided to sell the land and cattle to a good neighbor living five miles away with holdings adjoining Prairie Gem ranch.

It may have been an error of judgment not to concentrate at once on writing. But I did not foresee that time gained from not having to care for the cattle would so soon be wiped out by added plant demands. When at last the listings of plants and seeds were in the main discontinued, I used my new freedom in part for a wider exploration of the region's geographical limits, elevations and topography, species range and habitat, and variations in flowering seasons over the immense south-to-north range of latitude. I traveled extensively from Saskatchewan into Texas and from the Rocky Mountains to beyond the Missouri.

I knew that for my book to be of ultimate value, it had to present a vivid description and outline of garden value for every species of the region, so that appreciation of these unique plants could be more widespread.

To prepare such a comprehensive survey of the flora of a region, I had to consult books and herbaria where descriptions, pictures, and preserved specimens have been brought together by many workers over many years. The great herbarium of the University of Wyoming, at Laramie, known as the Aven Nelson Herbarium, houses the largest collection of Great Plains plants readily accessible from Prairie Gem Ranch. The herbarium welcomes investigators, and gives them generous assistance in comparing and identifying new or dried material. Since 1966, I have spent more than a month all told in study there. The shortest route from the ranch to Laramie is 230 miles. But by taking alternate routes, which did not add too many miles to the trip, I was able to collect many valued specimens, photographs, and habitat data.

Now and again, I wrote articles on the distinctive native perennials and shrubs of value to gardens for local periodicals and for the *American Rock Garden Society Bulletin* and the *Brooklyn Botanic Garden Handbook*. In 1958 the South Dakota Horticultural Society awarded me the John Roberston Memorial Medal for "the study and commercialization of the Great Plains plants." In 1965 I received a citation from the American Rock Garden Society for "study of the native flora and contributions to rock and alpine gardening." In 1973 the first Edgar T. Wherry Memorial Award was presented to me. This was particularly appreciated because Dr. Wherry, an authority on phloxes and native plants, visited Prairie Gem Ranch on two occasions.

Incidentally, Prairie Gem Ranch was named for its spot of emerald where crops and young windbreak trees so often in midsummer stood out against the rolling monotony of drying prairie grasses with their ripened seedheads.

To create for you an impression of the climate and soil in which we work, I invite you to come with me into the garden. It is July 3, with growth and bloom somewhat advanced for the date. This year a bountiful measure of heavy wet snow came in March; in April more than two inches of gentle rainfall, and shortly thereafter an inch or so more. With this deep soaking, the garden had a wonderful start— and to tell the truth, the flowers still doing well at this date seem to exist on the remnants of that early moisture.

*Penstemon glaber* in fine deep blue, its typical color response to moisture, hot sun, and dry atmosphere, is about gone, a few days ahead of schedule. The first few perennial four-o'clocks—dark red *Mirabilis multiflora*—have opened in the last week. There are bush morning-glories; the first one out yesterday was *Ipomoea leptophylla*, reddish pink with a darker throat. These large bushy plants with deep, moisture-storing roots, four-o'clocks and morning-glories, are good for long weeks of bloom. The pink 'Dorothy Perkins' rambler rose is in full cluster, and fading every day in the heat. The double, wild *Rosa arkansana* 'J. W. Fargo' is fine in much shade, fading elsewhere. The scarlet berries of the elder, *Sambucus microbotrys*, are in brilliant ripeness in a shady situation. From foreign fields, *Allium giganteum*, with its great globes of tiny, sparkling lavender-pink stars, is still lovely in my lath house.

The wonderful native *Echinacea angustifolia*, roots reaching deep for reserve moisture, is approaching full bloom, its expansive rays of pink shading to near-crimson about the glossy mahogany conical centers. It would take more than the day's 90 degrees to wither this stalwart, though in this drought it is reaching only two-thirds its usual stature. *Yucca glauca*, in cream-white or in greenish cream, and in selections with much mauve-pink or brilliant pink, is now fading.

Cactus plants, ever impervious to the vagaries of moisture, have nearly finished their riotous display of bloom. The yellows, apricots, deep pinks, and red ephemeral blossoms lie pleated and shrunken for the most part, though a few stray blossoms still entice green, solitary bees.

Yesterday almost at dusk, neighbors brought their guests to see the garden. Although some white evening primroses were out, the large-flowered yellow kinds were at best just showing the promise of color between the rupturing calyx segments, a full hour beyond normal opening. Fifteen minutes later, when alone, I took another turn about the garden, to find many of the yellow ones displaying a dozen or more wide open suns—or moons if you like—though their color is a far more intimate tone than the most brilliant moon, and about them is an air of softness and generosity which dispenses a breathable atmosphere suitable to our earth.

The scant rainfall of May and June was a great letdown after the promising conditions early in the season. It is a disappointment we are accustomed to on the Plains, especially in the "gumbo" which dries out so terribly.

A definition of "gumbo" should be provided for those who have not experienced this soil. It is an extremely fine-textured clay derived from the mud-shales laid down by the late Cretaceous sea over the Great Plains and wider regions. The "tight"-textured gumbo takes moisture slowly, but becomes very soft when wet. It erodes rapidly on any degree of slope and accumulates little humus. It is rich in minerals, especially potash and other alkaline salts. In its purest state it supports a sparse cover of grass and a surprising total of adapted flowering plants. At any stage of drying beyond the softest mud, gumbo clings tenaciously to footwear or to feet, and to metal or rubber tires. At critical stages there is no travel on the gumbo, or "in" it. If you have occasion to use a digging tool, you must also carry a putty knife to dislodge the mud with each lifting. If disturbed while wet, gumbo can dry to bricklike hardness. In short, the gumbo is an impossibly difficult soil at times. However, with favorable rainfall and light cultivation when moderately dry, a soil-mulch may be maintained to conserve a useful content of moisture.

Of course, the joys of gardening are to be experienced on the road as well as in the garden. In the early years it seemed to me that every new road of a stretch of miles must disclose some new species. Today the thrills of exploring have hardly diminished. To set a goal of seeking a certain described but unknown plant at a distance is very likely to disclose others along the way, and the surprise of a new find, whether species, color variant, or superior form, lends high pleasure to the adventure. Seldom have I settled for an ordinary plant if an extraordinary one was available. Those selected have unusual color and sizes or perhaps double flowers. With good fortune, one may happen upon a long-sought and diminutive bright treasure, or a wide field of bloom, unexpected and unscheduled.

In investigating a neglected region, its evolving environment and its resources, I have benefited from a willingness to make the best of often difficult situations and from a determination to carry through. The intimate understanding of the native plant-life's stresses, responses, and adaptations, which could hardly have been gained otherwise, has been a valued reward. The search for unusual forms of plants has given me skills in close observation and discrimination, and has lent a sense of purpose and zest to this best of all hobbies.

# Acknowledgments

The author wishes to thank his many friends, correspondents, and fellow gardeners who have given him encouragement and support over the years and who have shared his love of the Plains natives. While many contributors are acknowledged where appropriate in the text, there are a number of people whom the author wants to thank here. Among the gardeners and others who as friends have exchanged plants and information with the author are: Darwin M. Andrews, Rupert Barneby, Neva Belew, F. L. Bennett, Ralph Bennett, Lyman Benson, K. F. Best, Stuart Boothman, Kay Boydston, Mrs. Floyd Brown, A. C. Budd, Winnie Considine, J. W. Fargo, Bernard Harkness, Mrs. J. Norman Henry, Alberta Magers, Kathleen Marriage, B. Y. Morrison, Mrs. L. B. Nelson, Gladys Nisbet, W. R. Reader, Clara Regan, Lena Seeba, O. A. Stevens, Myrtle Thissen, Glenn Viehmeyer, Edwin F. Wiegand, and Louise Beebe Wilder.

The author is especially grateful to Norman Deno for his advice and friendship and to Mrs. C. I. De Bevoise, one of the founders of the American Rock Garden Society, for all her help during the establishment of his plant business and his subsequent botanical work. Ira Gabrielson's *Western American Alpines* provided the inspiration for what the author has envisioned as a similar volume for the beautiful and adaptable native plants of the Great Plains. Laura Louise Foster and H. Lincoln Foster have been continually encouraging.

The author is indebted to several curators of herbaria for their kind attention and to Ronald Hartman, A. C. McIntosh, G. L. Cross, S. F. Blake, Edgar T. Wherry, E. J. Alexander, Ivan M. Johnston,

H. Hapeman, Elzada U. Clover, Herman C. Benke, Aven Nelson, and J. F. Brenckle for their help with specimen identification. He is grateful to Tanja Jung, Linda Rector, Joyce Hardy, Donna Norton, Gene McDowell, Daniel Schneider, Barbara Weedon, and Ronald Weedon for their general assistance in preparing the manuscript; to Morton Greene, James Aber, and Betty Ann Mech for their help with the chapter on the geography of the Great Plains; and to Dorothy Hansell, Betty Ann Mech, Ronald Weedon, and William Wood for their editorial guidance. Earl Brockelsby, Betty Ann Mech, Marianne Beel, and others generously shared their color photographs of plants for the book. Grateful thanks are also extended to Gerald Ownbey and David Holden for reviewing the manuscript.

Most important, the author recognizes with a special thanks the personal support of his friends and neighbors close either in presence or in spirit to the setting of *Jewels of the Plains*, particularly Ray, Helen, John and Judi Sides, and Earl Brockelsby, for the many thoughtful and kind things they have done for him during the progress of this book.

# Publisher's Statement

The plant entries in this book are arranged alphabetically by scientific generic names, except for the cacti, fern, and orchid entries, which are by common family names since the horticultural requirements of plants in these families are similar. Common names are provided wherever possible, but not for every plant. This is because in many instances gardeners simply do not use common names or use so many common names that no one name (or even small group of names) can be safely applied to a given plant. Species within each genus are presented in order of importance to gardeners.

The color photographs in the plate section were taken by the author except as follows:

| Plate Number(s) | Photographer |
| --- | --- |
| 89, 90 | Marianne Beel |
| 4, 39, 40, 46, 48, 51, 52, 71, 74, 87, 92, 96, 98, 101, 114, 117, 118 | Earl Brockelsby |
| 1, 2, 3, 5, 6, 7, 16, 30, 35, 47, 49, 55, 57, 70, 79, 88, 99, 107, 108 | Betty Ann Mech |
| 58 | Richard Redfield |
| 59 | Richard Van Reyper |

Publication of this book has been greatly assisted by many people determined to see Claude Barr's great knowledge of and love for the wild flowers of the Plains brought to print. The publisher would like to thank especially Earl Brockelsby, Betty Ann Mech, and Ronald R. Weedon for their support in this respect. Betty Ann Mech also provided invaluable help with proofreading and by preparing the index.

# Contents

# The Great Plains

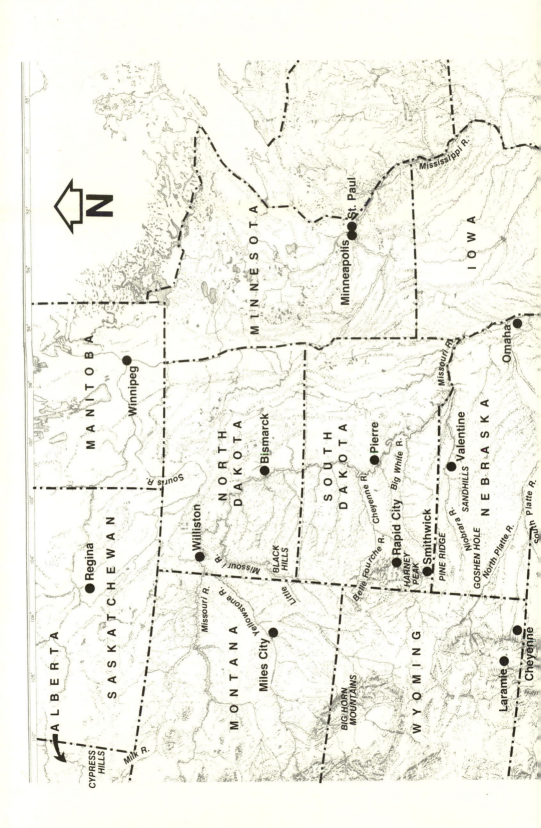

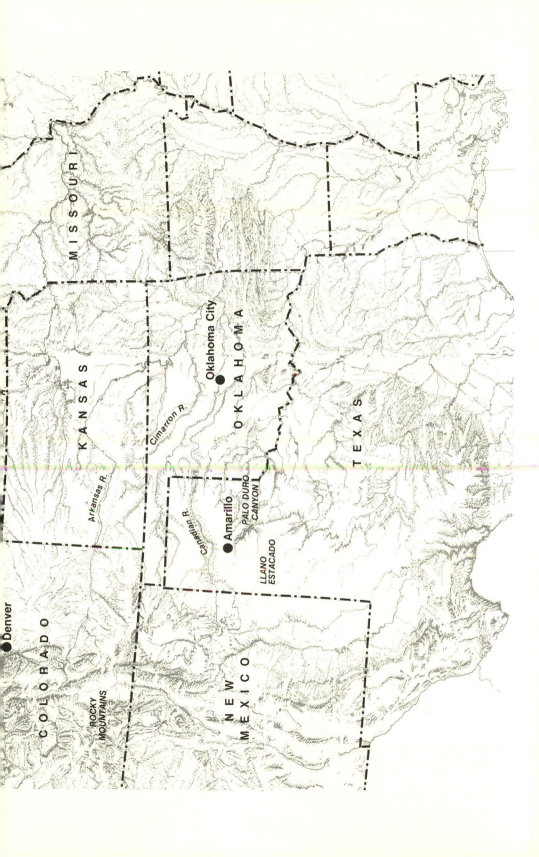

# The
# Great Plains

This chapter provides a brief description of the Great Plains region to help readers better understand how and why the unique plant species of the Plains evolved their special features and distribution.

The Great Plains comprises a vast and distinctive portion of North America lying west of the 90th meridian, about the midline of the continent, between the central lowlands and the western mountains. Characteristics of the region are relative flatness, moderately high elevations, low rainfall and much sunshine, and low winter temperatures that ensure plant hardiness adequate for most regions where ornamental gardening is practiced. Predominently prairie land, lacking trees except along water courses and on scattered, rugged areas of upland, the Plains constitute the original or adopted home of numerous races of native flowering plants of great beauty and value for the gardens of the world. Seasonal responses to warmth and cold, to the times of growth and dormancy, and the many instances of retention of live foliage color in winter adapt these plants to a wide variety of gardening situations.

In delineating the boundaries of the Great Plains, we start with the foot of the Rocky Mountains, at 5,000 or 6,000 feet, which forms the western barrier. The eastern boundary is not so readily distinguished. In places there is a low, eastward-facing escarpment marking a definite drop to the lower levels of the central lowlands, but in other reaches there appears only a continuation of the gentle slope that describes the general lowering of the region. The eastern boundary has been variously set at a certain meridian such as the 98th, or on a line determined by the annual rainfall, such as an average of 20 inches, or on the irregular line of the 1,800-foot contour. For our purposes, the third designation is preferred. It marks with close accuracy the edge of the higher, drier region to the west with its short-grass prairies and its very noticeable change in flowering plant types. It also runs in a northwesterly direction in North Dakota and Saskatchewan, which parallels the considerable offset to the west of the middle and northern Rocky Mountains from the strict, north-south line of the southern Rockies in Wyoming and Colorado. This delineation of margins gives the Plains a breadth, in the main, ranging from less than 400 to a maximum of 450 miles.

As an indicator of the rate of eastward descent of the Plains, the North Platte River, issuing onto the Plains from the montane region in Wyoming and continuing eastward through the length of Nebraska, drops uniformly at about ten feet per mile. Elsewhere, the agencies of wind and water, and crustal movements in the earth, have constructed a more rugged terrain.

Describing the northern extremity of the Plains, the curving North Saskatchewan River flows northeastward from the Rocky Mountain border to Edmonton, Alberta, and beyond to its turn toward the southeast. Not far from the river the northern forest takes over, to stretch away to Alaska and the frigid reaches of northern Canada. The forest likewise marks the northern boundary of the Plains across Saskatchewan.

By the strict measure of elevation, the Plains do not extend eastward to the Saskatchewan-Manitoba line, though the prairie vegetation does reach such longitude and beyond. Occasional hills and "mountains" rise out of the generally flat plain. They are well above the 1800-foot contour, agreed on as delineating the Great Plains. But numbers of typical Plains plants such as astragalus and cactus continue, even into Manitoba. This extension is also commonly called the Great Plains. In contrast, there are places where the "Prairie steppes" present lines of increased elevation, just as there are patches of "bush" — thickets of aspen, silver-berry, and willow, chiefly — 100 miles or more within the drier area, relics from changed environments.

From north to south with remarkable uniformity of terrain and climatic factors, the Plains extend 1,600 miles to the Llano Estacado (Staked Plains), or "High Plains," of northern Texas and adjacent

New Mexico. This is the practical southern boundary of the Great Plains, as far as plants are concerned.

Llano Estacado refers to the lines of stakes driven by early occupants of this large area of phenomenal flatness to mark directions and trails. Here some 20,000 square miles of prairie, almost without slope, continued age after age almost without drainage other than to the numerous local *playas*, or lakes. The one major disruption of the pattern is the Palo Duro Canyon, to be referred to later. The typical landscape closely conforms to the earth's normal curvature, and the typical horizon, without landmarks, appears from eye level at three and a half miles. When traveling, one experiences the sensation of approaching the rim of a vast shallow bowl which always recedes. And when driving slightly uphill, one gets the impression that all the world beyond the visible rim lies below, and the effect is unreal. Before trail marking and settlement, the unlimited flatness of the area bore fatal implications for wanderers unable to determine orientation by sun or stars.

In northern Texas and bordering New Mexico, the term High Plains is applied to the higher flat country whether above or below 4,000 feet, whereas the neighboring area to the north, crossed west to east by the Canadian River, is called Rolling Plains. North of the Canadian, the terrain again becomes high and smooth. The general flatness continues across the narrow Oklahoma Panhandle and into Colorado and Kansas, except for the trench of the Cimarron River.

North of the Arkansas River where the 4,000-foot contour closely follows the Kansas-Colorado line, there is much flat country. But numerous small undulations open the view to distances of eight or 10 miles, and sometimes beyond to a low skyline at 20 miles or more. The distant view has a lovely, quieting effect, bringing a sense of things as they ought to be and a wonderment that any portion of the earth's surface could be so perfect. Traveling this seemingly endless grass-and-sky country, the initiated bear ever in mind that meadows of the right type, and rocky pastures, bluffs, and breaks of all descriptions harbor the flower jewels which at frequent intervals deck the Plains.

The Black Hills cover some 6,000 square miles in southwestern South Dakota and northeastern Wyoming. The highest point is Harney Peak in South Dakota, with an elevation over 7,000 feet. The structure of the Hills is that of a truncated dome, with steep rock inclines to the east and more gentle dips on the west. A core of very ancient rocks forms the center containing many mineral deposits.

Nebraska presents a varied topographic picture, with the Republican River, the South Platte, the North Platte, and the Niobrara Rivers, the vast Sandhills, and the Pine Ridge escarpment. Here, the high and level areas are more infrequent and the northern margin of the High Plains is marked by the Pine Ridge. This prominent feature, a precipitous escarpment in places, is for much of its length a series of rugged remnants of the original smooth plains reaching out from a narrow tableland. From higher levels in Wyoming, the Ridge curves across a broad corner of Nebraska into South Dakota, then eastward overlooking the White River Badlands. It reflects in a widening arc, at a distance of 30 miles and more, the elliptical uplift of the Black Hills.

Although the Pine Ridge is, on the average, 1,000 feet above the surrounding plains, this elevation represents only a stage in the long process of the wearing down of the Plains. To the north, the Plains have everywhere suffered deeper erosion, owing to several factors, mainly to increased tilt occasioned by the last great uplift of the Rocky Mountains. Evidences of former levels are seen high upon the shoulders of the Black Hills. The Cave Hills and Slim Buttes farther north are similar kinds of remnants. Beyond the Missouri River, eastward and northward, instances of remarkably flat terrain can often be credited to the smoothing work of glacial ice; some are bench remnants of old river bottom lands.

Northward from Nebraska the notable streams are the White River, which has its source within the Pine Ridge; the Cheyenne, skirting the Black Hills at the south; the Belle Fourche at the north; the Little Missouri, coursing northward through the Badlands of North Dakota; and the Yellowstone. All are tributaries of the Missouri, which drains ultimately into the Gulf of Mexico. From Alberta comes the Milk River, draining the southern slopes of the Cypress Hills, with several small tributaries from Saskatchewan, to join the Missouri. From Saskatchewan the Souris River dips into the flat country of North Dakota for 60 miles, returns to Canada, and with all other Canadian plains drainage, chiefly by the South and North Saskatchewan Rivers, at last reaches Hudson Bay.

Among the numerous remnants of High Plains spread upon the more deeply eroded northern portion of the region, only the Cypress Hills can be compared in extent with the Black Hills. Nearly a third of their 100-mile length including the highest and widest portion, at approximately 4,800 feet, lies in Alberta. The more broken portion stretches eastward in Saskatchewan. The general rate of descent is 16 feet per mile. The effects of differential erosion and perhaps tilt account for the rapid descent. In exposed places a surfacing of small boulders, cobbles, and pebbles aids in preserving contours and identifies this highland, purely a Great Plains structure, as the course of a strong river during the upbuilding of the Plains.

In the Cypress Hills there is no evidence of glacial action above the 4,400-foot contour, but eastwardly the ice passed over the area and exercised its reducing power. On northern slopes and in valleys there is dense forest, composed of lodgepole pine, aspen, and the northern white spruce. The surroundings above the 3,000-foot contour are considered part of the Cypress Hills plateau, which widens to 40 miles or so, though the higher portions are much narrower, 15 to 25 miles. The general area includes forest reserve and provincial park lands. With its variety of environments, the Cypress Hills provide habitat for hundreds of flowering species, including some not elsewhere found closer than the western mountains. For its full length the area forms a portion of the divide separating the Hudson Bay and Gulf of Mexico drainages.

Western Montana's major streams, the Missouri and the Musselshell, have achieved as much as 1,000 feet of downcutting. The topography is further roughened in effect by high terraces and numerous flat-topped interstream uplands, often lying level for a dozen miles. In addition, and distinguished from High Plains remnants, there are several small isolated mountains rising 2,000 to 4,000 feet above the general level. Of these, the Little Rockies and Big Snowies are structured like the neighboring Rocky Mountains; some others are of volcanic origin. Unfortunately, only sketchy checking of the floras of these outlying high points has been done; the flower display in the Little Rockies is reported to be fine.

Over the Great Plains generally, the wearing down and roughening of the once beautifully graded surface has gone on without interruption since the last great uplift of the Rockies. Stream erosion, even to the smallest volume runoff from pouring rains—which come at times even to the areas of lowest rainfall—has been the chief agency in reducing the land to the stage of complete drainage, known as geological maturity. Wind rates second as an erosive force on certain materials. Intermittent but often powerful, the wind is highly effective wherever dry barren soil occurs, in excavating, in transporting, and in upbuilding. Often the wind moves immense volumes of soil where strong water action is lacking. It is obvious that the wind played a large part in the excavation of the Goshen Hole lowland along the North Platte River in eastern Wyoming and western Nebraska.

Goshen Hole is an immense widening of the North Platte valley by combined forces of wind and water upon earth material of suitable texture. The basin is 50 miles wide at the state line, 700 feet deep at the west where hard strata leave off in bluffs. One hundred and fifty miles from its beginning the excavation tapers to the normal width of the stream valley. Along with the seemingly inexhaustible sand burden of the river, Goshen Hole itself has supplied much of the material that the wind has distributed over 23 counties and parts of counties to build the famous Nebraska Sandhills. In places the sand is piled 300 feet high, which is typical of dune topography. Elsewhere there has been excavation to the water table level and below. Extensive flat hay meadows and small shallow lakes are frequent. Under the present climate most surfaces are well stabilized by grasses and sedges. The area is mainly a grazing district. Only rarely can the cover be disturbed without initiating new blowing.

A novel and characteristic erosion pattern in the Sandhills and in other sandy areas of the dry Plains is the blowout. On a northwestern slope the prevailing winds find an unprotected spot in which they cut a small hollow in the almost hourglasslike fine sand. The blowing may last for days with no rain to firm the loose particles. When a pit is formed, the wind tends to whirl within the pocket, lifting and carrying away the loosened sand grains; any weak binding roots may be undermined and the pit enlarged. In the somewhat circular excavation the windward side may become an abrupt drop, the upsloping "floor" a steep slope on which the coarser particles are dropped, to trickle back as the force of the wind permits, or to be carried up and out, often to be dropped close beyond the margin, to build the apex of the dune higher. At length the pit may be enlarged 50 to 100 feet. It may cut into dormant blowouts or remnants, and in an area where the formations are frequent it may result in the most wind-tortured topography imaginable—with more bare sand than pasturage—a veritable high chop-sea of sand. With seasonal moisture, seeds begin to sprout in the lower, more sheltered portion of the blowout. One of the earliest adventives, the rare and endemic *Penstemon haydeni*, is large-flowered, milky blue, and delightfully fragrant. Depending on soil texture, moisture, and time of year, the Sandhills display many colorful associations of flowering species.

East of the Sandhills district much of Nebraska has a smooth covering of loess, a wind-shifted dust derived in part from the sand, in part from wind-removed glacial drift, in a long dry period of perhaps thousands of years, during the last glacial period. In places the loess is deep, and remains of the extinct hairy elephants called mammoths are found where the typical vertical-sided ravines have exposed them. Sometimes the loess covers the glacial debris; it reaches the Missouri River and across into Iowa, briefly into Kansas. This excellent farming soil extends to the most easterly portion of the Great Plains border contour of 1,800 feet, and at this latitude the region reaches its greatest width.

On the very level prairie of southeastern Colorado stands the small Carrizo Mesa of volcanic origin. Almost a perfect circle, three miles wide, nearly level on its 500-foot summit, it has a warty excrescence of lighter brown lava near one margin, justifying the local designation of "Potato Butte." The mesa has the appearance of being built in a long series of eruptions when the aggrading Plains provided a restraining mold for each new lava flow. Habitats that shelter quail and deer are notable, and in ravines to the southeast a light growth of pine appears. Yuccas and cacti are interspersed with tall grasses on the steep bordering slopes. Nearby to the south begin the few miles of breaks, with both piñon and ponderosa pine, leading down and across the Oklahoma line to the canyon of the Cimarron River.

Twenty miles or more to the southwest of Carrizo lies Mesa de Maya, a similar structure of dark lava, built mainly on a foundation of Dakota Sandstone. Mesa de Maya rises 500 feet above its base; its summit is relatively level, its length some 20 miles. Still farther west and in part based upon the Dakota is Raton Mesa. Over this eminence a highway crosses from Trinidad, Colorado to Raton, New Mexico, and to lower ground. The Raton Mesa rises to 7,000 feet above sea level. The volcanic features continue west for 40 miles to include the high Spanish Peaks, which by position are within the Great Plains province and by structure do not conform to the Rocky Mountain system — they are a sort of no-man's land.

Of special interest are the histories of the Cimarron and Canadian River which rise among these volcanics of the Plains. The Cimarron, a small stream in a deep and anomalously wide trench, flows eastward for 80 miles in New Mexico and Oklahoma, then crosses the tip of Colorado and into Kansas. There is ample evidence that the Cimarron's trench once belonged to the Canadian, and that the Canadian was forced out of its channel by a dam of lava. Near its headwaters the Canadian now flows in a newer and narrower canyon. It turns southward for 90 miles, then eastward to find its way through the rolling plains of the Texas Panhandle.

The continually eroding and receding borders of the High Plains are nowhere as conspicuous as in Texas. Here the extreme flatness of the terrain, the texture of the soil in many places, the character of the rock below, and possibly the ready erodability of the Triassic and Permian red clay beds, still deeper, combine to produce a margin that drops precipitously. The process is initiated by the undermining of the softer lower strata, leaving the upper layers without support, sooner or later to slump. The outstanding example is Palo Duro Canyon which has been cut to great depths for 40 miles back into the High Plains. Its maximum depth is 1,200 feet, its greatest width 20 miles. This remarkable scenic feature is manifestly the work of water and wind. A small stream bearing the name Palo Duro Creek in its upper reaches, Prairie Dog Town Fork of the Red River in its lower course, served to carry away the immeasurable burden of excavated material. The present annual rainfall of the area is about 20 inches; it is estimated to have been 45 inches when the recurrent Pleistocene glaciers were present a few hundred miles to the north and northeast, and much closer in the mountains to the northwest.

The 15,000-acre Palo Duro State Park is readily reached from Canyon or Amarillo. It includes the descent into the canyon and many remarkable and scenic erosion remnants in the depths. The general aspect of the canyon's vegetation reflects the relatively dry climate. Flowering species like *Opuntia leptocaulis* are numerous, finding much habitat free from grass competition. At the canyon the view across from rim to rim strongly accentuates the contrast of abyss and extreme eye-level flatness. From the farther rim, the earth curves away, leaving only the most simple and abstract skyline.

The foregoing listing of topographical features has been presented to depict novel and attractive characteristics of the region, as well as to correct the common concept of the Great Plains as a featureless expanse of monotonous and insignificant flatness. A second purpose has been to point out that ruggedness of every sort provides habitat for the gentler flowering jewels which there find freedom to pursue their independent and decorative ways, relieved from the often over-powering competition of the ubiquitous grasses.

No discussion of the plant life of the Great Plains is complete without touching on the geologic history of the region. The ebb and flow of great seas that alternately covered and exposed the plains, volcanic activity, and wind-deposited soil—all changed the face of the land. But perhaps nothing stirs the imagination more than visualizing glaciers advancing southward, then melting, leaving great river valleys and rock and soil deposits behind.

What were the effects of the Ice Age upon plant life? Each of the continental glaciers moved out from the general northeastern source to turn nearly the whole of Canada and much of the upper half of the United States into absolute desert. Yet in the last 10,000 or so years—less time in portions of Canada—nature's wonderful processes of clothing the earth have revegetated the entire area to the limit of cold adaptation in the Arctic against water courses, against westerly winds, against all other hindrances; and indeed as to forests, almost as rapidly as temperatures near the retreating ice front provided acceptable habitat. Studies of tree remains, soil layers, pollen grains, and carbon reveal many details of ice movements and revegetation. By such means, for instance, we know that toward the close of the last Ice Age, the Wisconsin glacier withdrew into Canada and that a spruce forest grew to large size at a place called Two Creeks, on the west shore of Lake Michigan. Then in a new advance the ice dammed the northern outlet of the lake, raising the water level and drowning the Two Creeks forest; then it shoved the trees down and moved on, taking 150 years to reach the latitude of Milwaukee, 100 miles south, before final withdrawal.

The statement that the great ice sheets did not move any plants but simply annihilated them applies only to individuals and localities, whether grasses, herbs, or trees. The vast extensions of the glaciers carried with them their own temperatures and rainfall. As environments changed in tempo with the slow forward advance of the ice, the various types of trees and other plant groups colonized by normal processes farther and farther southward and westward. So the pollen layers and other records indicate. As the Pleistocene was a time of heavy snowfall in the northern regions and the mountains, so it was a time of heavy rainfall over wide remaining portions of North America. Environments were suitable nearest the ice for mosses, sedges, willows, and alders, and other tundra plants; then in succession according to temperatures came spruces and firs, then pines and the hardier deciduous trees such as beech, maple, and birch, then oaks; the oaks finally reached to northern Florida.

With every warming trend the colonizing process tended to reverse. Even though plant successions are sometimes long and drawn out, in each of the warm interglacial periods relatively few years could have sufficed for complete revegetation of the vast regions. However, plant succession following the retreating ice lacked the compulsive factor of its approach, and in the northerly succession vegetation stayed more or less constant while moisture and temperatures remained congenial. Pollen and carbon-14 tests indicate remnant forests in Nebraska as late as 5,000 years ago. In the cool canyons of the Niobrara and its tributaries, near Valentine in northern Nebraska, the hazel-nut (*Corylus americana*), iron wood (*Ostrya virginiana*), and paper birch (*Betula papyrifera*) have found a sustaining environment to the present day.

The northern white spruce (*Picea glauca*) probably came to the Black Hills in a forced migration, finding acceptable habitat in the cooler and moister canyons as at present, but doubtless over the centuries it has adjusted to a drier environment. Its nearest relatives are found beyond several hundred miles of prairie to the north. The climate of the Black Hills, though moister in the extensive spruce belt, is largely determined by the elevation and general dryness of the wide surrounding Plains. But at 7,242 feet, upon the fissured granite tip of Harney Peak, grows a shapely spruce some 20 feet tall. The Bighorn Mountains 150 miles to the west, rising from similar levels of 3,000 to 4,000 feet, meet their timberline at about 10,000 feet.

In studies explaining the predominance of grass vegetation on the Plains, it has been customary to review the prominent factors of climate, topography, soil types, seasonal and annual moisture supply, and fire, whether set intentionally or by lightning, and then to disregard the prime factor of adaptability. Adequate tests of trees of hardy and drought resistant species have been made throughout the period of settlement, extending 100 years and more. It had been found that the normal moisture supply will support trees into advanced maturity in groves about farmsteads and in extended shelterbelts for field protection. Early care is given until approximate forest conditions of ground shading and root establishment are attained, or cultivation is continued indefinitely.

Why, then, do we not find upon the open prairie, especially on the better soils, natural groves and forests? The explanation is very simple: for every type of soil and for almost every situation there is a grass or several species of grass so well adapted as to survive the most extreme droughts or prairie fires, when the last tree or shrub has been subjected to stress beyond its powers of endurance. Drought is a much greater enemy of trees than is fire, which has become so rare as to be almost inconsequential. Only in areas unsuited to the grasses can trees maintain a footing without assistance from people.

Habitat for trees on the Plains consists of streamsides where extra moisture is available and rugged places, either eminences or low breaks, to which the root systems of the dry-climate grasses are not adapted.

Many flowering herbaceous species successfully compete for moisture, where the turf is not too dense or overshading, by flowering early and spending the season of maximum heat and dryness in complete dormancy. Both grasses and flowering plants have incorporated another essential faculty, that of prolonged drought endurance. Other prairie flowers are more dependent, as are the trees, needing a definite space of their own, provided by soils of special texture such as residual gravel beds or even rocky crevices.

The present hardy flora of the Great Plains has obviously acquired its character and variety through a very long history of adjustment to changing phases of heat and cold and of extreme drought alternating with unscheduled periods of abundant moisture. In the genera consisting of many species such as phlox, penstemon, aster, cactus, evening primrose, the pea family, and others, the very noticeable differences between species indicate the following up of successful lines of differentiation. Adjustment and change lead to variation and continuation; failure to adapt to a changing environment means extinction—with plants as with animals. During the stresses of the last million years, and of earlier epochs, surely far more kinds of plants have perished than have animals. The survivors, including our native Great Plains plants which are cultivated in gardens today, have demonstrated the greatest ability.

# The Great Plains Native Plants

# The
# Great Plains
# Native Plants

### *Abronia*. Sand verbena, prairie snowball

The broad dark leaves and sprawly form of *Abronia fragrans*, an occasional denizen of sandy areas from South Dakota to Texas, are readily overlooked while the wide, rounded umbels of closely set buds await the hour of lessening light. As evening approaches, the neatly modeled snowballs appear. They last well into the next day, and they appear recurrently from June to late fall. Although white through most of its range, in parts of the South the flowers of sand verbena take on a lavender-pink tinge and apparently more color at times, for it is reported that nice color selections can be made. In the garden the plant is not exacting about soil. Not of dense habit, it may grow 30 inches wide while only a foot tall. It has a pleasant fragrance in the open air, but an overpowering pervasiveness when brought indoors.

The mythical or very rare *A. carltonii*, narrow-leaved and with flowers of white to rose, dwells in southern Colorado and ranges south into Texas.

### *Achillea*. Yarrow, milfoil

*Achillea lanulosa* is a straight-stemmed, feathery-leaved plant with a wide head of small flowers of uncertain white, on stems usually 16 to 18 inches high. It is often found on the Great Plains, indeed almost anywhere across North America. The difficult-to-distinguish immigrant, *A. millefolia*, has made itself at home on our continent, but recent chromosome studies show that over wide areas the native American *A. lanulosa* is far more frequent. To many a gardener the aromatic

*17*

milfoil, or yarrow, recalls pleasant memories; to others it is an intolerable pest spreading rapidly either by seed or by root, whether in the white or the more valued pink and rose forms.

Several young visitors asked me to lead them on a mountain climb. We chose the Harney Peak region, the heart of the Black Hills. We could not climb the rocket-form granite Needles at Cathedral Park, but a pathless, steep slope among pines brought us still higher to a broad rock top. We were at 7,000 feet, as we learned by the map, with Harney Peak only 250 feet above. There in a soil-filled, grassy depression grew dwarfed plants of purple harebell, and among them *A. lanulosa* made small carpets that were in full flower on stems only two to four inches high. The handkerchief load of small sods I brought home provided a gem for my prairie rock garden. Here it has remained dwarf, its dense, low mats advancing only an inch or two a year; its stems, five or six inches high, lift corymbs of fine white.

## *Aconitum*. Aconite, monkshood

The monkshood I was fortunate to find grew in the rich soil of a shady ravine contributing to Castle Creek valley of the more remote Black Hills. This species, **Aconitum ramosum**, or **A. porrectum**, may vary from 12 to 20 inches, as described. It has finely divided alternate leaves, and dark purple-blue flowers. It reminded me of delphinium until I noticed the prominent, arching, well-up-and-forward hood, or helmet. This plant requires shade and moisture. Another species, **Aconitum tenue**, was described by Rydberg among his fortunate, one summer's studies. This endemic was 12 inches high, with a varying shaped hood, and fleshy, fusiform roots.

## *Actaea*. Baneberry

The red baneberry, **Actaea rubra**, ranges from canyons of western Nebraska, mainly in the Wildcat Mountains of Scotts Bluff county and Pine Ridge in Sioux County, through the inner Black Hills and northwest into the prairies of Saskatchewan and Alberta, where Budd, in *A Key to Plants . . . of the Canadian Prairies*, reports it common everywhere in the woodlands and shady ravines. The species ranges in fact far east and west from the Plains to Alaska. Under cultivation it sprouts several stems up to two feet long, carrying wide, much divided leaves, small clusters of white flowers, and by midsummer shiny red berries. There is also a less common form with shining white berries. The shrub is long-lived and presents a neat appearance.

## *Agastache*. Hyssop

Anise hyssop, or giant hyssop, is called ***Agastache foeniculum*** and ***A. anethiodora*** — authorities differ. It is found on the Plains and to the north beyond the Canadian prairies, east to Ontario, and in the Rockies to Colorado. The northwestern corner of Nebraska is its southern limit in the region of low rainfall. It needs only a little encouragement to become established; it is not, however, a weed in the usual sense, since it travels only by seed and then requires some coolness and a not too rapidly vanishing moisture supply. To its credit are upright stems with many upright branches, each bearing a tapering spike well filled with purplish pink mint flowers. The stems, usually to 30 or 35 inches tall, are clothed with broadly ovate, prominently toothed leaves. The whole plant is pleasantly fragrant. The blooming period is from midsummer to frost.

Comment from a Minnesota correspondent: "Agastache grew four feet tall and took over the garden, the yard, the woods. The goldfinches loved the seeds and stripped each stem last fall. This spring Frank took all of the anise out of the 'South Dakota' garden and spread the plants through the edge of the woods. It is thriving."

## *Allium*. Onion

Wild onion species of the Plains are quickly enumerated, and only a few make the region their principal habitat. ***Allium cernuum (A. recurvatum)*** appears about midseason, with loose, nodding umbels on 12- to 14-inch stems, the florets pink with a pearly luster and not widely open. The leaves and scape are dark green. The new bulb, often reddish, forms on one side of the old one and leaves a thick, slowly decaying remnant which suggests a rhizome. ***A. cernuum*** maintains some green through much of the year, but even a completely dormant bulb can be recognized by this odd root feature. Under cultivation, clusters of bulbs may form and produce a generous display of bloom. This species has a continent-wide range and in our region is found from the rugged portions of northwestern Nebraska well into Canada.

***Allium textile (A. reticulatum), A. fraseri (A. canadense* v. *fraseri (A. mutabile)),*** and ***A. perdulce (A. nuttallii)*** have bulbs of a different type.

They have a netlike outer covering and grow into large clusters; they complete their annual labors before midsummer, producing bunched leafage and upright umbels of starry blossoms five or six inches above, then retire quickly to the cooler underground. *A. perdulce* does send up some fall leaves, if moisture is plentiful.

The white stars of *A. textile* are set off by smart green midribs, yet a pure glowing effect is lacking. The name *A. perdulce* means "especially sweet," and, strange as it may seem for an onion, the flower has the fragrance of a hyacinth. Moreover, its complexion is as pink as the well-known—or well-remembered—two-cent stamp, or even deeper with a hint of rose-red. Its preferred soil is a sandy loam; though drought-enduring and at home from southern South Dakota down into Oklahoma and New Mexico, it thrives in better than average moisture and makes good use of fall rains. *A. fraseri* occupies, to a great extent, the range of *A. perdulce*, whereas *A. textile* is found in the southern portions of Manitoba, Saskatchewan, and Alberta, and south to New Mexico; it also occurs in the mountains to the west. The bulbs of all the foregoing grow at a depth of four inches.

*Allium geyeri* bears dainty close heads of a clear, light pink. In exposed positions the scapes are from four to eight inches high, but in dense meadow grasses this species lifts its inviting color into the sun to 16 inches. It occurs from low meadows in the granite region to the highest portions of the limestone plateau of the Black Hills, and it has a wide range in the Rockies. The small, netted bulbs are found about two inches deep in rich soil. Requirements for the welfare of the bulb are coolness and never too-prolonged dryness.

*Allium stellatum* is a sturdy, upright, pink species which just brushes along the eastern border of the Plains until it reaches the northern Canadian prairies; then, following woodlands and cool nooks, it extends well westward.

## *Anaphalis*. Pearly everlasting

The broad, dense cymes of the very double, small flowers of *Anaphalis subalpina*, composed mainly of stiff, incurved, pearly white bracts, make a wonderful display above the velvety-whitened, green leaves. Among the Needles of the Black Hills, where this is a rare plant, the growth is usually a foot or so. The plant is not rampant in the wild, though its rhizomatous roots suggest that it might need to be controlled in the garden. In my garden, the pearly everlasting persisted only for

a time yet flowered readily—perhaps it needed better soil and attention. It is indeed worthy of extra care, and I hope to possess it again.
*A. subalpina* is sometimes rated a variety of the species *A. margaritacea*,
a more eastern one which did not persist in my garden and which I
found surprisingly grayer than the local plant. *A. subalpina* also occurs
in the Cypress Hills, and more extensively in the western mountains.

## *Androstephium*. Blue bethlehem, blue funnel-lily

To one unfamiliar with the Bethlehem-star, the name "blue bethlehem"
seems a borrowed name with little meaning; and careful examination
of the flower with six-segmented limb hardly suggests a funnel. In
the absence of a good popular name, the generic *Androstephium*
would serve well. *A. caeruleum* is a remarkably beautiful, willing, and
well-behaved native of central Kansas, adjacent Oklahoma, and the
eastern Texas Panhandle. Growing from a corm at about four inches
below the soil surface are a number of grassy leaves and a stout scape
(to about four or five inches), which bears an umbel of several light
blue or mauvish blue stars about an inch and a half wide. Growth starts
a trifle late, but the flowers come soon, to be followd by a generous
crop of waferlike, glossy black seeds and dormancy. The species is
fully hardy in the difficult climate of Prairie Gem Ranch. Under favorable conditions many stolonlike processes are sent sidewise from the
base of the corm, to an inch and a half or less, and new cormlets are
set exactly in the manner of gladiolus. In old specimens, the corm may
reach more than an inch in diameter and produce larger umbels.

## *Anemone*. Windflower, anemone    plate 8

*Anemone canadensis* shows no hesitation in dragging its white of
great purity into road ditches for the sake of extra moisture, where no
one can perhaps justly object to its energetic colonizing. But *A. canadensis* and I are not on friendly terms. For my average care, it pretty
well sits and does nothing, while a sister species at its side, *A. sylvestris*,
wins enthusiastic regard. My good garden friend, Mrs. Harry Crisp,
who supplied me with it, wrote: "There is quite a bunch of *Anemone
sylvestris*, of European origin, which is far nicer than *A. canadensis*.
Both are most invasive, look out for them."

The two are alike in much-divided leaf and upright stance to 10
or 15 inches, and it can be no disfavor to anyone who knows *A. canadensis*, with its plain flower an inch and a quarter wide, to point out

that the cupped and ruffled segments of the other, in white of equal purity, reach two inches or more, a very handsome product of June and sometimes later. *A. sylvestris* forms a dense, low, leafy cover and flowers freely, needing only a good degree of shade to remind it of an original woodland haunt.

In its Plains reaches, *A. canadensis* is mainly found in the North, especially across eastern South Dakota and Montana to Saskatchewan and Alberta, at edges of woodlands and in low, moist places.

*Anemone caroliniana.* When the name? I find no published record crediting this flower to Carolina. On the contrary, its range extends from the central midland states westward to the 3,000-foot contour in South Dakota and Nebraska and Kansas. And in this higher, drier country, on its favorite rich loam untouched by the plow, *A. caroliniana* spreads its jewellike blossoms over pastures, golf courses, cemeteries, and reserves.

The unfenced, "unimproved" 320 acres where I walked in May amid untold thousands of these brave and dainty flowers were bordered on one side by a hard-surfaced road, on the opposite by a thriving field of wheat. In this chance refuge, the competitor-protectors of the anemone were low forage plants, mainly buffalo-grass, blue grama, and some small sedges. The land lay nearly level, held against serious erosion by the sparse turf; but in the near distance a limestone-tipped tepee butte told the story that in an earlier age the general level of the ground stood higher than at present. The flowers, by no means omnipresent, followed some sort of colony pattern. There were none in any low place. Most flowers were white, but here and there appeared a smaller colony in magnetic sapphire-blue. From other areas, blues in various lighter tones, some with white eye, and some rarer pinks have come to my garden.

Flowers of eight to 20 sepals in daisy pattern, four inches or so above ground, develop from a small tuber or rhizome an inch or two down. This half-inch or shorter, delicate structure is the vital part of the plant; in the dormant period, from seed ripening until fall, all other parts including roots are absent. During lush spring growth, thick, short stolons are sent out horizontally from the rhizome, each to form a new rhizome at its tip, thus slowly developing a colony. Leaves return with fall moisture to remain all winter, and healthy leaves ensure good flowering. *A. caroliniana* is surely one of the world's prime treasures.

*Anemone cylindrica* and *A. multifida* have become adapted to the Plains, though they originally occurred in the cooler northern part of the continent. *Anemone multifida* has the familiar synonym *A. globosa*. The general impression of these not-too-beautiful plants is of stiff uprightness to 12 inches or more, much-divided leaves toward the ground, and smallish flowers, the eight or 10 sepals as naively and carelessly fashioned as if outlined by a single swinging stroke of a child's pencil. Moreover, the blooms are not plentiful. Yet various gardeners and garden writers have referred to them charitably. *A. cylindrica* hardly deserves praise, producing flowers varying from greenish white to a bit more noticeable color. *A. multifida* through its different color forms does better, finally approaching a somewhat dull, dark red or occasionally a bright or vivid red. It can be counted upon to carry for some weeks a wide, short knob of cottony seeds of some interest. The behavior of *A. multifida* in the garden is acceptable.

## *Antennaria*. Pussytoes, ladies'-tobacco, antennaria  plate 9

Many are the low, gray mats of the ladies'-tobacco, many the varied leaf forms and patterns in different regions, and many the attitudes of gardeners toward these useful and beautiful subjects in garden design. The late Clara Regan of Butte, Montana, who had the most intimate appreciation of all natural beauty, was quite indifferent to antennarias, because they had been all too common in the western mining camps of her early days. In contrast, it was the velvety, silver-green mat of an antennaria which etched the first indelible impression of a wild plant on my mind and turned me into an ardent admirer of them.

But how shall we assign identifying names to the antennarias? As an everyday name, "ladies'-tobacco," intriguing, distinctive, might satisfy those uncritical ones who shy from Latin designations; but it does not make any distinction between the many species and forms, of varying tones and textures, which the gardener will wish to employ as ground covers for small spaces. A few of the dwarfer and readily distinguished kinds to be found on the Great Plains are listed in the following paragraphs.

*Antennaria aprica* is one of the choicest. It is often found on exposed and dry prairie as well as in dry shade. All-gray leaves are oblanceolate to spatulate, with a short, sharp tip, and five-eights to three-fourths of an inch long. Overlapping in close pattern, they make a complete, very flat mat which is maintained through the winter and summer. In June many stems, to four inches tall or so, lift the small clusters of furry pussy-toes of light gray or pink—a pleasant show. A very bright pink one has been found, also a deeper pink, verging on magenta. As do most antennarias, *A. aprica* accepts light but never smothering shade.

*Antennaria campestris* departs from the usual gray of the genus with leaves twice the size of those of *A. aprica*; these are deep green or sometimes a bit grayish above, white below, broadly oblanceolate. Stems rise to eight inches, and the toes may be gray or brownish. The mats are very low. In *Wild Plants of the Canadian Prairies*, Budd and Best list a bright, light green antennaria from southwestern Alberta and Cypress Hills under the name *A. howellii*. A bright green one is also the staminate relative of *A. campestris*. Its broad, short, clear white bracts, which resemble rays, are held horizontally.

Silver-green in all parts, *Antennaria microphylla* lays down a perfect half-inch mat of leaves smaller than those of *A. aprica* and broadly spatulate in a charming, readily recognized pattern. Its stems and inflorescence are never anything but gray, except that the seldom-seen staminate form displays white bracts.

*Antennaria obovata* and *A. oxyphylla* are larger kinds, spreading mats of looser texture, with gray-green toes. The first one is a frequent resident of the dry, hot prairies; the other prefers much shade. There is little to distinguish these two, but *A. obovata* appears much like a larger *A. aprica*, its running mate in the open, whereas *A. oxyphylla*, of whose identity I am not sure, has leaves more spatulate and often with rounded tip.

*Antennaria rosea* forms a low, dense mat, but is somewhat loose in texture; its leaves are narrower and more pointed than most. The common color of the toes is pink, but occasionally they are light gray; in certain favored habitats with rich soil, cool shade, and ample moisture, the color is a rich rose-red.

*Antennaria parvifolia* is a name in this troublesome genus which has been bandied from specific status to synonymy and back again. Now, in some herbaria, the variety of forms and types filed under it suggests the name has become a convenient catchall for any unidentified small-leaved pussy-toes of low stature. No one should venture to apply a name to an antennaria unless he or she observes mature summer forms, preferably in flower. But plant hunters may safely take into their gardens any antennaria that appeals to them, with the assurance that it will be tractable and valued. On the Plains, antennarias are less frequent southward from the latitude of South Dakota. To the north they become more common and are seen more in the open. In portions of Canada *A. parvifolia* seems to be the most common kind, and pistillate and staminate plants are about equal in number. As usual, only the pattern of the little gray leaves and their size, consistently smaller than in *A. aprica*, tie these strange brothers and sisters to the name *A. parvifolia*. In this species sisterly toes are gray, brotherly toes tawny, larger, and lacking the petallike bracts noted in other species.

Much needs to be known about the genus *Antennaria*. The plant commonly seen is pistillate, bearing no stamens and producing seed by a process called *apomixis—parthenogenesis* in this case. In many species the pollen-bearing plant is very rare, has a lower stature, and is recognized only by leaf form and habit; in some the staminate form is unknown, if indeed it exists. Yet the familiar, versatile virgins go merrily on, spreading their gentle bits of carpet over the earth in the seemingly invariable pistillate forms. What of the "little brothers"? It would seem that some pollen-bearing or male plants must result from virgin-produced seed. But to what end? These plants put up their shorter stems, carry their distinct and peculiar flowers, and cast their unwanted pollen upon the winds. Is that the whole story? Perhaps not. Rydberg, in *Flora of the Prairies and Plains*, referred to "Staminate, or rather hermaphrodite, flowers with tubular, 5-lobed corollas, sterile, their styles and stigmas rudimentary." But another authority has mentioned that a normal staminate plant will at times throw a functional ovary. Very well, then it need not seem too strange if staminate plants, of *A. aprica* and *A. microphylla* at least, are discovered producing seed copiously, good seed to all appearances. Viable seed? To produce more male plants—or what? Who has made the test?

## *Aquilegia*. Columbine, aquilegia

*Aquilegia brevistyla* is a small species that is rare on the Canadian Plains until it becomes plentiful near the northern Canadian border, then goes on to the Yukon. The course of plant history has also brought it to the Black Hills where it is frequently found on cool, north-facing slopes. The flower is quite small, of rather dull blue and white, the short spurs hooked. It usually grows 10 to 18 inches tall.

*Aquilegia latiuscula* (or *A. canadensis*) occurs in canyons that penetrate the Pine Ridge escarpment in Nebraska, probably in Wyoming as well, and in many places in the nearby Black Hills foothills. Whether considered synonymous or as separate species, these two dainty and distinguished, red and yellow columbines are much the same. Yet there are differences. One fancies *A. canadensis* as among the handful of immigrants, along with bloodroot and downy yellow violets, that worked their way from the east to the Black Hills and no farther at a time when a continental ice sheet maintained a humid climate across the Plains; and that, in the 10,000 or more years since then, it has become accustomed to the area's increased dryness, started flowering earlier, and become *A. latiuscula*. It stands commonly at two feet and, among all aquilegias attempted at Prairie Gem, is preeminent in drought endurance.

## *Arctostaphylos*. Bearberry, kinnikinnick

Some of the most charming roadside pictures in the well-wooded Black Hills are the brief vistas of the rich, dark green carpets of kinnikinnick under medium-growth pines. Whether in areas many rods in extent or as beginning patches, *Arctostaphylos uva-ursi* is the prime evergreen ground cover of all the Plains region. Its habitat is generally northern. Southward it reaches sparsely into the Sandhills of Nebraska and in the mountains into Colorado; it occurs in shady places in rough areas of Montana and North Dakota, and more frequently on north exposures throughout the Canadian Plains. It is to be found also in many parts of Alaska and in Eurasia.

In fall and well into winter, kinnikinnick mats are liberally adorned with bright crimson beads, to as much as three-eights of an inch in diameter. These round, smooth berries are gradually taken by certain animals and birds, but they last well.

The secret of the kinnikinnick's reluctant germination remains hidden. Seedlings and plants small enough to be moved are hardly ever found in the wild. This accounts, in part, for the absence in gardens of this very desirable shrub. But where a branch has taken root in suitable ground, a transplant may be lifted in a good spadeful of firm soil. The branch is severed two inches back from the selected root and headed back a few inches beyond. It must be set in moderate shade, in well-drained, neutral or slightly acid ground, and have no deficiency of moisture for a year.

The occurrence of *A. uva-ursi* on limestone is surely not to be taken as indicating an adapted strain. There are limestones upon which the elements act very slowly; and a humus-filled fissure, aided by a minimal accession of acid material, seemingly is able to maintain a micro-environment agreeable to the plant. It has been observed that a readily soluble lime reacts at first as a growth stimulant to *A. uva-ursi* for perhaps a season, then as an unendurable poison.

In a perfect environment the kinnikinnick is very restrained in its annual growth. It delights in modeling the irregular surface of rocks with its advancing stems, and there displays at their best, in early spring, its brief clusters of tiny, pendant urns of pink and white. Is there a finer, four-season, low shrub to be found?

### *Arenaria*. Sandwort       plate 10

*Arenaria hookeri* is a typical Great Plains rock plant of southeastern Montana, eastern Wyoming, and western South Dakota and Nebraska, reaching somewhat into Colorado and the adjacent mountains. Its cushions of dark green needle-leaves are widened by underground branching of the crown that surmounts the taproot, reaching at best an 18-inch diameter, whereas the height seldom exceeds four inches, even when in flower. *A. hookeri* grows next to other species that also form cushions, such as silvery *Astragalus tridactylicus* and lighter green *Paronychia sessiliflora*; they often occupy mutually exclusive sections of a quite symmetrical cushion, whose leaves remain on the plants throughout the winter. Sharp-tipped white stars, about half an inch wide, crowd each other on *A. hookeri* in June. The species propagates only by seed and is very long-lived, reaching maximum spread where it has a narrow, limy crevice to itself.

*Arenaria (Sabulina) texana*, principally of northeastern Kansas and of Nebraska south of the Republican River, but extending into Oklahoma and Texas, scatters small tufts of mildly prickly leaves in suitable stony places and puts up spreading stems, to five inches or so, with open panicles of dainty white stars. Its free blooming and long season have earned it a place in the rock garden. This taxon is now considered to be a subspecies of *A. stricta*.

### *Argemone*. Sand poppy, pricklypoppy, argemone       plate 11

One handles *Argemone hispida*, an all-gray plant with villainous prickles, with tongs when mature, but cherishes it for its rare silver color and its fresh white flowers borne over a long season. The flowers, two and a half to more than four inches wide, are marvels of crinkled silk which flutter without fainting through the hottest of summer breezes. Four to six wide petals flare from a prominent yellow center. The plant, which seldom exceeds 20 inches, is very long-lived. In Wyoming and Colorado *A. hispida* stays rather close to the mountains, then crosses the westernmost portion of Oklahoma into New Mexico. Many taxonomists now consider reports of *A. hispida* to be *A. squarrosa.*

Widespread over the Plains from southeastern Montana into Texas and New Mexico is *Argemone polyanthemos*—long known as *A. intermedia,* a name first given to seedlings of another species. Its prominently lobed and prickly leaves are more glaucous green than gray, their ribs whitish. As with the flowers of most argemones, this has the wide, crinkled petalage of pristine white which endures intense summer heat. Often small plants from seed will flower, but full maturity, branching, and heavy production come the second year; with adequate moisture for the formation of new buds just below ground, plants will survive a third year. But this is not a long-lived subject. A common height is 24 inches.

Frequent over much of western Kansas is *Argemone squarrosa,* a coarser species with similar summertime flowers of purest white, and distinctive larger seed capsules with strong, recurved prickles, whence its name. Its range extends into portions of Colorado, Oklahoma, and New Mexico. Several other species of prickly-poppies that might be mistaken for any one of ours may be found beyond the Plains, well to the east and to the south and southwest.

## *Arnica.* Arnica

In years of plentiful moisture when the prairies are covered with flowers, *Arnica fulgens* contributes accents, grand displays, and panoramas from mid-Wyoming and the Black Hills into Saskatchewan and Alberta. Its rich golden or orange-yellow daisies, upheld regularly to 12 or 14 inches, are so fine that it has been remarked, "They hardly seem like wild flowers." Elegantly finished, a bit pinched and notched at the tips of the rays in the fashion of the genus, the flowers, one to three to the stem, gleam in striking contrast to the all-gray plant with heavy foliage near the ground. The leaves are long-lanceolate, parallel-veined. This plant circumvents the Plains climate by going completely underground when heat and drought come, and does not show itself again until the following spring. Short rhizomes build a crown to four or five inches in width, from which portions are readily taken for propagation. *A. fulgens* likes a good loam.

I found *Arnica rydbergii* in a deep gulch in the Black Hills and brought it to my prairie garden, where it flowered charmingly in deep yellow for several years, indicating that, unlike many arnicas, it needed little or no acidity. Its stem was low, its foliage deep green; but because I ignored its single-stemmed appeal for better soil and more moisture, it passed on.

*Arnica cordifolia*, a reputed acid lover, which I have not chanced upon, dwells in the Black Hills and Cypress Hills. It bears flowers in a lemon-yellow. *Arnica arnoglossa*, *A. chamissonis*, and *A. sororia* also occur within the northern Plains.

## *Artemisia.* Sage, sagebrush

Of the sages of perennial habit, *Artemisia frigida* and *A. longifolia* are the only ones I know which may be safely taken into the garden. Even if low and of intriguing appearance, others I tried began at once to gain ground with frightening speed.

The little sage, or northern sage, *Artemisia frigida*, is always conspicuous because of its clean, silver-green softness, like coarse velvet, in low pillow-form. Stems touching the ground do strike root, but the plant never spreads to an unwanted distance. It is agreeably fragrant and has a pungent taste, which led to its use in the early days as a flavoring for sausage. For that purpose, a much lighter amount was needed than of the common seasoning salvia, known as garden sage. In summer *A. frigida* sends up numerous, gracefully arching stems with pendant bells, green-silver tipped with dull yellow. After this pleasant display has been enjoyed, the plant may be sheared back to the cushion for an all-winter effect.

*Artemisia longifolia* is entirely deciduous and somewhat rhizomatous, makes a dense root-crown, and sends up many stems, to 28 inches or thereabout, well clothed with linear leaves four or more inches long. The inflorescence is not conspicuous but, like the rest of the plant, gray-green. A winning feature is the delightful fragrance of a crushed leaf. *A. longifolia* belongs to badlands and exposed clay slopes from western Nebraska into southern Canada and westward, whereas *A. frigida* may be seen, often at roadsides, throughout the northern Plains.

*Artemisia cana*, usually a low, upright shrub, here and there becomes gnarled and picturesque and 40 inches tall. It has small, entire, light gray leaves and an all-season effect to recommend it, and a moderately running root as a demerit. It is common from Nebraska north, especially in Montana. *Artemisia filifolia*, found in sand ground from southern South Dakota to Texas and New Mexico, is one of the most beautiful of the grayish shrubs. Its silvery green, hairlike leaves and silver inflorescence stand gracefully erect or bend with the breeze. *Artemisia tridentata*, the big sagebrush of the farther West, is common on the Montana and Wyoming plains and touches North Dakota, South Dakota, and Nebraska. Here it is generally low but under cultivation readily reaches four feet. Densely clothed with tiny, three-tipped, gray leaves, the shrub carries some foliage through the winter and is a desirable bushy ornamental. Both *A. filifolia* and *A. tridentata* have a delightful and stimulating pungent fragrance.

## *Asclepias (Acerates)*. Milkweed     plate 13

*Asclepias angustifolia* is a pleasant find for those who admire green flowers. The stems, often single, a foot or more tall, are sparsely furnished with rather small umbels; the flower is pale green with a nearly white center. As observed in the wild, the species does not seem to be of weedy habit. It ranges from South Dakota to Texas.

*Asclepias ovalifolia* is a neat, clean, and attractive milkweed, to 10 inches or so, with good-sized umbels of a pure light green.

*Asclepias pumila* belongs strictly to the Plains, is relatively rare in Montana and the Dakotas, where it grows to six or eight inches, and more frequent south to Texas where it may reach 14 inches. Everywhere it flowers freely and with its close-colony habit produces masses of attractive, honey-scented blooms. Its slender stems, thickly set with tiny, linear leaves, often branch and bear two or three relatively large umbels of white flowers. Usually the white is tinged with green, but in a ravine of badland clay I have noted light brown flowers and in a few widely separated localities flowers with a definite tinge of pink, the buds conspicuously pink.

The showy butterfly-weed or orange milkweed, *Asclepias tuberosa*, typically of the eastern United States, reaches the Plains region in Kansas, crosses Oklahoma and Texas to New Mexico and Arizona, and occurs in Colorado in the foothills. Where this magnificent plant stands alone, its intense coloring raises a cheer; and with harmonious colors, such as those of the monarch butterfly, its effect can be thrilling. As grown at Prairie Gem Ranch, stock from southern Kansas shows dependable drought resistance.

I have been unable to find the name of a plant I observed in western Oklahoma which must belong to *Asclepias* or a closely related genus. In late July, one or two stems a foot or so long, each with a typical large milkweed pod or two, may be seen lying flat on barren ground at the roadside, as if utterly weary or, perhaps, broiled by the unrelenting southern Plains heat. The color of stems and pods is fascinating, a dull but vital pathological red, at that stage of "ripeness" a startling novelty, curious rather than repelling. In the garden, one plant stays in its place, with no hint of troublesome roots.

## *Aster*. Aster     plates 14-16

For some miles along a road in central northern Kansas, I noticed one September, low, arching stems of light blue asters. Where a dozen plants appeared along a cut bank, a single stem held out its brief, crowded raceme of sparkling blue and gold as if especially prepared for that fortunate moment of discovery. And it was love at first sight. In my garden this aster, *A. batesii*, thrived beyond expectation and from a rock garden prospect grew to 24 inches and more, with many slender stems rising from a compact crown and bending over with the load of blossoms—a veritable mound of color. For a few years the newcomer seeded moderately in its regular tone; then began to sport, throwing deeper-toned blue, and finally deep purple, with light pinks and attractive intermediate tones.

For all of 20 years at Prairie Gem Ranch, the white *A. ericoides*—which does not belong in anyone's garden—and *A. kumleini* grew in close proximity to *A. batesii* without exerting any perceptible influence on it, and none at all on each other, though they have been suspected of giving rise to *A. batesii*. Be that as it may, over the range of *A. batesii* from central Kansas to the northwestern corner of that state and to central Nebraska, the species present a remarkable uniformity; while over the hundreds of miles outside that range, where the putative parents reside side by side, nothing resembling *A. batesii* occurs, though occasional plants of *A. ericoides* show a little color.

On the Great Plains, *Aster conspicuus* occurs in the Black Hills, the Cypress Hills, and the northcentral, northwestern, and western portions of the Plains in Canada. It is also native to the farther West.

Rather heavy-stemmed, with large, coarsely toothed leaves, it flowers in August, often at 16 to 20 inches; or branching widely to 24 inches or more, it presents its pinkish violet or bluish violet heads, each an inch to an inch and a half wide, in a flat-topped show—a very handsome plant. A few wide-reaching rhizomes are put out, with no prospect of forming a thicket.

*Aster arenosus (Leucelene ericoides)* is a small, white daisy with the intriguing habit of forming not tufts but a sparse colony, from widely ranging roots, of many separate plantlets to four or five inches, little-branched and few-flowered. Its home is on rather barren slopes, particularly in Kansas and Colorado, from western Nebraska to Texas and New Mexico. Short, needlelike leaves create a sparse effect, giving accent to the half- or five-eighths-inch, gold-centered flowers. What its garden use might be is yet to be learned; my efforts with it proved unsuccessful.

The late Dr. H. Hapeman, who built up as a hobby the largest private herbarium in Nebraska, took me one early September to one of his favorite collecting grounds, his "Table Mountain," a prominent limestone-capped knoll of a few acres in sight of the Kansas line. The find of the day, in cracks in the slabby limestone of the summit, was the prime rock aster of the Plains, *A. fendleri*, in full flower at four to 10 or at most 12 inches. Many-rayed, cupped heads of light lavender-blue with small centers were everywhere. Small plants grew upright, larger ones put out many branches from the base and presented their flowers in corymbs; the leaves were small, narrow-oblong or lanceolate. This aster does not form a wide crown; some branches, however, come from below ground and bear roots of their own, so that the plant is easily divided for propagation. Its range from southern Nebraska takes in most of western Kansas, crosses the corner of Colorado, reaches to the rim of Palo Duro Canyon in the Staked Plains of Texas, and goes also to New Mexico. Blues of deeper tone are seen in some areas.

*Aster geyeri* of the Black Hills has an interesting history. Apparently it originated in the northern Hills and may still be there in the wild. It must have been taken into gardens early, for it is now seen in every town in the Hills and in many other gardens. Years ago, all attempts to trace it led back to a gardener of still earlier years. Rydberg gives the range as Alberta, South Dakota, Colorado, and west to Washington. In *Wild Plants of the Canadian Prairies*, Budd and Best report *A. geyeri* in wooded valleys and forested areas, west and northwest on the

Alberta Plains, but with flowers only an inch and a quarter wide. (Most flowers of the species are an inch and a half wide and a few are fully two inches wide.) The species must be rare. The great herbarium at Laramie, Wyoming, had no specimen until I supplied one. Any plant of *A. geyeri* is spectacular. Bold, glossy, dark green leaves, entirely hairless, are attractive on strong stems that reach 40 inches or more when in flower. Then all the upper parts are wide panicles of blue, radiant in shade or a lovely softer blue in sunlight. The heads are long-rayed, with small, golden centers. The plant increases by short, strong rhizomes and in time builds a wide clump. Long culture in the garden has not destroyed its ability to endure drought.

*Aster kumleinii* and *A. oblongifolius* seem often to be involved in controversy as to their taxonomic status in reference books. The gardener, who needs a simple name for a plant, will readily subscribe to the opinion of a noted English taxonomist that "an entity which can be satisfactorily defined on the morphological-geographical basis should be given a binomial." *A. kumleinii* could then be *A. kumleinii* — without reference to its uncles and its cousins and its aunts! Our local *A. kumleinii*, usually blue and gold, was identified at a state institution and the name so appears in *Hortus Second*. Years ago, when I was attempting to gain botanical footing, I purchased a plant under the name *A. oblongifolius* to learn what it was; resembling *A. kumleinii* in many respects but taller, scraggly, and blooming in October rather than September, it is still with me. *Aster oblongifolius* 'Campbell's Pink' of similar loose habit was hastily discarded, because its color was inferior to the clear pink of the local selections. Synonyms, such as *A. oblongifolius* v. *rigidulus*, can be disregarded, for they are really not a gardener's concern.

*A. kumleinii* of the prairie is, under cultivation, rather stiff-stemmed, with small, rough leaves and repeated branching to give space to every purple-blue, gold-centered floret of the dense mass. The plant is eight to 15 inches tall and compact when not influenced by much moisture. Short rhizomes are freely sent out, enlarging the clump and requiring frequent division. On the open prairie, the presence of *A. kumleinii*, though frequent, is often never suspected, for in a dry fall there is no bloom and to find the stems, well scattered among the grasses, necessitates a close search. Perhaps no other native plant is so much improved by cultivation. It has been called the finest native aster. The range is from the High Plains of Texas to Montana and North Dakota.

With a wide range both east and west, **Aster laevis** ventures on to the Plains in Nebraska in shady places. Then it stocks the Black Hills from end to end and continues northward well into Canada. Variable in stem growth and leaf form, in the wild often consisting of only a single, low, few-flowered stem, *A. laevis* is always glabrous and sometimes glaucous. In the garden it may build a crown several inches wide and send up many stems to produce at 36 inches, rarely taller, a wide mass of fine medium blue. It is weedy by seed.

The ancient migration trail of **Aster meritus**, also known as *A. sibericus*, whether from the western mountains to the Black Hills or the reverse, is conjectural; but, under the present dry Plains climate, the species is safely confined to the two retreats. In its rough-textured foliage and in the way it spreads its masses of flowers in a sheet, this aster suggests *A. conspicuus*; its color, a light violet with a hint of pink, is also somewhat reminiscent of *A. conspicuus*. But *A. meritus* hardly reaches 10 inches, and its close colonizing qualifies it as a ground cover. It flowers in July.

The beautiful and stately **Aster novae-angliae** is rather an anomaly on the Plains; yet it has traveled to Colorado, South Dakota, and Montana and now haunts favored nooks, avoiding the wide open spaces.

**Aster ptarmicoides (Unamia alba)**. Mainly an eastern species but found in dry, rocky places in western South Dakota, through North Dakota, and into Saskatchewan. It is a graceful and attractive daisy, white-rayed and cream-centered. As it appears in the wild, it is often no more than seven or eight inches tall; but in better footing or in the garden, it increases to a close clump reaching 16 inches and carries an abundance of flowers. This aster is easily recognized by its narrow, light green leaves that are oblanceolate, parallel-veined, and stiff.

**Aster saundersii** is sometimes included in the widely varying or group-species *A. ciliolatus*, and thus with close relatives is found throughout the continent. In the Black Hills, *A. saundersii* is readily distinguished by its broad, half-heart-shaped leaves, medium to low stature, and small, light violet heads. Out of curiosity I brought this species to my garden, where it showed its true capability and produced wide, dense columns of color. It spreads moderately.

Numerous other asters that inhabit the Plains are better left to the roadsides and out-of-the-way places; however pleasant there, in gardens, as far as is known, they are weedy.

*Astragalus*. Milkvetch, locoweed, buffalo pea,
orophaca, astragalus     plates 17-24

Of the vast and worldwide genus *Astragalus*, more than a score of
species have established homes on the Great Plains, and these include
some highly desirable garden material. Colors vary widely, and growth
forms range from the most intriguing of rock garden "buns," to ground
covers, to bold and strikingly colored specimen plants. Some, perhaps
most, bear nitrogen-gathering bacteria in nodules on the roots and
so require an alkaline footing and freedom from overwetness or, more
simply, lime and perfect drainage. As small plants, before roots have
become woody, they are usually amenable to transplanting.

*Astragalus agrestis (A. goniatus, A. hypoglottis)* appears as a wide
patch of color close to the ground, often in a low place where rain-
water collects briefly. The delicate pinnate foliage is hardly noticeable
among the low blades of grass. Cloverlike heads of fresh, light lavender
accented with purple, the florets larger and in looser cluster than in
the clovers, are borne from May through summer, if moisture lasts.
The network of roots spreads freely and must be confined. The range
is from mid-Colorado and Nebraska northward. Well into Canada the
color deepens to purple-blue. The plant may be recognized out of
season by the small burrlike, though not prickly, double seed pods,
containing few seeds.

On the Plains, *Astragalus alpinus* is confined to the higher Black
Hills and Canada, and there mainly northerly. It ranges across the North
American continent and to the Arctic Ocean in Alaska, and across
Asia and Europe. An *A. alpinus* sent to me from Wisconsin flowered
in bright purple of varying rich tones. But flowers of the local form,
borne in short, wide heads, are only murky white shading to an uncertain blue toward the petal tips. The low carpet of *A. alpinus*, of
dark, broad, oval leaflets, with the complement of good flower color,
is delightful. A colony forms by running roots.

*Astragalus barrii*, Barr's milkvetch, red orophaca. Twenty to thirty
miles to the southeast from the Black Hills and as many miles short
of the Pine Ridge escarpment lie scattered limestone-capped buttes,
remnants of badland formation, which stand above the gumbo clays
and shales of the lower ground. On a carefree, balmy, sunlit morning
in May, I was descending, by a well-worn cattle trail, one of those
happy hunting grounds where no discerning botanist had ever trod

at that season. As the ground steepened, away from the turfy crest and among isolated tufts of grass and tumbled blocks of limestone, tufts and buns and small cushions of the familiar *Astragalus gilviflorus* appeared. I stepped slowly, attempting to savor the beauty of every assembled mass of glinting white blossoms; then suddenly I stopped. Just ahead, scattered among the white-flowered plants, were seemingly the same little tufts and cushions smothered in soft, silvery rose, with more and more of them farther down the slope in harsher badland clay, until the white left off entirely.

The small, triparted leaves of the two plants were not at once distinguishable. But in the strange new plant, the blossoms were borne, two or three to the tiny scape, or stem, just above the foliage, whereas the white blossoms of *A. gilviflorus* were stemless, single in the leaf axils, and gained their place in the sun mainly by virtue of lengthened banner petals.

At first the new plant was identified for me as *Astragalus tridactylicus*, a species of southeastern Wyoming and northern Colorado. I had in my possession, however, a pressed specimen sent from Montana by a garden correspondent, Winnie Considine, and later I discovered the red orophaca of three other badland buttes in my own corner of South Dakota. Then I learned that specimens of the unnamed or misnamed plant, from northern Wyoming and southeastern Montana, were available in herbaria, and Dwight Ripley and Rupert Barneby found still another station in Montana. Barneby distinguished the new species from *A. tridactylicus*, and by his courtesy it became *Astragalus barrii*, as recorded in his monograph of the genus *Astragalus (Atlas of North American Astragalus*, Parts I and II, 1964). An added note: *Astragalus barrii* was recently discovered some 50 miles to the northeast of other known stations, in the Badlands National Monument, by a Canadian visitor and identified by Barneby. It was also found on two other closer badland buttes by Earl Brockelsby.

Since *A. gilviflorus* and *A. tridactylicus* have been mentioned, it will be well to consider all members of the orophaca group.

*Astragalus gilviflorus* is the current name of the white-flowered *Orophaca caespitosa*, also called *A. triphyllus*. This species has the widest range of the group, from extreme northwestern Kansas far into Canada, and possibly the greatest adaptation to soils, being frequent on gumbo clay but little modified from the primeval shale, on fractured limestone, and on lime sandstone, though it is possible

that other orophacas chose their particular habitats for surer freedom from encroachment by other vegetation. Introduced into many
gardens east and west, *A. gilviflorus* has been reported to ripen
seed as far east as Pennsylvania. Its color is not always white, sometimes pinkish or purplish keel petals may be noted, and, rarely,
all petals have a charming flush of pink. In my garden a plant of
*A. gilviflorus* attained a spread of 14 inches, though eight is the
usual maximum in the wild. (At its best, *A. barrii* widens to perhaps
20 inches.)

*Astragalus hyalinus (Orophaca argophylla)* is almost exclusively
of the Plains, from eastern Colorado to southern Montana. It makes
as neat and tight a low mound of foliage as any rock garden plant,
with a faint bluish tinge to its silver green. This astragalus is capable
of long life, for a single plant may cover a space of 16 inches. My two
trials lived to flower only once, and I lost interest because the flowers
did not make a show; they were small, almost colorless. They appeared
about July.

Unlike other orophacas, *Astragalus sericoleucus (Orophaca sericea)*
sends out long, sinuous main stems with adequate side branches to
make a perfect carpet of irregular outline and generous extent. In
season, mainly early June, the entire plant dons a purple robe. The tiny
florets have an astonishing roundness in the banner, and they lie close
upon the very low, silky, silvery, fine-textured leafage. The finest
display I have seen was on an expanse of light tan sandstone near the
Niobrara River in western Nebraska. Many of the plants had the rock all
to themselves, and their compelling color was visible from a distance.
The range of this orophaca is northeastern Colorado, western Nebraska
to the Kingsley Dam on the North Platte River, north to the White and
Cheyenne River drainages, and following the North Platte into the
Wyoming mountains.

*Astragalus tridactylicus* follows the usual pattern of close-foliaged,
rounded mounds and is reported as vivid purple in flower. In an instance or two, it has been found well out on the Plains; otherwise, it
is known in the foothills and on the Laramie Plains, which lie beyond
the Laramie Range, at 7,000 feet. Ardent plant hunters may welcome
the word that there is another orophaca of brilliant and varied coloring,
*A. aretioides*, hiding in the mountains of Wyoming and Montana,
and still another, *A. proimanthus*, little known and farther west, as
described in Barneby's monograph.

All the orophacas are strictly taprooted. All branch from below ground to widen their crowns; and as the branches do not put out roots, divisions cannot be made. Propagation is by seed only, and seed is by no means a certain crop.

Returning to alphabetical sequence: *Astragalus bisulcatus*, two-grooved milkvetch, may strike one as a hulking weed when not in flower. It grows upright to 12 or 24 inches or more, and a single plant may have several rather coarse stems. The dark, glossy leaves are of no special attraction. But when in flower, mid-June to mid-July, a colony or a lone plant achieves the spectacular. In its gala attire, upper stems, flower-stalks, pedicels, and calyxes wear a glossy purple-red, mingling effectively with flowers of purple-blue in massed clusters, six to 10 inches long. Driving by extended roadside displays, one views the clanging parade with cheers—and listens for the calliope! Brilliant and rich displays are also to be seen against the bright verdure of prairie pastures. *A. bisulcatus*, so named for the double groove on the upper side of the pendulous pod, is plentiful at intervals, most often on eroded soils, from New Mexico well into Canada. The plant pictured in plate 18 was growing near Centennial, Wyoming. Seed is the only means of propagation.

The bird egg pea, *Astragalus ceramicus* v. *filifolius (A. longifolius, Phaca longifolia)*, is a hardly noticeable plant, except in close-colony formation in favored spots of loose sand or when in fully developed green pod. The real feature of the plant is the large, inflated, papery seed pods of light green, streaked and dotted with red, pink and purple in startling exotic pattern. The slender stems of *A. ceramicus* are but five to eight or 10 inches high, and, with such extreme skeletons of leaves, reduced to mere veins, are even hard to see when mingled with other vegetation. The blossoms, small and pale pinkish, also are of little consequence. Very slender roots and stolons steal about to form colonies in especially sandy areas from the Oklahoma Panhandle to North Dakota and Montana, but especially in the vast reaches of the Nebraska Sandhills.

The buffalo pea or ground plum, *Astragalus (Geoprumnon) crassicarpus*, an early spring-flowering plant, grows from a strong taproot. It has broad, oblong leaflets in pinnate arrangement on radiating stems, a foot or so long, which lie flat on the ground except for the tips which turn up a bit. Upon this rather loose mat, also lying quite flat, numerous wide racemes of longish, raspberry-pink to purplish, pea florets, varied in hue in various petal parts, compose a pleasant picture. A month or more later, plump pods like small plums, red cheeked on the sun-touched side, replace the blossoms and, crowding for space, make the better show for some weeks. As with apples, when rain and sun alternate just right, the fruits take on brilliant coloring. These plums, with more tough fiber than juice, are not unpleasant to taste. As a matter of note, they served the early settlers of the Plains for pickling and preserving.

Typical *Astragalus crassicarpus*, with notable variations, occupies practically all our region and extends to markedly lower altitudes in Oklahoma and Texas and especially into Iowa and Minnesota. Distinct variations under varietal names are found in bordering areas. Propagation is by seed, which is glossy black, very hard-coated, and slow to germinate.

*Astragalus drummondii* is an upright bushy plant, grayish in all parts with white hairiness, and bearing several erect racemes, of creamy white. It occurs from northeastern New Mexico into Saskatchewan and Alberta and prefers sandy clays. *Astragalus racemosus* is suited to tough gumbo, usually in low sites that have an abundance of alkali. Mostly glossy in stem and leaf, it forms a sprawly, wide mass with a great show of creamy blossoms in spring. Where it is much in evidence along roads, it occasions inquiry; but it is an untidy plant and short-lived. The sometimes wide colonies of *Astragalus gracilis* with airy, pink-purple racemes at 15 inches or less, above hardly noticeable slender stems and skeletonlike leaves, also lend interest to the roadside. In the garden this astragalus has not become weedy, but in general lacks color and presence.

Belonging to the group that Rydberg called *Xylophacos* or, commonly, sheep pod, *Astragalus missouriensis* (though it is not one of those with really woolly pods) gives its prominent clusters of pods a covering of short, appressed, gray hairs suggesting, rather, a well-shorn sheep. Close upon the ground small rosettes of neat, pinnate, grayish leaves, from a several-branched crown, are in evidence through much of the year. In early spring horizontal branches radiate to eight inches, to be dressed in late May or early June with an abundance of up-arching racemes of magenta-purple—often more bluish purple—creating a luminous effect of pleasing color. The rare sight of a short-grass pasture slope thickly set with hundreds of these plants at their height of bloom gives a high rating to *A. missouriensis*. In the garden a plant seldom lasts beyond the third year, but there are usually young ones to carry on, and never any undue number. The species dots the Plains from Texas and eastern New Mexico to southern Canada and extends into the mountains to the west.

Woolly loco, *Astragalus mollissimus*, is gray-white with silky hairs over its long pinnate leaves which are disposed in a beautiful low rosette. In some localities its low, upturned racemes of crowded medium peas are vivid pink-purple. Its more usual color, unfortunately at least in the northern reaches of the species, just touching South Dakota, is accurately described as "tawny yellow suffused with lurid purple." Or it may be the pale tawny yellow with a cast of green that sometimes frustrates the hopeful collector, even in Texas where I first saw the luminous purple form. This is another astragalus that grows a deep taproot; therefore it must be moved when small or grown from seed. The name, loco, is Spanish for "crazy," referring to the effect on pasturing animals when they consume quantities of the herbage.

One of the more beautiful of the moderate-sized *Astragali* is *A. pectinatus* with its fresh medium green, made up of slender stems and long, linear leaflets, and its large, upright trusses of white or slightly yellowish pea-blossoms. Although *A. pectinatus* grows freely on some nearby badlands, the one trial in my garden did not persist. Can it be that the plant must have selenium in its diet, the mineral that it can absorb from certain badland soils, and that poisons foraging cattle? Other species addicted to selenium thrive in the garden here. Did my treasured plant suffer from encroaching tree roots? Seed regularly escapes my occasional visits to its badland haunts, and small plants are seldom seen. *A. pectinatus* is mainly a Plains species, especially frequent in Colorado, western Kansas, Wyoming, Montana, extreme western North Dakota, and southern Canada.

Tufted milkvetch, *Astragalus spatulatus* (*A. caespitosus, Homalobus caespitosus*). It would be difficult to blueprint a more perfect plant for the dry, sunny rock garden. Indeed, nature with lavish hand has employed thousands of this plant to drop a veil of light purple across a mile of prairie; or hundreds to decorate, in honor of the month of May, a series of rocky tepee buttes with a frosting, thicker toward the top, of royal purple which varies with the cast of light; or, more modestly, dozens to scatter some color into the upper crevices of crumbling limestone cliffs where few other plants can maintain a footing. At close view the small, loose clover heads of *A. spatulatus* hover well above the tufts or eight-inch wide cushions of slightly hoary, sharp-tipped leaves. Banner petals disclose varying markings; wings are conspicuously tipped white. At a short distance, with side or back lighting, all blend into a solid rich tone of purple. The natural range of *A. spatulatus* on the Plains includes the Cypress Hills and some beyond in Alberta and Saskatchewan, western Nebraska, and northern Colorado, and it extends well into the Rockies, especially of Colorado and Wyoming. In the garden this gem is long-lived in a scree of almost any mixture containing limestone and a little humus.

From a stout taproot *Astragalus adsurgens (A. striatus)* forms, in full development, a cushion of numerous stems and foliage 20 or more inches wide and six or eight inches tall, and is covered in July with short, wide, upturned heads. A fine show can be seen when one happens upon a hillside sheeted with its light pinkish or bluish purple flowers. In the garden one might wish for greater definition in color. The species is frequent from Nebraska northward.

*Astragalus tenellus*, with an abundance of straw-yellow in a bouquet, and *A. vexilliflexus*, in a 10- to 15-inch, low cushion of plentiful spikes of very dark purple, do not make good garden subjects because their color is of inferior quality.

## *Atriplex*. Saltbush

A prominent shrub in olive-gray on alkaline soils from Wyoming and South Dakota southward on the Plains, as well as westward, *Atriplex canescens* maintains a well-dressed appearance throughout the growing season. It branches widely from the ground and above, clothed densely in oblanceolate leaves as much as two inches long, and conveys a desert atmosphere. Short terminal spikes of flowers and conspicuous four-winged seed pods appear, with slight variation in coloring from the leafage. In late fall the foliage is ripened to a dull light brown, and much of it is retained while small new leaves are put out along the twigs to carry the olive-green note throughout the winter and to renew general leafiness very early in the spring. The result is far from evergreenness, yet a bare-stem effect is avoided. In the wild the plants, not usually over two feet high, are much eaten down by rabbits and other wildlife for their salt content.

## *Bahia (Picradeniopsis)*. Bahia

*Bahia oppositifolia* is an energetic, small composite related to the eriophyllums of the farther West and, like them, is a harmony of gray-green and brilliant yellow. The members of a colony are of uniform height, four to eight inches. From June to September, this bahia is often seen in spreading masses along shoulders of roads—one of the few colonizers that venture right up to the wheel tracks or to pavement. A single flower-head has a relatively wide disc and short, wide rays; but there are too few rays to compose a pleasing rounded, daisy-like flower, and so one must depend on mass for effect. Although roots and stolons are hair-thin and seemingly fragile, bahia is to be taken into the garden with caution because it may become weedy. Its range is from Canada to Arizona.

## *Balsamorrhiza*. Balsamroot      plate 25

*Balsamorrhiza sagittata* advances far on the Plains from the Rockies in Montana and Alberta, but its separate occurrence in the Black Hills marks an interruption of the immigration route of earlier days, because of the present dryness of the Wyoming Plains. It is possible that for the same reason the northern extensions are receding.

Radiating from the crown of the plant are bold, silvery gray leaves that are partly folded, sagittate, and as much as eight inches long; above, on upright stems at 12 inches or so, a few to many somewhat stylized sunflowers of vibrant yellow are posed. Their rich color contrasts, yet harmonizes with the deep velvety blue of *Delphinium bicolor*, where they flower together in June. Quite small plants are successfully transplanted. Perhaps in most gardens, they should be given half-shade.

## *Baptisia*. Wild indigo, baptisia

The baptisias occur in the extreme South and Southeast. Just one, *Baptisia vespertina (B. australis,B. minor)*, has become adapted to the Plains climate. It ranges across western Oklahoma and into the high, sandy portion of the Texas Panhandle, and into a few counties west of the somewhat vague Plains border in Kansas. This is a plant of distinctive appearance, about 20 inches tall, with sparse, trifoliate leafage and upright racemes of pea-blossoms of a striking indigo-blue. Remarkable, too, are the wide and short pods which blacken on drying and become, with their loose seeds, good rattle-pods. The coarse and deep root, said to reach six feet, indicates a permeable soil, such as sand, a rainfall sufficient to penetrate to that depth, and equally good drainage. The species is grown with some success in the North. *Baptisia leucophaea*, cream-colored, and *B. leucantha*, white, of similar habit to *B. vespertina*, extend a little way into the drier portion of Kansas.

## Cacti    plates 26-36

The various cacti provide some of the major floral spectacles of the Plains region. Especially notable are the tree cactus, *Opuntia imbricata*, and the prickly pears, *Opuntia*. Many others, observed at close range, charm with their novel forms and sparkling colors.

A score of cactus species have discovered a land to their liking in the wide open reaches of the Great Plains. Here they find excellent drainage and abundant sunlight, and some plants come upon an uncluttered freeway to expansion northward. From the beginning of the course, doubtless, it has been through the eternal quest for territory and adaptation that they have acquired the essential mechanisms of hardiness. A half-dozen kinds endure the worst of the cold of Wyoming and South Dakota, the extremes of summer heat, the interminable droughts, and, on occasion, periods of soaking wet as well. Montana and North Dakota each know four kinds, and in Alberta and Saskatchewan three species are very much at home. The little hitchhiker, *Opuntia fragilis*, has gone to the end of the course and flaunted its flower by the Peace River in far northern British Columbia, as photographed by Mrs. J. Norman Henry.

Hardiness in the Plains species, and in others accustomed to high elevations and cold situations, depends largely on the equipment of adjustable pores in the epidermis which close for moisture retention and open in the short days of fall to expend moisture from the tissues to avoid rupture by freezing. This latter process results in great shriveling and wrinkling, the marks of safe wintering facility.

In the garden an exposed and sunny, well-drained position is preferred; if possible, drifted snow and drip from trees and roofs should be avoided. When rainfall is heavy, extra drainage is required, even to the extent of nine parts of sand and bank gravel to one of rich loam. Some lime is needed, and some of the smaller cacti may relish added richness. A favored soil mixture consists of two parts fine sand,

and one each of good loam, limestone chip, and peat moss. The plants prefer the drying care of open sun through the winter.

The technical names employed in the following descriptions conform to common usage. I am awaiting confirmation or correction to agree with Dr. Lyman Benson's *The Cacti of the United States and Canada*, soon to be published.

One of the most widely distributed of the Great Plains cacti and one of the most admired is *Coryphantha (Mammillaria) vivipara*. It is a somewhat elongated ball, covered with spirally arranged mammillae, or teatlike processes, which are armed at the apex with clusters of short and sharp spines, brownish tipped on the newer growth. From the bases of upper mamillae come from one to a full circle of radiant flowers in June. Flowers grow to two inches and have many narrow, sharp-tipped petals, sometimes pale but more often a deep carmine pink, and rich yellow centers. The smooth fruits ripen at the end of summer. They are green with dull purplish tints, and are filled with a tasty, sweet pulp and countless tiny, reddish brown seeds. Some plants of *C. vivipara* remain single-stemmed indefinitely; others "give birth" to new ones from basal mammillae and, after several years, may form mounds of closely crowded stems. This faculty of "live reproduction" may depend on location, food supply, or other factors. One of my plants was brought from a gravelly pasture knoll as a cluster of three; it is now a mound of 17, most of them two inches wide or less. Occasional individuals measure four inches or more. Especially on loamy and sandy soils and on humus-filled rocky knolls, *Coryphantha vivipara* ranges the High Plains from Texas and New Mexico into the drier southern portions of Alberta and Saskatchewan and includes portions of North Dakota and Manitoba east of the lower Plains levels.

In southwestern Oklahoma are two areas of low granite mountains. The more extensive Wichita Mountains rise above 2,000 feet; the Quartz Mountains, some 70 miles to the west, are lower. These related areas seemingly embrace the range of *Echinocereus baileyi*, which locally is extremely plentiful. It flourishes in granite sand and the humus contributed by a thick, coarse moss, its chief associate. Both are benefited by the runoff from bare exposures of the rock. Seedlings find the environment to their liking, thriving either in the moss or in sandy crevices. *E. baileyi* is a barrel five or more inches high, with a lacework of short spines from areoles closely set along the many low ribs. The glossy spines vary remarkably from plant to plant through shades of brown, notably a pinkish brown. The flowers, borne freely in June, are short trumpet-shaped and purplish pink. The species branches moderately at or near the base.

A similar small barrel, type, *Echinocereus reichenbachii*, branches somewhat from near the base. Its very short, light-colored spines spread sideways from the closely set areoles to accent the rib pattern. The flowers, two or more inches wide, range from pink to red-purple. It is common in scattered localities from Texas through western Oklahoma to the bluffs of the Arkansas River in Colorado. It flowers and ripens seed regularly in my garden in South Dakota.

Even though ribs and spines are prominent in *Echinocereus trig-lochidiatus*, the interminable specific name refers to the microscopic stickers about the base of the spine clusters, seldom explained in descriptions. The type variety, or subspecies, has strong spines and about nine wide ribs; variants have more ribs and more numerous and lighter spines. There is even a spineless form. All bear cup-shaped flowers in abundance, an inch or more wide, from light to intense scarlet, and, in contrast to the ephemeral life of many cactus blossoms, remain open for three days. The species ranges chiefly through the mountains of the southwestern half of Colorado, briefly on to the Plains, and to New Mexico and western Texas. The form I have from the southern Plains extension has more ribs and many more spines than the type. Individual stems are only a few inches high; the faculty of proliferating into mounds probably is inherent throughout the several varieties. King's-crown, hedgehog, and claret-cup are popular names for this cactus.

Many narrow ribs and short spines mark *Echinocereus viridiflorus*, a near ball or squat barrel, at its best lengthening to four inches. Surrounding bands of varicolored spines on the newer growth are an attractive feature. The inch-wide flowers are freely borne, high or low, on the ribs in late May. The color of the flowers is an unimpressive yellow-green if the season is warm and dry, but in a cool, wet period it is a clear, pale, and luminous traffic-signal green, startling at first acquaintance. *E. viridiflorus* occasionally multiplies into clusters. It belongs mainly to the Plains from western Texas and eastern New Mexico to South Dakota and into the Black Hills.

As far as can be learned, no trick of wintering in climates where frost strikes deep or remains for long periods can accommodate

*Homalocephala (Echinocactus) texensis*, the devil's head or horse crippler, though in portions of its native range temperatures briefly drop to below zero. A veritable show piece, nearly a foot wide and commonly no more than half as high, *H. texensis* has pink trumpet-shaped flowers and brilliant cherry-red spine-free fruits. It is coveted by every admirer of novel form. From western Texas and southeastern New Mexico, this cactus extends into southwestern Oklahoma and northward across the High Plains of the Texas Panhandle into the drainage of the Canadian River—and thereby breaks the rule of complete hardiness for denizens of the Great Plains. Wherein lies its fault? Specimens of *Coryphantha vivipara*, dug from within a colony of *H. texensis*, are weather-proof here.

The handsome ribs of the devil's head widen from center toward perimeter. At moderate intervals they are set with strong, thick, and curved spines which, supported by a firm interior structure, can penetrate the underside of a horse's foot or puncture any ordinary car tire. This firm and tough inner part shrivels in drought but is not proof against deep cold, and repeated trials in my South Dakota garden have failed in the first or second winter. The degree of cold adaptation of *Homalocephala* is unknown. It is reported to have grown and flowered for as long as four years in Denver.

The small, mammillaria type *Neobesseya missouriensis* prepares for extremes of winter, into Montana and North Dakota, by reducing its volume by half and withdrawing to ground level. With the warmth of spring it quickly becomes turgid and by late May bears a ring of light straw or orange-tinted blossoms about its center. Its near-white spines are soft and readily handled. This kind occasionally attains a diameter of two and a half inches. It sometimes forms clusters. The flowers arise from the bases of the teatlike extensions, and the small, round, green fruits form in summer to ripen in April of the following year in a charming display of crimson or bright scarlet. These catch the eye of northward migrating birds and soon disappear, but somehow the species has failed to spread into Canada. Southwardly it ranges to northern Texas.

*Pediocactus simpsonii* is a somewhat flattened ball, with a veritable network of short, sharp spines which fairly obscures the spirally arranged, low tubercles. Even when quite small, it produces flowers in the early days of May in a compact corona of shining light pink. In time the stems may reach a diameter of four inches or more, the common dimension being less than three inches. Clusters are occasionally formed. The spine color, usually gray to reddish brown, approaches black in some individuals. Some specimens have white spines and these are called "snowballs." For the cold season the species shrinks remarkably; with spring warmth and moisture it quickly doubles in volume and very early presents its bright pink flower buds.

The *Pediocactus simpsonii* of the Plains is the variety sometimes designated as *P. simpsonii* v. *minor*, which in the mountains climbs above 8,000 feet in Wyoming and Colorado and reaches to New Mexico. It is reported to have been found formerly to the east and to the north of Denver. At Laramie it is at home on land adjoining the University campus. Eastward from the Laramie Hills it continues on the Plains to the vicinity of Cheyenne and for some miles northward—this represents a northern range extension. (Records of *P. simpsonii* for the State of Washington refer to the heavier-spined varieties, *robustior*, which grows into a 10-inch cylinder, and *nigrispinus*, a ball type, whose coarse, dark spines become black with age. Their flowers are a deeper pink than those of *P. simpsonii* v. *minor*.)

In older manuals the name *Opuntia compressa*, properly an eastern species, was applied as the specific for a number of western, yellow-flowered prickly pears which were given varietal ratings such as *macrorhiza* with plump, short tubers; *tortispina* with long, twisted spines; and even *humifusa*. All these western plants have much thicker joints, heavier spining, and different flower characters than the eastern species has. The western prickly pears are now generally accorded specific status.

Jointed and cylindrical-stemmed, closely and diversely branching, *Opuntia davisii* is spectacular in its many long, amber, light-reflecting spines. Its distribution is localized, ranging from southeastern New Mexico into western Texas and up into the Panhandle and southwestern Oklahoma. But the species has proved adequately hardy for southern South Dakota. Its showy spine effect is attained as a plant reaches maturity. From closely set areoles the spines extend in every direction, and, fairly hiding the green of the stems, they contribute character and beauty. The deep green flowers, two inches wide, come later than those of many other species. *O. davisii* produces some slender tubers to a depth of several inches, a characteristic to be considered when transplanting.

From a Colorado cactus club member came my largest, widely ovoid, flat-bladed prickly pear, *Opuntia engelmannii*. The length of the joint is up to nine inches. A plant that goes by the same name and that covers wide reaches of the High Plains of the Texas Panhandle has a blade two-thirds this scale. I have been unable to distinguish between the medium-size yellow flowers of the two, the spine patterns likewise, but the areoles are less widely spaced in the smaller type. Throughout its history *O. engelmannii* has worn many names. It is, indeed, a species that the taxonomists have difficulty in determining, possibly because large populations have had hybrid origins. My larger type plant often suffers winter burn, but flowers freely. The large, pear-shaped ripe fruits are a lustrous carmine-maroon.

With a penchant for traveling, the diminutive member of the Plains prickly pears, *Opuntia fragilis*, has equipped itself with sharp and pronged spines which so effectively hook onto the hide of animals, or to the dry and tough leather of footwear, as to detach the end joint from the older stem. Thus it hitches a ride of indefinite length and surely by this means has enlarged its territory. Beyond its well-stocked supply base on the central Plains, it reaches Texas and all northern Plains states and provinces; eastward it ranges to Wisconsin and Manitoba; and westward it has added much ground from Arizona to northern British Columbia.

In relation to the scale of the stems, the flowers of *Opuntia fragilis* are enormous, two or more inches wide, with a strong yellow tone. For the dormant period the joints shrivel remarkably. When turgid in growth, the joints vary from half-inch globes to elongate-terete or obovate and flattened; an inch and a half describes the length of practically all. Larger-jointed specimens may be suspected of being hybrids, locally either with *O. humifusa* or with *O. polyacantha*, and some interesting forms are found. They are often free-flowering and regularly retain the dry-ripening, small, prickly fruits of *O. fragilis*.

The largest of the three prickly pears of South Dakota and Nebraska and most of prairie Wyoming is *Opuntia humifusa*. While not reaching farther north, it extends to Oklahoma and Texas. The blades are rather thick, the areoles rather widely spaced, and the prominent spines cover most of the blade, or, in some strains, are much reduced or absent below. The abundant, often crowded flowers are large, brilliant yellow, silken-textured; the perianth orange, tinted or crimson toward the base, with correspondingly colored filaments; the anthers golden; and the stigma knob yellow-green. The flowering season is June. The pears are deep red when ripe in late summer and are pleasant to eat, provided the few clusters of tiny stickers are removed.

Hardy and substantial, a spectacle in the wild and in any garden, *Opuntia imbricata* is treelike or bushy, with dark green, roughly cylindrical stems and barbed spines which should be avoided. Not often does it exceed five feet, but it may reach 10 feet. Its carmine-red flowers are profusely borne, after the plant has reached two feet high or so; and when the short and wide, tubercular fruits are well ripened, they provide late-season ornament in light yellow. *Opuntia imbricata* is native on the Plains from the latitude of Pikes Peak southward through the western portions of Oklahoma and Texas, and into New Mexico, Arizona, and Sonora. In a Dakota garden a large specimen has endured cold to −27° F. This cactus has a definitely woody framework. With the death and decay of the outer tissues, the inner structure with its handsome network pattern, resists weathering for many years. It has been used for walking sticks and to make furniture.

*Opuntia leptocaulis* is a very slender-stemmed cholla, at home in southwestern Oklahoma, the Palo Duro Canyon country of the Texas High Plains, minor lowlands cutting into the High Plains, and in regions farther west. This rather weak-structured plant branches to form a wide bush, 30 inches or so high in open areas. In light shade, to which it is agreeable, it clambers for support on a low-branched tree or shrub and may reach five feet, while remaining typically slender. Numerous small, greenish yellow flowers line the upper stems early in the season; for the balance of the year very small pears, of the same dark green color as the stems, remain inconspicuous. The second season the fruits double in size, take on a beautiful crimson hue, and require the rest of the year to mature seeds. The decorative display has prompted the local name of "Christmas cactus." A well-branched plant that had grown 10 inches tall in my lath house was badly broken during a late snowfall. Many short twigs lay neglected upon the ground and by fall had taken root. Some are being wintered indoors until large enough to be experimented with. Might *O. leptocaulis* succeed in the North with proper shelter?

A collector of rare cacti in California sent me more than a score of strains of *Opuntia phaeacantha*, of scattered origins, for hardiness tests. These had many characteristics in common: the areoles were more widely spaced than in the more common prickly pears of the

Plains, the spines rather longer and most prominent upward, the blades somewhat larger, most of the flowers a lively deep yellow. I found that five of the lot were well suited to this environment, among the yellows a selection from Oklahoma, one from Colorado, and one reportedly from southern Wyoming. The species reaches into Kansas, but its principal range and greatest frequency are in Arizona and neighboring states. Among my real treasures are an *O. phaeacantha* flowering in pink-scarlet and one in soft crimson. The pears of all are large and edible, with a fascinating gloss and a color best described as maroon-carmine. These data refer to the better-known variety *major*.

The typical variety, *Opuntia phaeacantha* v. *phaeacantha*, is apparently much rarer. Its spines are well distributed over the joints and its most conspicuous feature is the brushlike glochid cluster, huge and light tan, at their danger-warning best on the marginal areoles. I had climbed the high volcanic Carrizo Mesa, on the flat plains of southwestern Colorado, "to see the country." Excited by the discovery of this "new" cactus, but armed with only a pocket knife, I took a small joint and rigged a sling of tall grass blades to carry it down to the car. It has increased to a dozen joints. The flower is yellow. The identification was obligingly made by Dr. Lyman Benson.

Among prickly pears on the northern Plains *Opuntia polyacantha* is always distinguished by its closely set areoles and spine clusters well distributed over the blade—certainly not by any uniformity within any population! Observe any hundred plants in close association or scattered: it will be unusual to find any two that are closely alike in size of joint, in spine length, and in color of the corollas. Spines vary from a half inch to two inches, their color from white to dark brown, through neutral tints, clear amber, yellow-brown, and rich glossy auburn; all spines turn gray within a year. Flower color is not coordinated with spine color. But whether they are large and brilliant or small and of indifferent color, the flowers always attract by their silken or crystalline texture. One may have to survey thousands of plants in their Maytime bloom over some miles of pasture lands to find outstanding pure yellows, strong yellows with crimson base and filaments, the rarer light yellow with greenish cast, or a lone one with a definite orange tone. Hardly to be found beyond the confines of Colorado, a flamboyant, all-carmine flower becomes common between the foot of the mountains and the Kansas line. In a field of such flowers it is a difficult task to pick the one with the most beautiful color.

*Opuntia polyacantha* ripens its green prickly fruits, tightly packed with large seeds, to dry straw-color in late summer. The species covers all the Plains states and the drier portions of Alberta and Saskatchewan, reaches sparingly into Manitoba, Minnesota, and Wisconsin, and also occurs farther west.

## *Callirhoë.* Poppy mallow, wine cups, buffalo poppy     plate 37

*Callirhoë involucrata*, whether wild or cultivated, is one of the most faithful in the production of rich color; its season continues unbroken from spring to fall when moisture is favorable. Its five, inch-long petals of glossy wine-crimson, which are centered by a stamen and stigma column of light yellow, are disposed as a flaring cup and effectively displayed well above the lengthy, procumbent stems and the masses of digitate leaves. If permitted to colonize by seed, small to huge parsniplike roots are established here and there, and their long stems crisscross, unrestrained, with their neighbors to thicken the ground cover and concentrate the broadside flower effect. In suitable sandy soils, the poppy-mallow sometimes paints acres with gorgeous color. Nature readily disposes of the deciduous stems and foliage, and the winter phase is, at best, a small rosette of green readying for another springtime. Doubtless every county in the western two-thirds of Kansas harbors *C. involucrata*, and it moves in full panoply northeastward to the Platte River in Nebraska, and more sparingly into South Dakota; in the opposite direction, to Oklahoma, Colorado, Texas, and New Mexico.

## *Calochortus.* Mariposa tulip, scgo lily, calochortus     plates 38, 39

*Calochortus gunnisonii*, sometimes known as Rocky Mountain mari-posa, and *C. nuttallii*, sego lily or mariposa tulip, are closely associated in their ranges on the Great Plains. They grow side by side in the Pine Ridge country of Nebraska and Wyoming and in grasslands of eastern Montana, with *C. nuttallii* preferring the higher, drier ground. In the Black Hills the species segregate, *C. gunnisonii* occupying the higher elevations, except where it comes into the foothills at the northeast. *C. nuttallii* surrounds the other, then advances eastward for 100 miles along the White River drainage and northeastward for 60 miles to the Slim Butte country. In North Dakota, *C. nuttallii* covers buttes and badland ridges in the extreme west; there, as everywhere, it selects slopes where the winds pile deep snow, an environment that provides extra moisture during the growing season and sufficient dryness during the long months of dormancy.

One who has not seen the beauty of these delicate flowers cannot picture it. Like most of the other mariposas of farther west, *C. gunnisonii* and *C. nuttallii* have three petal segments, deeply cupped, then gracefully reflexed to form a wide, flaring rim on the completely rounded chalice. The three narrow, lanceolate sepal segments, of glowing white, fill in between the petal claws. *C. gunnisonii* has a flush of blue-lavender on the exterior and a prominent crescent of greenish hairs across the lower part of the petals within. *C. nuttallii* also has some tinting on the reverse, and a yellow base within and a showy brownish maroon crescent. The blossoms, with a spread of two to three inches, are borne on stiff stems above a few grassy leaves; flowers of *C. nuttallii* grow about 10 inches high and bloom in early June, those of *C. gunnisonii* are taller and usually appear three weeks later.

Although these bulbs have been flowered all across the United States to Washington, D.C., and in England and elsewhere, they are not easy to manage away from their native climes. Their inveterate enemy is wetness during dormancy or excessive wetness at any season. Every measure favoring dryness must be taken: a relatively humusless soil, with a close-textured soil, not sandy; drainage above and below; enough sun for quick drying; and excellent air circulation. Even then, failure may result from days of continuous rain. Perhaps the most effective safeguard is a stratum of several inches of gravel, no more than three inches below the bulb. The bulb should be planted about four inches deep. Tales of impermanence or irregular flowering reflect lack of knowledge of the performance of these plants in the right environment. At Prairie Gem, bulbs of *C. nuttallii*, grown from seed, have maintained themselves for more than 30 years and flower regularly. Similar performance is attested by growers with other species in other climes. *C. gunnisonii* persists in this dry prairie garden in conditions of half-shade and delayed evaporation provided by the lath house, while *C. nuttallii* accepts either half-shade or full sun.

## *Campanula*. Harebell, campanula

Harebell? Bluebell? In the melting pot of the Great Plains, few are aware that a choice of names stirs mild jealousy among those of English and Scottish descent. "Harebell" is the more precise name, for many different kinds of flowers have been called "bluebell," and it at once relates our lone Plains campanula to a particular type in its genus. As a technical name, *C. petiolata* serves to distinguish our type from the numerous and varying forms gathered under the name *C. rotundifolia*.

This name, *C. petiolata*, continues the usage of respected horticulturists of other days, including Mrs. G. R. Marriage of Colorado Springs and D. M. Andrews of Boulder. Our harebell is large and floriferous. The foliage is firm, reflecting the drier habitat; rotund basal leaves are often lacking, upper leaves reduced. The flowers average larger and longer; their color is purple, not often lighter. With great rarity a near-white one is found, accented by a pink-lavender stigma knob. The true albino, even more rare, has a creamy stigma. *C. petiolata* is rhizomatous, in sun strongly so. Full flowering comes in June, and with good moisture a scattering of bells is borne throughout the summer. As a Plains denizen, *C. petiolata* occurs in wooded portions of western Nebraska, then becomes increasingly frequent northward.

## *Castilleja*. Indian paintbrush, castilleja     plate 40

Indian paintbrushes are doubtless destined to be admired at a distance, however frequently some covetous garden maker is impelled to challenge their hardly debatable characteristics of parasitism and "stand-offishness." The Cypress Hills and other favored places, as far as the central Canadian Plains, locally provide forests where the gaudy *Castilleja miniata* and *C. rhexifolia* are at home. The paint-dipped bracts, leaflike parts carrying the color and almost hiding the small, true flowers, are scarlet or brick red in *C. miniata* and crimson, scarlet or rose in *C. rhexifolia*. The latter species also hides in Spearfish Canyon and other deep gulches in the northern Black Hills. Mrs. Floyd Brown of the Homestead Mine town of Lead, South Dakota, whose garden could provide a suitable haven for almost any desired plant, reported that she had repeatedly tried to grow *C. rhexifolia* without success. But why—if gardeners really desire to possess the paintbrushes—should not one of them, or a phalanx, in the light of the miracles being performed daily in chemistry, investigate the magic-sustaining forces of the castillejas and concoct a synthetic "pill" to induce these brightly pigmented tribesmen to adapt to civilization? Or must gardeners always be hit-or-miss to be happy?

Compared with the brilliance of almost any other paint brush, the anemic pallor of **Castilleja sulphurea**, which occurs in many localities in the Black Hills, is a subject for commiseration. *C. sessiliflora*, often growing on dry, open hills from Texas northward into the southern portions of Canada, departs radically from the normal paint brush manner. Several hairy stems, ascending rather than erect, produce green or yellowish or pinkish bracts and prominently exserted two-lipped flowers. Usually pale, they often carry a flush of pink or salmon to hint that one with good pink coloring may occur somewhere. In mid-June I found one such specimen among many paler-flowered plants far out in Montana—too far to return for seed. There is evidence that this species is less dependent than others on host plants. A plant brought to my garden with undisturbed roots lived for a couple of years and flowered; some years later a seedling appeared and lived for a year or two.

*Castilleja integra*: In eastcentral Colorado, to the northeast of Colorado Springs, lies a prominent high area. It is 60 miles across, and at an elevation of 6,000 feet to well above that. Its formation is typical Great Plains outwash from the mountains, including Pikes Peak. From opposite the United States Air Academy it stretches eastward, then southward in upside-down "L" shape; this Black Forest of ponderosa pine is bordered and penetrated here and there by grassland. From this high habitat Mrs. G. R. Marriage once sent me a special deep-colored **Phlox longifolia. Geranium fremontii (caespitosum)**, a clear pink, is frequent here, along with more distinctively prairie kinds, such as azure **Penstemon angustifolius, Opuntia polyacantha** in a carmine-flowered form, and **Echinocereus viridiflorus** with color-banded spines.

Seeking the latter cactus on a thinly grassed slope, I came upon some short, dry stalks with seed pods resembling penstemon capsules. The plants showed no life, nor were green plants found which might have borne such fruits. Within the hour, however, my companion and I visited a friend's garden in a sunny spot in the forest, where many of the native plants are valued. Here a lone, low plant flashed clusters of softly glowing crimson, and some of its stems bore ripe capsules duplicating those I had so lately failed to recognize in the pasture. This showy Indian paint brush, to all effects comfortably at home, had been brought to the garden in a large spadeful of earth.

*Castilleja integra*'s specific name refers to its mostly entire leaves, narrow and of moderate length. Leaves, stems, and paint brush bracts are invested with a soft hairiness, or tomentum, varying to intensify the color impact of the wide brushes, which reportedly range to rose, or pink, or even orange-yellow. The real flowers, kept safely hidden by these dazzling bracts, are insignificant, small, and green. The species grows a foot or so high. It is found in southern Colorado, New Mexico, Arizona and Mexico, in dry plains and tablelands.

## *Cerastium*. Mouse-ear chickweed

Perhaps *Cerastium arvense* (*C. strictum* and others) should be regarded with suspicion for the common name suggests bad companions, not only animals but also plants of ill repute. However, *C. arvense*, increasingly frequent northward from the Pine Ridge country of northwestern Nebraska and adjacent Wyoming into Canada, has valuable attributes for the garden. A strain selected from a sunny Wyoming slope for its half-inch-wide, white flowers of especially pleasing petal notching forms a dense creeping mat, hardly more than an inch above the ground, of tiny oblong to oblanceolate leaves. The great show of blooms on erect stems four to five inches tall comes mostly in June. This differs from what is generally known as *C. arvense* in that it has glandular-viscid stems and foliage with no hint of grayness. The name *C. arvense* is now considered to cover several variants which have at times been given specific names. C. W. Wood remarked of the local form, "*Cerastium strictum* makes a pretty green carpet for a difficult shady spot." But Louise Beebe Wilder warned strongly against letting *C. arvense* into the rock garden. If your plant find pleases you, you may want to take the risk and try growing *C. arvense* in your garden.

## *Cercocarpus*. Mountain mahogany

With numerous slender, upright to arching stems from the ground, *Cercocarpus montanus* bears small, faintly grayish leaves and greenish, petal-less flowers. It remains an unobtrusive but pleasant novelty until fall, when its plentiful seed plumes draw attention. The long glossy plumes, which are spiraled, feathery, and light-reflecting, become more conspicuous as the leaves are shed in late fall, and at length serve as whirling parachutes to disperse the heavy seeds to no great distance, the shrub's only attempt at propagation. Where *C. montanus* forms a chapparal, as on lower slopes of the Black Hills, it grows four to six feet. In favored places it may reach eight feet. It is long-lived and drought-resistant. The mountain mahogany occurs also along river bluffs in northwestern Kansas and commonly on the lower slopes of the mountains from Montana to New Mexico and as far west as Utah.

## *Chrysanthemum*. Field daisy, ox-eye daisy

The beautiful white-rayed, gold-centered ox-eye daisy, which stars the environs of the golf course south of Lead, in the Black Hills, is unquestionably a lovely ornament. Visitors ask, "Isn't that the same daisy that grows—well, everywhere?" The excuse for mentioning **Chrysanthemum leucanthemum** here is to bow to a long admired and beloved friend. The story goes that an elderly Englishman, marooned in the Hills in the goldrush days, scattered the seed to relieve some of the rawness of the wilderness. Naturally, the daisy has spread; but because the climate of the Plains is dry, the daisy is not a weed there. Of course, I brought it to my garden. In much shade and with some extra moisture from the eaves of the house, it thrives and necessitates only a little extra weeding.

## *Chrysopsis*. Golden aster, chrysopsis

Handsome or plain, admirable or weedy in appearance, these plants occupy the Plains, especially in sandy areas, from New Mexico and Texas to Saskatchewan and Alberta. They can be recognized by their moderate height, usually 12 inches or less, often pressed down by the weight of bloom, and by their grayish green, hairy stems and leaves. Many forms have been named and gathered under the specific **Chrysopsis villosa**, a generalization with which the gardener need not differ, for their value is in their masses of softly glowing gold, principally in September. Most agreeable in appearance is the typical form with soft, silky leaves that are oblanceolate to obovate. This form, too, spreads nicely for flower display.

**Chrysopsis hispida** grows on rocky ridges around Dinosaur Park at Rapid City, South Dakota. Its stiff stems are covered with bristly hairs. Although the flowers are as brilliant as those of *C. villosa*, the heads are more open. The name is rather generally accepted for this outstanding type. Years ago, I received a plant of *C. stenophylla* from the South. It remained few-stemmed, carried the expected very narrow leaves, flowered with a poor furnishing of spindly rays, and was discarded. But when at last I visited Oklahoma in July, the flowering period of *C. stenophylla*, I found most plants of this name with rays as wide and beautiful as any. To have the best, one must select from the best source.

The compact spatterings of golden-aster, seen in September along roadside shoulders that have been mowed, give us a hint for keeping the plants at a low stature: head them low in early August. Propagation is by seed, and the plants should be moved before taproots become stiff and woody.

A new name involving *Chrysopsis* has appeared and seems to be gaining some currency on a "fide" (believe it or not) basis: *Heterotheca*. Vote No!

## *Chrysothamnus*. Rabbit brush, chrysothamnus     plate 41

A very large group of autumn-flowering shrubs of the Great Plains and farther west, *Chrysothamnus* belongs to the Composite family. The species and varieties attain distinction by their magnificent production of wide, terminal, and massed inflorescences of golden yellow. The closely clustered flower heads, composed only of disk flowers, provide a textured richness unequaled at their season. This flower display is supported by gray to whitish stems thickly foliaged in gray-green. Wind-borne plumed seeds are the rabbit brushes' only means of spreading. Sometimes abundant in a given area, the colonies often show definite limits, determined perhaps by aggressive competitors. Although roadside or pasture colonies may be large, miles may intervene before the readily recognized gray and gold are seen again.

It is easy to distinguish a chrysothamnus, but to apply a definite specific or varietal name is troublesome because there are many similar species and varieties within the genus. Some 40 species were once described; recent systematists have grouped closely related forms into "twelve clearly defined species," a valuable simplification in which it is still convenient to designate numerous subspecies or varieties.

For the gardener, criteria other than botanical relationship may well apply. Some precocious species begin heavy flowering at six to eight inches, then take a number of years to attain their maximum of 30 inches or less; the taller kind flowers from a foot upward. The gardener's choice will depend on available space or desired effect.

Small plants of all the Plains rabbit brushes are readily transplanted. They will doubtless thrive wherever moisture is not excessive, and their chief practical use is to beautify the landscape or the garden. They are little browsed by wild or domestic animals; jackrabbits make use of them for shelter from weather and winged enemies.

A well-worn name, *Chrysothamnus nauseosus*, is now applied to most variants of the Great Plains. The species is subdivided into three groups, *C. nauseosus* v. *nauseosus, C. nauseosus* v. *albicaulis*, and *C. nauseosus* v. *glabratus*. These varieties all have dark to light gray bark on the older wood, pale green to white bark on the new growth, whether glabrous or tomentose at the start, and have narrow, plentiful leaves that are green or more or less grayish. All the better strains produce astonishing masses of late-season golden blooms. They differ in growth habit, in maximum height, and in native range. Together they are found from the southern and southwestern portions of the Canadian Plains to northern Texas and New Mexico.

The gem of the tribe is surely *Chrysothamnus nauseosus* v. *nauseosus*. This is described in the manuals as not reaching above 24 inches. Only a few years in my garden, it has not yet exceeded 12 inches, and its wide clusters of bloom often outweigh the strength of its many slender whitish stems. Possibly on a par is the lovely low form of *C. nauseosus* v. *albicaulis*, formerly called *C. baileyi* or *C. pulchellus*. In southwestern Kansas and southeastern Colorado where it occurs in great colonies over many miles, I have not seen it much taller than two feet, and young plants begin their careers of bountiful bloom at six to eight inches. One must beware of forms that have been known by other specific names, such as *C. plattensis*, and that are now classified under the heading *C. nauseosus* v. *nauseosus*, whose narrow and pale blossom clusters do not conform to the high standards of its associates.

The name *Chrysothamnus albicaulis* has been applied since early in the century to taller rabbit brushes of certain type. Now as *C. nauseosus* v. *albicaulis*, the former *C. speciosus* and *C. pulcherrimus*, noted for their spectacular flowering and others, low or tall, have been added. Their combined ranges extend almost throughout the Great Plains and into Arizona, Mexico, California, and to British Columbia. In a Colorado garden where I firest recognized *C. albicaulis*, in several mature specimens to 45 inches tall, each shrub had a sturdy, branched framework two-thirds of the way up, then intricate fine branching to build a smooth dome of its golden wealth in a spread equal to the height, a naturally neat and impressive result. Other lower forms of *C.*

*nauseosus* in several varieties construct a wide framework of finer branches from near the ground, then send up numerous slender branches to form the compact florescent cover.

*Chrysothamnus nauseosus* v. *glabratus* includes the familiar *C. graveolens* and some less prominent names. It is the most frequent on the northern Plains and reaches west beyond the Rockies. Although greener than some strains, the variety exhibits a fine white feltiness on new twigs and leaves, which lends a gray effect that does not quite depart with maturity. Two habit types are common. In broken ground or sheltered places, or even in seepy ground with good drainage, the larger type often attains five feet or more; whereas in some large colonies in open valley flats, observed over many years, a height of two feet to 30 inches marks the maximum. These *C. nauseosus* v. *glabratus* forms branch to display their brilliancy at lower levels as well as in less formal upward concentrations.

A different group, *Chrysothamus viscidiflorus*, is known as the green rabbit brushes. There are some seven varieties or subspecies. *C. viscidiflorus* v. *lanceolatus* inhabits much of Montana and Wyoming; other varieties are more western. My plants, which were collected when quite small, have branched widely from ground level and flowered at eight inches, then at 12. The leaves are dark green, narrowly lance-olate, to two inches long, distinctly twisted, and plentiful, hiding the stems. The heavy terminal flower clusters, patterned like the best in *C. nauseosus*, are somewhat muted by a tinge of bronze. This variety is said to reach 20 inches, seldom more.

## *Cirsium*. Thistle

Anyone who admires the wide, symmetrical, light rose-purple heads of thistles can well attempt to grow *Cirsium undulatum*, which ranges over the length of the Plains. It is a low plant, commonly under 20 inches, and its flower is one of the more beautiful wild flowers. Flower heads are large, ranging from two and a half to three inches across. Foliage and stem are a harmonious gray-green. Leaves have clasic un-dulant margins; and all leaf extremities, stems, and involucres are well armed with stiff and sharp spines. When handling the mature plant, tongs or heavy gloves are required. In my garden it has proved reliably perennial. With its free but not troublesome stolonizing, new rosettes appear here and there each year, though the original rosette dies after it has produced one to several fine flowers.

## *Claytonia*. Springbeauty

To quote Arch C. Budd: "Our earliest flowers are always *Claytonia lanceolata (C. rosea)* from the Cypress Hills, where it is found flowering in large patches shortly after snow melts in spring." It is also common along the margin of the Alberta prairies and between grassland and wooded areas in the foothills of the Rockies. The late Dr. F. L. Bennett found a colony of this charming little plant in a ravine on the Wyoming side of the Black Hills. He gave me three small, round corms which I planted close to a north wall, a spot which in retrospect was far from suitable, for it is subject to extreme drying out and to deluges of rain. There, nevertheless, the delicate waifs held out for several years, blossoming freely—with lines of deeper pink on the pale pink ground of the five cupped petals. Several stems come from one corm. The few leaves are relatively shorter and wider, darker and less glossy than those of *C. virginica*, the common spring beauty of the eastern woodlands. The general habitat of *C. lanceolata* is in the mountainous West.

## *Clematis (Atragene, Viorna)*. Leather flower, virgin's bower, clematis      plates 42-44

*Clematis columbiana* is a low vine with long-stalked, triparted leaves which clambers over bushes. The base of the plant is usually shaded. The light blue to lavender flowers are of atragene type. The principal stronghold of the species is in the Rockies, but it maintains colonial footing more than 150 miles out on the Canadian Plains, in the Cypress Hills. My seeing it flowering in the Hills in late June was one of those bits of luck that come to the inveterate plant hunter. Ascending a north slope, from Battle Creek, I had stepped out from the road to look closely at a wide patch of *Viola rugulosa*, under light conifer shade. Up the slope, hovering just below eye level, three lovely flowers of the clematis reached out, face upward, to invite admiration. No description can convey their character, grace, and refinement. The sepals, two and two opposite, forming a simple cross, were centered by a brush of pale yellowish stamens. I spent several moments in rapt attention. Then I remembered the call of the road, and, without seeking the vine's footing or identifying the supporting shrubbery, I turned from the rare clematis with a sigh.

Native to northcentral Kansas is **Clematis fremontii**, a viorna type. Several stems 10 or 12 inches tall grow from a stout crown and support a close mound of unclematislike, broadly ovoid leaves that are somewhat grayish and rough. Appearing in May are numerous leathery-textured, gray-purple urns with widely recurving, light yellowish lips. Clusters of large, short-plumed seeds follow. This species thrives on full sun and a lean and alkaline soil.

A hardy, woody vine of excellent appearance is **Clematis ligustici-folia**, which will grow to 20 feet or more, or create a tumbled mass on any low support. It is much like the more eastern *C. virginiana*. Wide clusters of small, cream-white blossoms of wonderful fragrance cover the upper portions of the plant in summer, and masses of light-reflecting, silky seed plumes provide ornament until winter. From Saskatchewan to Texas and to the foothills of the western mountains, ravines and streamsides are its native haunts. When well established, even in dry or exposed locations, this plant has remarkable endurance. Indeed, all **Clematis** species of the Great Plains are very long-lived.

Now known as **Clematis occidentalis**, the prize rock garden clematis of the West, perhaps of the world, has formerly been burdened by the "false" name **pseudoalpina**, likewise by the name **tenuiloba**. It is a low, deciduous perennial with flowers of atragene type. The four, long-attentuate, blue-purple sepals are poised in a nodding position and of thrilling grace and carriage. The stems are ascending or erect to five or six inches; longer stems are trailing, leaning for support on neighboring vegetation or rocks. This species is not a vine; it has no climbing faculties. On rare occasion, a stem may stretch out, lightly buried in soil and duff, to 30 inches, putting out few or no roots or top growth short of the tip. Similar rootstocks or rhizomes move about, sparsely, several inches underground to extend a colony; but the habit is compact when nutrients, moisture, and light are right. A ground cover of attractive texture is formed of twice-divided, smooth and slightly glossy, medium green leaves. Rarely, whitish flowered forms are found. Depite much searching, I have not seen a true albino. Plants are handled with ease. They thrive in humus, clay, and limestone rubble and prefer half-shade. *C. occidentalis* is very much at home on the great gray limestone of the Black Hills and in the small Killdeer Mountain area of North Dakota, and seems to inhabit the Rockies sparingly from northern Montana to New Mexico.

*Clematis pitcheri* is a climbing viorna to 10 feet, floriferous over most of the summer. My strain at Prairie Gem Ranch hails from central southern Kansas, where the species margins the Plains, its general habitat being more eastern. It bears urns that are grayish purple on the outside, clear dark purple within the four sharp-pointed, recurved tips. In northwestern Arkansas, I once saw *C. pitcheri* in pearly white and in delicate pink, and lavender—which I recall here to suggest that one need not be content with vague color in this neat, glossy, clean vine. *C. pitcheri* dies to the ground in the fall.

*Clematis scottii (C. hirsutissima)* is a marvelously free-blooming leather flower with viorna urns, or old maid's bonnets, in soft violet-blue to deep purple, or a rare delectable pink. The leaves are pinnate, partly divided, and slightly glaucous. The flowering season is May, often beginning by the first. In the wild, a plant consists of one to several stems; under cultivation, well-developed specimens form a veritable mound as much as 20 inches wide, densely foliaged, with a corresponding bounty of blosssoms at 10 or 12 inches. Rootstocks with coarse, deep-reaching roots and a crown with dormant buds may be divided. *C. scottii* is usually dormant in the summer. The species has a restricted, discontinuous range from the eastern foothills of the Black Hills, southeastward across buttes and open prairies to Pine Ridge in Nebraska, then across eastern Wyoming to the mountains and down to New Mexico.

## *Coreopsis*. Coreopsis, tickseed     plate 45

A flower that seems to enjoy spreading glorious color over the landscape, especially on the dry, sandy loams of Nebraska and portions of Kansas, but also across the continent, is *Coreopsis tinctoria*. Wide rays, cleverly cupped and notch-tipped, of a lovely richness between orange and gold, compose a flower of two inches or less. Herbage is pinnately compound and further divided into narrow parts, dark green and glossy. A single plant branches widely to provide space for each of a multitude of heads, and the common height is 10 inches. One wishes that *C. tinctoria* were perennial. It flowers the first season and is usually rated as an annual, but it makes its maximum show in my garden in the second year; then, sometimes sprouting new growth near the base, it tries for a third season and too often meets defeat.

## *Cornus*. Bunchberry

*Cornus canadensis* occurs in the Black Hills and in Montana, in the Turtle Mountains of North Dakota and Manitoba, and commonly over the Canadian prairies, wherever bits of woodland have provided *acid soil*. It is a colony-forming dwarf of four-inch stature. A strong little stem supports a wide stage of broad, ribbed, green leaves and, at the center, four prominent white bracts around a tiny cluster of flowers; for the second act, a pretty mound of shining crimson berries out does the flowers.

## *Crepis*. Hawksbeard

In scattered occurrences from northwestern Nebraska and adjacent Wyoming to southern Saskatchewan, *Crepis occidentalis* makes a very good impression in June. A rather stocky plant with several upright stems eight to 10 inches high, it covers its flat top with inch-wide, rayed, deep yellow blossoms. The lower leaves are bold, four or more inches long, much-lobed, with sharp but not prickly tips. The fleshy, deep-reaching taproot is not divisible; propagation is by seed. The common name, hawksbeard, does not seem to apply to this one, but other Prairie species of *Crepis* are all for the birds.

## *Cryptantha (Oreocarya)*. Candleflower, cryptantha     plate 46

Two of the best-known cryptanthas are biennials: *C. virgata*, or miner's candle, principally of the foothills and mountains of Wyoming and Colorado, and *C. bradburyana*, now known as *C. celosioides (Oreocarya glomerata)*, or butte candle, of the Plains from Saskatchewan to Nebraska and far to the west. The first year these form rosettes of narrow, oblanceolate leaves, grayish with stiff hairs; the second year they lift to eight or 12 inches one to several "candles" of tiny, white florets, each with a fleck of gold at the center. These flowers are as delicately modeled as fine jewels and betray the close relationship of the genus to the forget-me-nots, *Myosotis* and *Eritrichium*, the latter generic name having once been applied to *Cryptantha*. The candles are much alike, except that *C. virgata* has a number of leaves among the lower blossoms, while *C. bradburyana* has none. In early bloom the spikes are simple; in advanced anthesis small, arching branches strike out from the column in scorpoid fashion, extending, as more flowers open, until an all-around candelabrum is achieved.

*Cryptantha thyrsiflora*, a short-lived perennial of this group, has a main stem breaking into many slightly divergent branches, which carry a mass of smaller florets than other cryptanthas and of not so clear a white. The plant is even more bristly and not of garden interest. It ranges from western Nebraska and Wyoming south to New Mexico and west.

The cryptanthas might be passed over except for one outstanding gem, the perennial *C. cana*. This forms upon a deep taproot a wide, low crown of small, oblong leaves, grayish with short appressed hairs. Several upright candles, to six inches or less, of pristine whiteness, each finely fashioned floret with its minute glint of gold, are lighted from June to August. *C. cana* is very choice—and difficult to grow, a challenge still to be met. Although not rare on its gypsum-bearing red beds and crumbling limestones, it is known only in western South Dakota and Nebraska, eastern Wyoming, and northern Colorado.

## *Cucurbita*. Wild gourd, buffalo gourd

*Cucurbita foetidissima* is a spectacular perennial vine. Coarse and trailing, this hardy plant is useful for masking and protecting banks or as a bold ground cover, capable of smothering other vegetation. The handsome, gray cordate leaves are partly folded or deeply chan-neled, long-tapering, rough-textured, and eight to 10 inches long. They are held at a uniform height above the radiating and crisscrossing stems. As a rule, neither the large, yellow blossoms nor the orange-sized fruits, striped and mottled in two shades of green, are in evidence until the leaves have been cut down by frost. Then the gourds turn bright yellow and remain for a long season. The reputed horrible odor of the plant is not released until some green part is crushed, and then it is not too unpleasant. Southern Nebraska, Kansas, and points south and southwest are the native abode of *C. foetidissima*. There it is not in favor in cultivated fields, for the enormous and deep-seated root will sprout up again and again. Otherwise, it is not in the least weedy.

## *Cypripedium*. Lady's slipper

*Cypripedium calceolus* v. *parviflorum* is now considered the correct name of the smaller yellow lady's-slipper. It occurs in certain canyons of the northern Black Hills and not elsewhere inside Plains borders.

This remotely isolated habitat possibly enjoys a favorable microclimate, but one certainly far different from that of glacial times, when there were no "dry plains" at this latitude and when, presumably, the dainty flower made its migration here. Whether the plant has acquired a special tolerance for dryness, its success here, as elsewhere, surely depends on its receiving a certain minimum amount of moisture. The group of six or seven flowering plants in the garden of Mrs. Floyd Brown in Lead, within the Black Hills, were in a seemingly dry location. The garden has much shade, however, obviously a suitable soil, and water supplied as needed.

## *Dalea (Parosela)*. Silktop, dalea

A plant of distinction and charm is silktop dalea, **Dalea aurea**, of scattered distribution in South Dakota and more frequent southward to below the Texas Panhandle, in especially well-drained footing of gravelly or shaly content. The habit is much the same as that of the prairie clovers (see **Petalostemon**). From a thick taproot, one to a dozen slender stems spring up, branching a little, to describe a loose dome. At the tip of the lightly foliaged stems, broad spikes or elongated cones, circled with airy, light gold *Papilios*, open progressively from base to tip over several weeks in June or July. Small leaves (of five to nine leaflets), stems, and especially the prominent cones are gray-green with appressed silvery hairs. Silktop accepts heavy or lighter soils, but is especially dependent upon drainage.

Plume dalea, **Dalea enneandra**, is attractively different in many ways: glabrous, dark green or reddish stems, single or few, erect to gently arching; very slender, simple up to 15 to 25 inches, then branching widely in a bursting-rocket effect to display numerous, narrow plumes or tapering racemes of silvery calyxes and pearly white corollas. Flowering time is mainly July, though the bright calyxes prolong the floral effect for many weeks. The glossy, pinnate leaves are small, giving an airy note, and by flowering time are frequently absent from the main stem. The species is found from central southern North Dakota to Texas, often in wide, sparse colonies. Propagation is by seed.

Rare in southwestern Kansas, southern Colorado, and south to New Mexico and neighboring Oklahoma and Texas, **Dalea jamesii** is a dwarf that may have garden possibilities. It is described as ascending or with flat-on-the-ground stems, with shaggy, silky, cloverlike heads of bright yellow. It has escaped my search.

There are several other daleas, including **D.** *frutescens*, an intricately twigged, spreading, desert-type shrub to 30 inches, frequent about the breaks of the Palo Duro Canyon of Texas and east into Oklahoma. Its scattered, tiny blossoms, which I did not observe in full bloom, were a luminous purple, the leaves tiny and dark green.

## *Delphinium*. Larkspur     plates 47, 48

*Delphinium bicolor* is abundant in the Black Hills and across the northern half of Wyoming, extreme western North Dakota, the Montana plains, southwestern Saskatchewan, southern Alberta, then far to the west. It is low, 12 to 14 inches, with a few widely divergent branches and characteristic divided leaves, mainly basal. The flowers are an inch wide, rich dark purple-blue, rarely lighter; in some areas, flower color is occasionally an unpleasant mauve and a dull white. *D. bicolor* appreciates a humusy soil in shade or full sun. The plant flowers in May or early June and, shortly after ripening seed, dies down to a shallowly set cluster of diminutive dahlialike tubers. It has been called a "perfect plant," but, however beautiful and well mannered, it leaves a vacant space because of its early dormancy. *Bicolor* is rather a misnomer, for the "bee" is often blue like the sepals instead of yellowish or white.

*Delphinium geyeri* is arresting in the intensity and depth of its textured blueness. The flowers are borne in dense spikes on one or more upright stalks 10 to 20 or more inches high. The leaves are much divided, light green, and slightly grayish with fine hairs. Several dark, thickened roots develop from the crown and strike directly downward. *D. geyeri* is at home from Colorado to Utah and Montana; it spreads its wondrous color in repeated accents across pastures and along roadsides from southern Wyoming to Nebraska in late June. My trials show excellent drought-resistance and a need for good soil and moisture for maximum bloom.

*Delphinium nelsonii* occurs chiefly in Wyoming, Colorado, and the Nebraska Panhandle, and in the Black Hills on the Wyoming side at least. It is said to cover whole hillsides in favored spots.

Common on the Plains and to the east, *Delphinium virescens* is a tall, spindling, white-flowered species that impresses one as just recovering from a mud-spattering storm.

## *Disporum*. Disporum, fairy bells

*Disporum trachycarpum* is a woodland member of the Lily family, adapted to rather dry places as well as to rich soils and shade, from Manitoba and northwestern Nebraska far to the northwest, and in the mountains to New Mexico and Arizona. In dry areas eight inches represent a quite uniform height, but the species grows much taller elsewhere. An arching stem, with several very broad, pointed leaves, ends with a few small, white, deeply notched bells and later on a pretty raceme of light green, dark-striped berries. In ripening, the berries take on highly decorative tones of soft luminous yellow, then orange, then red, all three colors in the same raceme. Although the plant is rhizomatous, I have never seen many in one place. My trials of *D. trachycarpum* in much shade and in the half-shade of the lath house resulted in no returns; it was planted right before a dry winter. Doubtless any motherly gardener could coddle it to success.

## *Dodecatheon*. Shooting star, dodecatheon (emblem of the American Rock Garden Society)     plate 49

*Dodecatheon pulchellus*. Note that the Latin masculine ending "us" is here used in simple agreement with the Greek masculine "on" of *Dodecatheon*.

This widespread and variable species has accumulated a string of synonyms, one of which, *pauciflorum*, I am told, more properly belongs to *D. meadia*. Other names, which have been used for the dodecatheon of the Great Plains, *radicatum*, *salinum*, and possibly *cylindrocarpum*, are all referable, as far as I can learn, to *D. pulchellus*. The variations are exceedingly minor in garden effect.

Throughout the year, our shooting-stars react to the vagaries of the weather, growing quickly and flowering by early May in a headlong spring or later, if snow and cold hold unseasonably. They wither and close shop for the year without flowering if moisture fails. After the year's fruitions they sidestep the heated hours of summer by going completely underground. There they remain until the warmth and probable abundant moisture of another spring invite a hopeful return. Is the shallow subsurface retreat a safe haven? Oh, yes! Although the last perceptible vestige of moisture may vanish from the horizon of the roots in an exhausting drought, and the facile plant members react correspondingly until only discolored and brittle traces of crown and spreading roots remain, within 48 hours after a rain the normal, fresh, white turgidity of good health is recovered. This sleight-of-hand trick of survival does not, indeed, distinguish *D. pulchellus* from other dodecatheons. What does set it apart is the ability of the Plains strains to spring back to full performance and to sprinkle or wash shaded slopes, open hillsides, and treeless ridge tops with sparkling color—this with an average rainfall of under 15 inches. The Plains range of the species includes western Nebraska and South Dakota, eastern Wyoming and Montana, and lower Canada.

Rosy mauve or lavender-rose describes the color in many localities. On the favorite haunt of the Minnekahta Limestone belt, as at Gobblers Knob at the south entrance of Wind Cave National Park, the varying tones run more closely to red. Very occasionally, pure white ones are seen. For long years I have devoted many a jealously sought holiday to jaunting among the "stars" in search of finer form and outstanding colors; the finds, and memories of the hours spent in search, are equally guarded treasures.

It is a truism that the shooting-stars enjoy coddling, though it be only an extra share of humus in the bit of clay in a limestone fissure; and their response is wholehearted. Several hours of midday shade is acceptable, along with many hours of sun. Be sure to provide drainage: no "wet meadow" for this one. Under good care, crowns widen to send up veritable clusters of flowering stems, scapes rather, for masses of bloom. Dividing the plant for purposes of propagation is easy—simply dig up the whole clump and divide it—and is best done in late fall.

### *Dyssodia (Boebera)*. Fetid marigold

I hesitate to disclose the common name of this genus and the species *Dyssodia papposa* because it denotes prejudice. This small, unequivocal annual weed is listed here to apprise those devoted plant hunters, who are also lovers of marigold fragrance, that an inconspicuous, four-to-eight-inch, underfoot plant has provided a reminiscent whiff. The leaves are twice pinnately parted into linear lobes, the flowers are hardly noticeable; but a plantlet of a mere inch can make its presence known, and the faculty persists into late fall when the decadent remnants have turned a bright reddish brown.

## *Echinacea*. Coneflower      plate 50

*Echinacea angustifolia* is bold, spectacular, and beautiful. To create this impression an upright stem of 12 to 20 inches rises from a basal cluster of longish, rough, parallel-ribbed leaves and supports a wide daisy-type head of widely spreading or drooping, rose-pink rays about a prominent cone of glossy, mahogany-colored prickles. A mature plant may put forth a dozen flowers, each on its own stem, a welcome sight on its native uplands and equally acceptable in the garden. Breadth, length, and color-depth of the rays and their angle from the horizontal are matters of selection. Pure glowing crimson at the base of the ray is sometimes seen. An albino with greenish yellow cone is known, as well as a marvelous variant in which the brown cone is replaced by a wide, full pompon of pink rays.

In some books the designation "purple coneflower" is used for *E. angustifolia*. Let's be honest and call it "pink coneflower." Also, it is sometimes indicated as a western variety of *E. pallida*. It may be seen from southern Saskatchewan to Texas for some weeks beginning in July. Gravelly or stony soil is a considered preference of the plant in the wild; in cultivation a measure of freedom from crowding affords the same result. Propagation is usually by seed or, in collected plants, by a few inches of root of a young plant. With controlled moisture, four-inch sections of the thick taproot, set upright with an inch or so of cover, will strike both new roots and top growth.

## *Erigeron*. Daisy, fleabane, erigeron      plates 51-53

*Erigeron* is a genus of mostly small, daisylike or asterlike flowers, some beautiful and valuable in the garden, and some notably transient. And there are others, only technically related, plain weeds that never show a recognizable flower to the eye. These unworthy kinds are welcome to the common name of "fleabane." But "fleabane" is no name for a plant I care to have in my garden, and I never hear the word but that I think, defensibly, of pyrethrum, malathion, even chlordane! The erigerons listed below are all beautiful, and the recommended ones are worthy of the best of care.

*Erigeron asper* has for long years been a "lost-my-way" character, because a poor cadaver on a herbarium sheet had so lost individuality, color, stem, foliage, and root character as to be classified as a mere

variant of the very distinct *E. glabellus*. The majority of texts, following this lead, so name it or ignore it. Canadian and North Dakota
authorities now agree that a pleasant daisy, which I first recognized
east of Saskatoon, Saskatchewan, then on the way to Regina, and
again south of the Missouri River, near Williston, is the true *E. asper*.
The erect stems grow to 12 or 14 inches. The little-branched leaves,
which are mostly basal, long-oblanceolate, and sharp-tipped, are three
or four inches long and as much as an inch wide. A few flowers are
displayed in June; they are about an inch wide and not densely furnished with rays. The rays of the traditional *E. asper* were described
as white, as they might well be after drying; in the three stations
where I studied the species the rays carried a definite tinge of blue
toward the tips. In North Dakota, *E. asper* has been reported as plentiful to near the southern border.

This resolved situation leaves a great void for one of the most
beautiful and permanent of erigerons—the one I have distributed for
many years under the name *E. asper*, on the finding of a well-known
botanist. *For the time being it must go without a name.* Its prominent
features include a flower of more than 200 very narrow rays of pure
lavender in a thick shaggy fringe for a disk of just the right tone of
gold; and slender stems erect from the ground, branching only to hold
the flowers in close clusters, at 10 inches or so. My stock came from
southeastern Montana. In my lath house it has maintained itself in
a colony of a few feet, for more than 30 years, by very slender rhizomes. Once in the wild I saw this species, south of the Devil's Tower,
in Wyoming also.

*Erigeron caespitosus* is distinguished among the small members
by wider rays of purer white—sometimes reported as pink. The gold-
centered heads are an inch or more wide and are held at seven or
eight inches. Stems are ascending, leaves oblanceolate, somewhat
hairy, dark green. Flowers come in July and August and are welcome.
Shade is acceptable, but *E. caespitosus* is intolerant of close crowding.
It spreads moderately. The Plains range is from the Pine Ridge breaks
of Sioux County, Nebraska, to central Saskatchewan; in the mountains to Colorado, Utah, and the Yukon.

*Erigeron canus* is an all green-gray plant with small, oblanceolate
leaves and a good show of white or sometimes pinkish or lavender
ray flowers. Its disk flowers open yellow but begin browning while
the rays are yet fresh, a serious demerit. The species belongs to the

Plains from the Black Hills to New Mexico, in sites of excellent drainage and sun. Its season is mainly June; it is not long-lived.

From the Oregon gardens of Dr. Ira N. Gabrielson, *Erigeron compositus* came to me over 30 years ago. I still have the stock; and when an old plant has died, there has always been a seedling or two to take its place. At present there are, perhaps, a dozen near a venerable plant. At a glance, its divided and redivided, tiny leaves suggest a tuft of velvety gray moss. The bevy of little flowers stands low above the cushion; they are white with wide disks of yellow, very neat. The flowers keep coming over a long period. Both this and *E. trifidus*, to be noted farther on, are reported either to be white or to have some color. These diminutives seek the cool regions from Greenland to Alaska or in the mountains as far south as Colorado. On the Plains they accommodate themselves to dry, rocky ridges in Saskatchewan, North Dakota, Montana, and the Black Hills. They dwell comfortably, however, in half-shade in my prairie garden at 3,200 feet.

*E. divergens* v. *arenarius* is found in southern Montana and southward. Sometimes flowering from seed late in the first year, it draws admiration with its great abundance of half-inch heads, purplish in the bud, a glowing white when open. The second year the plant attains proportions of 10 inches in width and height, is very diffusely branched and dense; and from June until after hard frosts in October, it is constantly a mass of blooms. In the coolness of late season, more and more color infuses the fringe of rays until they are a gay lavender. The promise of flowers for another year is seen in strong, neighboring seedling rosettes.

The most diminutive daisy I have found is correctly named *Erigeron eatonii* — now unfortunately omitted from certain technical lists. Its white and gold heads are a half-inch wide. Its stems send out many branches, a trait not found in some of the other small, linear-leaved daisies, and it continues flowering from spring into summer when moisture is available. It grows four inches high with some variation allowed. *E. eatonii* ranges from the Plains across the first low ranges of mountains and is plentiful along the road bordering the Rifle Range to the northeast of Laramie.

Whiplash daisy, *Erigeron flagellaris*, is always appealing along a roadside with its myriads of miniature flower heads, all upfacing at a general level of four or five inches. To achieve this pleasant and apparently restrained effect, the species must have full sun and a poor soil. It has its own peculiar method of forming the dense colony, essentially a ground cover, not ordinarily by seed but by arching, whiplash runners. Each plant, with a rosette of an inch and a half to three or four inches, sends up an erect stem to produce a solitary flower, and immediately from the axils of several small stem leaves there grow "whiplashes," to a foot or longer, which root down at the tip and establish new plants. In a season or two an extended colony may be formed, although individual plants remain tiny and shallow-rooted and are easily destroyed. In better soils, with more moisture and perhaps light shade, *E. flagellaris* can stretch higher and farther. The watchful gardener will quickly realize that it can be an overwhelming menace to small and defenseless plants.

The closely circling rays are usually white. In some strains the buds are almost red, but little of the color shows in the open flower. Typical leaves are small, oblanceolate, grayish with short pubescence. A strain with greener leaves, three-lobed at the tip, and with somewhat restrained whiplashing power was once found, but the colony was later destroyed by road widening. This strain has been dispersed under the name erigeron 'Prairie Gem'. The species is frequent in the Black Hills, but rare on the Plains southward, through Cimarron, the westernmost county of Oklahoma, and into New Mexico. In the Rockies it is one of the commonest of the little daisies at elevations up to 10,000 feet.

*Erigeron glabellus* is principally northern. It is common on the central and northern Canadian Plains and extends much farther north, also into Manitoba and Wisconsin. In North Dakota and Montana, it tends to seek the lower prairie and northern slopes. Farther south it is widespread in the Black Hills, coming down to below 3,000 feet in suitable soils, sometimes in quite dry exposures. In the Rockies it ranges farther south at increasing elevations.

Because of its general character, beauty, and appeal, *E. glabellus* has made itself a favorite. At first it is a low tuft or mat of glossy, oblanceolate, entire leaves, somewhat leathery in texture, almost evergreen; by June or earlier, nearly horizontal stems are put out, carrying incipient buds, later to turn upward, arching, seldom erect, and dividing to support several daisy heads which open over a long period. According to season and site, flowering will begin sometime in July; but it is not uncommon to find occasional blossoms in September. There is a nice balance between disk and ray flowers; disks are a rich golden, while rays in strong light and in the warmer months are apt to be nearly white. With shade and coolness the color deepens to a pleasing light purple. The height of the plant ranges from 12 to 18 inches.

*Erigeron montanensis* is one of many linear-leaved, little species native to the West. Although there are fewer such species on the Plains, it is often difficult to decide which is which. This one, however, has a character and an air of its own; its taprooted tufts, with many flowers at a time, on stems six to eight inches high, compose enticing pictures. The flowerheads, about an inch wide, are sparkling white and gold, the very narrow leaves dark green. In my garden, in soil of no particular preparation, it has made itself at home, seeding freely; yet it is not one to inherit the earth. I have discovered it in otherwise barren outcrops of sandy shale in northern Wyoming, and I have found it far up in Montana. It is reported for South Dakota. Some recent changes in herbarium labels include *E. montanensis* in *E. ochroleucus*.

Growing throughout the North American continent, the very weedy *Erigeron philadelphicus* occurs sparingly in the Black Hills, and in other especially moist portions of the Plains, particularly along streams. Somewhat ungainly in habit, though "not unpretty," as a child described it, this erigeron can be troublesome in gardens where much moisture is present. *E. pumilus*, a small, white-rayed species, grayish with glistening hairs, greets one unexpectedly here and there on some of the driest prairies in early spring. Although described as a perennial in most books, it hardly survives a second year, and has the additional defect of greenish tinged, yellow disks.

Of the little daisies of the Great Plains, *Erigeron scribneri* is the crown jewel. Its heads have a wide disk of molten gold and finely modeled rays of glowing white, all under an inch wide. They stand singly and in close array above a wide mat of linear or narrowly oblanceolate leaves that are softly downy and medium green. The taprooted mat may attain a spread of seven inches and support a score of the dainty blossoms at a uniform height of four inches or so, and all opening at once. There is no continued blooming. It is rare moment when one stands amid thousands of these gems along a limy ridge in the bright days of May or June. This erigeron is easily accommodated in a limy, sandy, or clayey soil, delights in sun, and is long-lived in the garden. It is at home, here and there in abundance, on the Greenhorn Limestone that margins the prairie surrounding the Black Hills, and also in the Pine Ridge table country of Nebraska. It is also found on similar limestone exposures in the Wildcat Mountains near Scottsbluff on the North Platte River; it extends into Wyoming and Colorado and was recently found on the Killdeer plateau in North Dakota—appearing for the first time on the state's wild flower lists.

Erigeron naming is truly a difficult pursuit and the most careful study still leaves conflicts of opinion. Plant characteristics, which are not evident morphologically, are of no use to the taxonomist. In the garden and among plants in the wild, characteristics are evident which cannot be transfered to the herbarium sheet; yet species naming is the sphere of the technical botanist, and in the genus *Erigeron* the genius who will speak last has not appeared. Suffice it to say that the entity here called *E. scribneri* is sometimes regarded as a variety of the vague *E. ochroleucus*, and that it was called *E. nematophyllus* by Rydberg, in his *Flora of the Prairies and Plains*. The *E. nemato-phyllus* of some authors was, some years back, called *E. eatonii*.

*Erigeron speciosus* and *E. subtrinervis* are closely related, large plants that carry their corymbose displays at 10 to 20 inches. They are prominent in the higher valleys of the Black Hills. *E. subtrinervis* is seen more frequently, often in extensive drifts. The plant is some-what grayish, with broad, lanceolate leaves and fine flowers, often an inch and a quarter wide, of crowded, narrow, pinkish or bluish lavender rays. *E. speciosus*, or possibly its variety, *E. speciosus* v. *macranthus*, has narrower, darker green leaves and rays tending strongly toward purple-blue. Both species make splendid shows well into the summer, are well behaved, and reasonably long-lived. *E. subtrinervis* also occurs sparingly in the canyons of northwestern Nebraska, and *E. speciosus* extends to southern Alberta; otewise, they are of the western mountains.

It was a memorable day when I first visited Flag Mountain, a forestry lookout point in the Black Hills, an isolated pinnacle capped by the gray Pahasapa Limestone, 6,937 above sea level, and first saw *Erigeron trifidus* in the wild. That narrow aerie appeared a precarious station for an important watchtower; on one side, above a precipice, some fissures had been filled with cement to provide a walk around the tower base. Yet in minute crevices, especially on the north and northwest, exposed to the reflected heat of the summer sun, to the worst of winter at that elevation, and dependent on such moisture as might penetrate the fissures in draining from the rock, grew numbers of the tiny daisy. And not another thing but wispy bits of grass.

It was late summer; there were a flower or two and ripe seed. A second thrill came soon after spotting the daisy, when I approached the yellow cross-mark of a helicopter landing site and found in looser crevices, with a bit of soil in evidence, numbers of a diminutive, unreported phlox, which proved to be pink-flowered. Close by were four-inch plants, in flower, of the shrubby *Potentilla fruticosa* and small rosettes of *P. plattensis*; a few steps down was *Clematis occidentalis*.

*Erigeron trifidus* resembles *E. compositus* but is green or lighter gray and has smaller parts. In cultivation its crown widens to perhaps five inches above a taproot, and it is especially generous with its dainty daisies. It thrives and self-sows freely in a scarcely tilted limestone scree in the coolness that my lath house affords. I now have specimens of *E. trifidus* from the Laramie Hills, from Alexander Butte in North Dakota, and from a prairie pasture at about 4,000 feet in western Montana—the last still in the form of seed. It will be interesting to compare them.

*Erigeron vetensis*, from the border of the Plains near the foot of the Laramie Hills, is a lovely little daisy of deep blue-lavender and gold. It flowers abundantly in June, well supported by dense leaves. The leaves, two inches long, are narrowly oblanceolate, almost velvety, more green than gray. The low, divergent habit displays the flowers attractively, from near the ground to about seven inches. This acquisition has flowered well at my Prairie Gem Ranch and now has a scattering of seedlings about it.

## *Eriogonum*. Sulphur flower, false buckwheat     plate 54

Travelers across the Plains, even serious searchers for plants that might enhance their gardens, may pass by sandy stretches of pasture land gray-white, or sometimes faintly pinkish in season, with the so-called *Eriogonum annuum*—which comes to fruition in its *second year*. Or they may pass by an occasional patch of shaly wasteland with even grayer flecks of *E. pauciflorum*, flowering in dusky white, and never suspect that these belong to a genus that embraces some startling beauties of perfect garden character.

An outstanding one is *Eriogonum flavum*, probably never to be seen again from a fleeting car on a superhighway, but not infrequently seen where byways traverse limestone ridges, from southern Saskatchewan and Alberta through the Plains states to Colorado. Look closely if you see a single rosette or an eight-inch mat of short, broadly oblanceolate leaves of dark green, velvety above, and felty white below. In late May and June, one to many umbels of lovely sulphur-yellow fluff will nearly obscure the foliage, four to six inches above it. The leaves are almost evergreen; the mat is built of many rosettes on a branching caudex from an indivisible taproot. Doubtless *E. flavum* chooses its stony dwelling places for the freedom from competition such terrain affords; but with similar freedom it is happy in the alkaline gumbo of my garden, where it increases moderately by seed.

*Eriogonum depauperatum*, now considered a synonym for *E. pauciflorum*, is a much rarer species of similar habit, the leaves smaller, gray or gray-green. The four-inch-high flower clusters, knobs of near white, take on tints of rust and pink after a few days. It has a cleanness of foliage and a certain squat charm in keeping with its favorite badland habitat—hardpan littered with gravel and shared with a few prickly pears.

*Eriogonum multiceps* is so close to *E. pauciflorum* that one may readily pass it without recognition unless the inflorescence displays its mature or, perhaps, weathered color. A long time ago, when tramping the Greenhorn Limestone along the Cheyenne River bluffs at dusk, I came upon a low, gray plant with a nicely rounded umbel of luscious pink. But what I have seen since in that area seems always to be the nonentity, *E. pauciflorum*. I find, in the herbarium at Laramie, that many specimens once labeled *E. multiceps* now bear the name *E. pauciflorum* v. *gnaphalodes*; as compared with the type, the variety is more compact, the leaves shorter and more densely white-pubescent, and the heads of bloom more uniformly knobby. Some display an enticing pinkness. Does there exist a strain in which attractive color is consistently developed? It should be sought from Saskatchewan to Colorado.

Very distinct in the form that reaches out from the west to well across Montana and Wyoming, following more or less barren, stony ridges, is *Eriogonum ovalifolium*. Almost white are its buns or narrow mats of crowded leaves of the size and roundness of a typewriter key, or longer and more oval. The tiny, sulphur-yellow flowers are carried plentifully a few inches above in wider balls, or umbels. The species is reported to have forms varying to white with rose veins or to purplish, often with the type color in the same patch. *E. ovalifolium*, which I have had from northern and from southern Wyoming, has not lived long, though for a year or two it flowered well. As happens often with plants I have lost, the most recent rather sudden departure occurred after months of deficient moisture, which leaves unanswered the question of the real cause of death.

On one of my many study trips to the Wyoming University herbarium at Laramie I found *Eriogonum umbellatum* in full bloom on gravelly prairie some miles to the northeast of Cheyenne; it had previously been unknown on the Plains. This species of beauty and distinction has been a treasure in appearance and in adaptation in my garden.

*E. umbellatum* widens its low mat of quite small, but broadly oblanceolate leaves of glossy rich green, often in rosettelike clusters tipping short, slender stems. From the mat arise many remarkably sturdy scapes to about eight inches long, to support wide compound umbels of bright bronzy gold, each with minor umbels in separate neat balls. The brilliant show lasts through June. The aging flowers take on hues of bright reddish bronze, prolonging the season, briefly. Still contributing color by late October, the mat of low foliage deepens to bronze. Like Rydberg, Gabrielson in his *Western American Alpines* of the early 1930s, gave the range of the species as "mountains and dry valleys; Wyo.-Colo.-Calif.-Wash."

Residing farther south are three other yellow-flowered species, *Eriogonum chrysocephalum*, *E. jamesii*, and *E. lachnogynum*, which I hope to see someday.

## *Eritrichium*. Forget-me-not  plate 55

For the beginner, every plant needs definition. To the well versed, the name "forget-me-not" brings to mind the tiny and dainty, intensely blue flowers of *Myosotis*. Only the widely read, or those who have had the fortune to explore in high alpine flower fields, will recognize the name *Eritrichium*. In far northwestern Montana there is a little valley, miles away from the mountains; at an elevation of around 4,000 feet; there nature has prepared an unbelievably wide garden spot in casual view, lying as smooth and level and suited for a fine farm as any land could but so completely rock-filled as to be unproductive even for pasture. Little grass or other forage grows in the spot. This river flood plain is entirely surfaced and filled to a depth, measurable in the road ditches, with coarse and fine gravel, sand and silt, and small, imbedded cobbles and boulders. Apparently no one claims this ground; there are no fences. It continues as an unencroached, made-to-order habitat for the hardly known dwarf forget-me-not, *Eritrichium howardii*. There it has occupied acre upon acre in an unbroken sheet of blue, the color dimming in the distance.

This species is a close replica of the high alpine that Farrer, with unbounded enthusiasm, called "the Crowned King of the Alps, the Herald of Heaven, Woolly-hair the Dwarf." It is something for the fortunate to see, but not for the general run of gardeners, nor even the greenest of "green thumbs," to grow. The plants themselves are so exacting that no gardener, so far, has been able to put together a workable substitute for their natural environment. So, about mid-June, see these matchless miles of one of the most wonderful blue flowers the world affords — if you can; and leave them in their inviolate seclusion. Otherwise, as Farrer mourned, the flowers will "have to sit content in the admiration of marmots."

Available information indicates that *E. howardii* extends to the mountains but does not reach the Continental Divide, relatively low in that part; extends into two counties still farther on the Plains; and is expected farther south in Montana and to the Bighorn Mountains of Wyoming.

The adaptation of *E. howardii* to low altitudes, however, is a characteristic not possessed by the high alpines and gives hope that the species can be further molded to garden purposes.

## *Erythronium*. Midland erythronium, deer tongue, fawn lily, trout lily      plate 56

What a list of names, familiar and common, these gentle and sweet-breathed, nodding stars of early spring have been burdened with! Combined names involving adder, trout, and dog have been employed, as well as deer and fawn, hardly indicating appreciative perception or understanding. William Chase Stevens, in his remarkably fine book *Kansas Wild Flowers*, explained that even the pleasant sounding name *Erythronium* is a borrowed one, first applied as a generic for *Erythronium dens-canis*, a rose-purple European species with a bulb, or corm, shaped like a dog's tooth.

*Erythronium mesochorium*, chiefly of Kansas, and credited also to portions of Nebraska, Iowa, Missouri, and Oklahoma, has a wide, thick corm, unlike a tooth, and its wide, short, and pointed leaves are green, slightly glaucous, and without mottlings to suggest the spots of fish or fawn. Stevens further pointed out that *E. mesochorium* differs from **E. albidum**, a much more widespread species which it resembles in size and color of flower, in making offsets from the base of the bulb in the manner of tulips, rather than by means of "rhizomes," and by habitat on the open prairies rather than in woods and thickets. The six segments of the flower, in both species, are mainly white, strongly tinted with light purple. Keeping to their respective haunts, both species extend westward to near the center of Kansas, at about the 1,800-feet contour.

*Erythronium mesochorium* definitely shows adaptation to dry plains conditions in my garden at Prairie Gem Ranch. In a few years the increase of corms produces as many as eight or ten flowers just above the clustered leaves: a nice effect, the very essence of spring. Heavy capsules of seed on lengthening peduncles are held out flat on the ground, on which the seed are soon emptied—the plant's maximum effort at spreading. Soon all is dormant.

*Erythronium albidum*, increasing readily by the long processes sent out from the corm, in time forms colonies so dense that they do not flower except around the margins. My present stock of two corms came from Texas. With the care I have given them, they have bloomed; but in the several years I have had them they have never reproduced.

## *Eurotia (Ceratoides)*. White sage, winterfat

A low shrub, much-branched and leafy from the ground up, *Eurotia lanata* has a striking appearance, its stem and leaf permanently coated with a soft and very short, whitish wool. Its abundant linear leaves are an inch and a half long. Its flowers are hardly noticeable; but in late fall, the shining white hairs of the seed tufts lining the upper stems enhance the light gray-green effect for many weeks. Much of the gray effect is retained for the winter garden. This fine-textured, rounded shrub, usually 24 inches or less in height, is a sage in name only, because it belongs to the Chenopodiaceae or Goosefoot family. It favors dryish, limy hills from Saskatchewan to Texas and more westerly regions. Small plants are readily transplanted.

## *Eustoma*. Tulip gentian

Shaped like a shallow-cupped tulip, the glossy-textured, light bluish purple *Eustoma russellianum* (now *grandiflorum*) is an anomaly on the Plains, requiring relatively constant moisture in the Nebraska Sandhills region and in meadows along the North Platte River to near

Casper, Wyoming. In southwestern South Dakota, it enjoys a restricted habitat near seeping springs. In Colorado, it is rare in moist meadows. In Kansas, it is found in the southwestern quarter; then, avoiding the drier Panhandle, it spreads far to the southeast in Texas where immense fields furnished ample florist supplies—perhaps still do. Dr. H. Hapeman, however, who made a hobby of selecting color forms from white to yellow and brownish purple, grew the plants in his yard in a 20-inch rainfall area. Not often attempted in gardens, because of the moisture requirement, and usually rated as annual or biennial, plants in flower have been observed with remnant stubs of stalks of the previous years, suggesting a four-year cycle with the first as a seedling rosette. Surely the flower is worth the effort; it is six-petaled, recurved, two inches long, and two inches wide. The opposite leaves are two inches long, broadly oblong or lanceolate, glaucous, in fine harmony with the flower color. The season runs from June to August; the flowers open in succession in terminal cymose panicles. In the North, the height is commonly 14 inches.

## Evolvulus

*Evolvulus nuttallianus* makes itself at home in especially sandy soil, and in other soils as well, where a modicum of free space permits. It is not aggressive, though it has the faculty of spreading by root, which it exercises moderately. It is a densely leafy little bush, more often five inches tall than 10, and silky hairy; the wide, pointed leaves are little more than half an inch long; the flowers, wide, tubeless trumpets of pinkish lavender, are so modest they must be observed at close range, yet so abundant from May to July that they fairly illuminate the bushlet. The typical *E. nuttallianus* is found now and then from southern Montana to New Mexico and Arizona, stretching east to cover almost the whole of Kansas and touching Missouri. The name *E. pilosus* may be given as a synonym in some references; but when I found a much hairier bushlet with smaller flowers of silvery white, a botanist gave it this name.

## Ferns

Ferns are exacting in their choice of habitat the world over. Shade, moisture, and near-neutral soil are the requirements of most. Rare seepy places, exposed rocks along stream bluffs or badlands, any terrain not vulnerable to the ever-searching grasses and other strong competitors may become fern habitat, however restricted or however isolated. Fern endemics are nonexistent on the Plains. Those species whose range includes the entire Northern Hemisphere occur so rarely on the Plains as to imply persistence as relics from an era of different climate. Spores are widely transported by many agencies, however, and numerous species now range the northern portion of this region where the lifeless deserts of the Ice Age once held sway. Ferns, even of the more plentiful kinds, are seldom to be seen from the roads, though a nearby cliff or shaded slope may shelter a well-populated hideout.

**The Smaller Ferns**

To simplify study and comparison, the rock ferns and other low kinds are presented in alphabetical sequence by their technical names. The larger species follow in like arrangement.

The southern maidenhair fern, *Adiantum capillus-veneris*, doubtless has enjoyed a timeless, though anomalous residence by the warm waters of Cascade Springs in the southern tip of the Black Hills, while its closest relatives dwell 600 miles to the south. Lining the water's edge and vertical banks with ribbons of rich green, this delicate and lovely fern grows densely from a network of creeping rootstocks which uphold the wet soil of the seeps, main outpourings, and the rushing stream for an indefinite distance below. Flexuous dark stipes and rachises lower the fronds upon the leaf mass, so that their form is indistinguishable except in a lifted frond. Broadly wedge-shaped, the structure is bipinnate, the leaflets irregularly fan-shaped. Stipe and blade together are commonly a foot or less in length. All change to dull brown as winter comes, except a few fronds which live through by lying flat upon the warm water. Locally, *A. capillus-veneris* is grown indoors, where it is said to require daily watering.

So that their occurrence may be known, I mention the following: *Asplenium septentrionale*, tiny, with linear blades that are merely lobed or toothed, in crevices in granite, in South Dakota, southeastern Wyoming, to western Oklahoma and New Mexico; *A. trichomanes*, tiny, with rounded pinnae, in the mountains of southeastern Wyoming, apparently extremely rare in the Black Hills, but otherwise occurring throughout the Northern Hemisphere; *A. viride*, somewhat like the last, occasional on moist rocks, in the northern Black Hills, northwestern Wyoming, and around the Northern world. Then, *Botrychium lunaria* and *B. matricariifolium*, diminutive and of little interest except to a fern specialist, in the Cypress Hills of Canada; and *B. virginianum*, entering the moister Plains in North Dakota and Nebraska, and common over much of North America. The last, which has a wide blade in elaborate bipinnate pattern, grows 10 to 15 inches high in shaded areas along streams.

Where the rugged country, draining to the Cimarron River, drops from the level plains of southern Colorado and the mesas of volcanic rock rise above, *Cheilanthes eatonii* is at home. It also extends westward to the mountains and southward across the extremity of Oklahoma, and as far as Mexico. With longer stipe and oblong-lanceolate, doubly or triply pinnate blade as long as 12 inches, this lip fern is much less compact than the more widely distributed following species.

*Cheilanthes feei*, one of the more common of the small Black Hills ferns, is found where north-facing or shade limestone provides a footing. A favorite site is a horizontal crevice with a thin wedge of soil. Sometimes a shallow lodgement of nearly pure humus on a sheltered shelf serves, with the lower roots outspread upon the stone. In any situation, access of moisture is the controlling factor, and the leaf masses of numerous crowns spread to fill the adaptable space. The doubly pinnate fronds are conspicuously compact. They arch to present much of the blade toward the horizontal, a very handsome picture in dark, textured green — evergreen when the moisture supply is uniform. *C. feei* is found in the eastern half of Wyoming and southward through the western Plains into the Texas Panhandle and New Mexico, also to the farther west and Mexico, as well as in localities in some Mississippi River states. Its drought-resistance is remarkable. The fronds may curl temporarily during a drought, then revive; but the maximum test it passes is to survive unseasonable and complete loss of green.

Distributed over much of the Americas and Eurasia, and common over several Plains states, *Cystopteris fragilis*, the brittle fern, is a delicate little thing of familiar pattern. With its textured fronds of light green, it makes a delightful carpet on a well-watered, shady slope in early season, becoming weather-worn or completely dormant in the heat and drought of August.

The beautiful dwarf oak fern, *Gymnocarpium dryopteris*, with three-parted blade and paired pinnae, occurs in a few of the moister places in the northern Black Hills.

Sometimes a crevice plant, but more often scorning its common name "cliffbrake," *Pellaea atropurpurea* seeks the advantage of moisture drained from rocks high or low, even undergoing submergence by flash floods. Where plentiful in its southern and eastern Black Hills haunts, it makes good use of humus and much shade. At Prairie Gem Ranch, well out on the prairie, it is content at the base of a north wall and provides a pleasant show in periods of ample rainfall. Its blades, rather narrow and long-tapering, vary from simple to bipinnate, the stipe in polished purple-black, the leaflets dark green, with a semigloss and only a bit of a bluish tinge. Absent over most of the Plains and the Rockies, it comes to Plains levels in central Kansas and is known in southeastern Colorado in the Cimarron breaks. *P. atropurpurea* should be found in the Cimarron drainage in Oklahoma and New Mexico.

Perhaps ever dependent on limestone fissures for a roothold, *Pellaea glabella* v. *occidentalis (P. pumila)* is a diminutive cliffbrake of the West, frequent on the Great Gray Limestone of the Black Hills and extending to central Wyoming and northwestward to Banff, Alberta. Like jewels of bluish green jade, the fronds, which seldom exceed two inches, and leaflets, which tend to be ovate rather than elongate, and have few and shallow lobes, lend distinction to the gray rocks that provide moderate temperature and an infrequent trickle of moisture. In a contrived similar environment in a friend's garden, this fern has continued for some years.

Worthy only of mention is *Polypodium vulgare* ssp. *columbianum (hesperium)*, with pinnately lobed blades eight inches long and less than two inches wide. It occurs in moist, granite crevices about Sylvan Lake in the Black Hills. This bears the borrowed name "Rocky Mountain rockcap fern," though it is said to be rare at 8,000 feet and above in Colorado and is known in only one locality in Wyoming. Northwesterly, it ranges to British Columbia.

*Woodsia obtusa*, the larger cliff fern, patterned much like the following species, is recorded as common in eastern Kansas and occasional to beyond the middle of the state and within Plains levels. It ranges over much of the continent, avoiding drier areas and exposures.

Mainly a western species, reaching to Mexico and British Columbia with scattered habitats as far eastward as Quebec, *Woodsia oregana*, similar to but smaller by half than *W. obtusa*, is well equipped to thrive under the regional heat and drought. Even when moisture is withheld for long periods and all green parts are reduced to haylike wisps, with good rains new fronds are put forth and persist until the plant becomes dormant in the winter. In the wild, good soil and cooling shade seem to fulfill its needs apart from rocks; it can produce some admirable clusters of greenery seemingly from nothing more than afternoon shade, very limy siltstone, and an occasional trickle of rain. In my garden it proves an enduring treasure when its simple needs are met.

(In conformance with recent revisions of the woodsias of the Plains region, and corresponding misidentifications, the taxon *Woodsia oregana* now embraces the glabrous form and the somewhat hairy form previously miscalled *W. scopulina*. *W. mexicana*, a smaller fern with distinct characteristics, credited to the Black Hills by Rydberg, has now been relegated to extreme southwestern Colorado and southwardly to Mexico.)

The true *Woodsia scopulina* is known to come onto the Plains only in the Black Hills. There it is much less common than *W. oregana* and occupies shady, rocky places at intermediate elevations. It is recognized by its frond length, up to six inches or rarely larger, and by its compact and heavy-textured appearance due, in part, to the rich effect of its velvety hairiness. It is deciduous. At the foot of a limestone foundation wall it has shown excellent adaptation to drought over several years. In the wild it may be found in black leafmold on granite ledges or in deep fissures in rich loam. The range is principally in the western mountains. There are outlying occurrences as remote as North Carolina, Quebec, and Alaska.

### The Larger Ferns

Frequent along French Creek and about Sylvan Lake in the Black Hills, and in the canyon of the Niobrara River near Long Pine, Nebraska, one of the larger ferns, the lady fern, *Athyrium filix-femina*, is a handsome plant, capable of growing, it is said, much taller than it does in these environments. Assuming that it could never be suited in my prairie garden, I have not tried to cultivate it. It is much grown in the Hills in the shade of buildings and reaches a height of about two feet.

*Dryopteris cristata*, narrow swamp fern, of medium height and attractive, is reported from wet banks of the Dismal River, in the Nebraska Sandhills, about Sylvan Lake in the Black Hills, and in damp, shady sites on the Canadian prairies. *D. filix-mas*, the male fern, with a handsome wide blade tapering to both base and tip, and long, slender pinnae, appears in ravines in the Harney Peak district in the Black Hills and in the Cimarron Canyon country of western Oklahoma at about 4,000 feet. It grows to 30 inches and is a favorite in gardens. *D. spinulosa (D. carthusiana)*, toothed wood fern, attaining 30 inches, dwells along the Niobrara and Dismal Rivers in Nebraska.

The ostrich fern, *Matteuccia struthiopteris (M. struthiopteris)* — with a novel assortment of synonyms — rises at its maximum to a majestic four feet and will furnish a spectacle in the garden if adequate shade and moisture are provided. The blade has very many divisions, holds a good width well toward the tip, and tapers narrowly toward the base. Along the eastern border of the Canadian Plains and in the Turtle Mountains, site of the International Peace Garden (a prairie swell across the Manitoba-North Dakota line), this great fern is at home and, again, with a long jump, finds agreeable habitat along streams draining eastward from the granite heights in the Black Hills. Its complete range includes Eurasia.

One of two wholly dominant, full-sun, marsh ferns of the Nebraska Sandhills, *Onoclea sensibilis*, with broad, undulate-margined blade divisions, has a distinctly plain effect, But it has a certain bold attraction in a Black Hills habitat with streamside shade and backed by highlighted or shadowed, rounded boulders. Elsewhere its range is eastern, from south to north.

The hairy bracken, *Pteridium aquilinum* v. *pubescens*, a chiefly western North American representative of a worldwide species, provides a rare sight where, for half a mile, the road climbs from Little Spearfish Creek toward the Cement Ridge forest lookout, across the line in Wyoming. The broad-bladed fern borders the trail closely and reaches the car windows. Aided by a few scattered pines, it furnishes all the visible plant cover of that north-facing slope. The rainfall for the locality is above the average for the region. This bracken appears also along the eastern border of the Canadian Plains on shaded slopes and in woodlands, and in shaded ravines in Wyoming at 4,000 feet and above.

Uniformity of moisture and mild acidity suitable to the marsh fern, *Thelypteris palustris* v. *pubescens*, enable it to team with *Onoclea sensibilis* and turn wide, low areas of the Sandhills into exclusive fern meadows. It has the familiar bipinnate blade pattern, the blade as much as 15 by six inches, set upon a lengthy stem that lifts the frond 30 inches or more. Principally eastern in range, it is rare west of the Mississippi River except where sand and wind have cooperated to create wide flats at near water level in Nebraska.

## *Frasera (Swertia)*. Green gentian

On the high reaches of the Pahasapa Limestone of the Black Hills may be seen the striking green-gentian, *Frasera speciosa (Swertia radiata)*; other haunts of the species are in the Rockies and to the west. No other plant of the Plains resembles it. Large, channeled leaves, up to a foot long, have a fine-textured, velvety surfacing—puberulent, to use a technical term—which one instinctively touches to test the attractive smoothness. A stout stem, with reduced leaves, rises three or four feet, bearing on a foot or two of the upper portion a broad column of four-petaled, wide-open flowers, which approach an inch in width. Their color is near white, with tints of green and dots of purple, and pale green stamens and pistil. The whole column is composed of many slender-stalked panicles arising from axils of the small, upper leaves. The plant has a large, dark root that goes deep. *F. speciosa* is probably not long-lived. Many large, black seeds are produced in straw-colored capsules.

## *Fritillaria*. Yellow bell, bronze bell, rice root

*Fritillaria atropurpurea* has a few longish, dusty-glaucous, somewhat twisted leaves on an erect, six- to 12-inch stem which bears one to four flowers of the most astonishing effect. There are three sepals, three petals, practically alike, three-fourths of an inch long, irregularly mottled bronzy purple and dull yellow, often with the darker color predominating. This somber combination is headlighted by six large anthers of brilliant gold. *F. atropurpurea* comes from a loose-scaly bulb at a depth of four inches or so, which must be handled carefully to avoid dislodging the scales; but it grows readily if transplanted when dormant. The bulb seems to propagate by stolons as well as by dislodged scales. Remaining within the United States, *F. atropurpurea* extends across western North Dakota and Montana to Washington and portions of northwestern Nebraska; in the Rockies, above 6,000 feet, to New Mexico. Once, just below a cliff of the Pine Ridge escarpment, I found a treasury of the species, probably a hundred plants in flower within a short space. Later, after cattle had trampled and bedded there during a storm, no trace of a plant was found. Although not many of the bulbs may have been destroyed, the apparent destruction was complete.

*Fritillaria pudica* formerly grew as far east as the center of North Dakota and may yet have hideouts in the Badlands of the southwestern part of the state, where it was reported some years ago by E. C. Moran. A lone flower was found on Cabin Creek in southeastern Montana, a once flowery area that has been pastured mercilessly for fifty years. Sixty miles farther west, almost in the shadow of the Bighorn Mountains, the yellow-bell is said to be still plentiful. It is obviously a receding species where human occupancy is a factor; yet Booth, writing for Montana, says it is common on mountain slopes and hills, of which features there are a number isolated on the Plains of that state. The yellow-bell arches its stem to hold one flower or several in a bell-like position at four to 12 inches. The bronze-bell hangs its head shamefacedly. Yellow-bell has a fresh and dainty air, as if made of "sugar and spice and everything nice"; by contrast, the bronzy "fritz" must have been concocted of "snips and snails and puppy-dog tails."

## *Gaillardia*. Gaillardia, blanket flower

*Gaillardia aristata*, lone perennial of a fair-sized genus, mostly southern, is itself a northerner but also occurs in several counties in central southern Kansas. It inhabits the Canadian Plains widely and is common in North Dakota and Montana and in the Black Hills. It also appears in the high mountains of Colorado and west to Oregon and British Columbia. The wild plants are usually lower and more graceful than the rigidly erect garden hybrids, and some nice choices may be made from the infinitely varied proportions in breadth and length of the rays, and in their red and yellow colors. The environment of the plateau of the Cypress Hills of southern Canada seems to favor large-sized flower heads. Flowers four inches wide have been measured there, as reported by August J. Breitung who made a thorough survey of that remarkable area.

## *Galium*. Bedstraw

*Galium boreale*, an unfailingly attractive species in a genus of numerous inconspicuous weeds, is itself possessed of such an excessively weedy root that I mention it chiefly to warn you not to bring it into the garden; it is very difficult to eradicate. Dense clusters of small, white, four-petaled flowers in an upright stance, usually 12 to 18 inches tall in my area, adorn a narrow-leaved bushlet, or rather colony in favored places, from western Nebraska northward and around the whole Northern world. It flowers mainly in late June and July. Its common name refers to the fragrant dried herbage, once favored as mattress filling.

## *Gaura*. Gaura, butterfly weed

*Gaura coccinea* and its companion species, or variety, **G.** *glabra*, differ in the plant in hairiness, the former being grayish with fine, short hairs, the latter almost completely lacking hairs; and in the flower which, in the fomer, opens white and turns in a few hours to pinkish, pink, or even scarlet, and which in the latter often remains white or takes on little color. These plants frequently grow intermingled, but the **G.** *glabra* form is much more common on heavier soils. **G.** *coccinea* and **G.** *glabra* occur from Texas into southern Canada and are frequent. They vary from a few inches to a foot in height, with narrow, lightly toothed leaves of two inches or less; the flowers suggest small butterflies and, graced with long-filamented stamens, are borne in close racemes over several weeks; the lower flowers open first. The genus is unquestionably attractive and with such fragrance that a friend "would not be without it in any wild garden." My own opinion? It spreads by deep rhizomes, which reach astonishingly far and are able to send up new growth after repeated hoeings!

## *Gentiana*. Gentian

The Plains region can make little claim to gentians of significant beauty. Those that occur are rare, for they dwell mostly along streams and in moist meadows, habitats resembling in degree their wider ranges east and west. A relative, Russell prairie-gentian, has been treated under the name *Eustoma* and another relative, the green-gentian, under the name *Frasera*.

The lone gentian in my garden, a recent acquisition, came as a gratuity. At the end of June I followed a lonely road, a 38-mile stretch without human habitation. By taking a wrong turn, I had come upon an acre-wide colony of wild iris, *I. missouriensis*, which was notably dwarf in foliage and had full-size, green capsules. Only the day before and a few miles away, at a lower elevation, Dr. Bill Solheim and I hunted for depth of blue color in a large expanse of the iris at its height of bloom. But now as I was backtracking an hour later to the right road, and still puzzling over the advanced maturity of the iris, I would have dug a plant or two. However, just at the iris colony, there had come the distracting sound of something breaking in my car and then a terrible clatter—a wrecked shock bracket. The car would run; I was several hours from home; I passed up the iris.

In October I went again and dug five large clumps of the iris in five widely separated spots, for the chance of variations. When removing grass and other unwanted material from the chunks of soil, several unidentified plant bits were left with the iris roots for development, while one small, thick root came free. It was entirely strange and was replanted carefully in good soil and partial shade, where snow would lodge as a cover. By the next July, five spreading stems six to nine inches long, well-clothed with small, narrow leaves, were showing racemes of dark blue buds. Crowded, overlapping, they opened through a month's time into thrilling, one-inch miniatures of the famous *Gentiana acaulis*. They were indeed gentian trumpets—*G. affinis*. The plant came from a sunny slope, well up, with at best only average dry-country moisture.

Stevens, of North Dakota, who gives *G. affinis* the name "northern gentian," says, "It was quite common, even on rather dry hillsides, near Williston." Best, writing of the Canadian prairies, says, "Fairly common in sandy areas and moist meadows, even saline ones, throughout most of the area." *G. affinis* goes far to the west, to British Columbia to California. Gabrielson, in *Western American Alpines*, mentions it as of "swampy places, in the Cascades of Oregon and Washington."

Pool, writing years ago of the Nebraska Sandhills, listed *Gentiana puberula* and *G. andrewsii*, the closed gentian, as prominent members of the rush-sedge wet meadow association. Possibly in those congenial environments, they are still plentiful.

## *Geranium*. Geranium

For some miles along the old "Happy-Jack" road out from the Laramie Hills toward Cheyenne, through rocky pasture country, *Geranium fremontii* presents charming flowers of clear, strong pink in June. Growing about a foot high, the airy and somewhat floppy stems have much-reduced leaves. The prominent, divided, and incised basal leaves provide a restrained balance for the well-displayed, inch-wide flowers. The fleshy roots go deep. The species is at home in Wyoming and Colorado, and to Utah, on plains, foothills, and mountains.

*Geranium richardsonii* and *G. viscosissimum*, native over a vast range of the western mountains, venture on the prairies very little but are to be seen in the Cypress Hills and the Black Hills. The flowers, opening almost flat, an inch to an inch and a half wide, are white with pink veins in the one species, pink-purple or purplish red in the other; they are attractive enough in themselves and are borne scatteringly from late May through most of the summer. Plentiful as they are in the high valleys, where the tall plants with much-divided leaves are not obtrusive, they make a pleasant contribution to the landscape.

## *Geum (Sieversia).* Prairie smoke, torch flower

Refinement and delicacy of mien mark this somewhat retiring plant, *Geum triflorum (Sieversia ciliata),* which lacks the brilliancy of its relatives. Leaves of dark green covered with fine down, oblanceolate in outline and deeply incised, form handsome rosettes upon the ground from a thick, branching rhizome. In favored, somewhat shaded spots of rich soil, these rosettes make small, irregular patches of cover. A common height of stem, with much-reduced leaves, is 12 inches; stems branch to carry three gracefully pendant flowers with pale petals that never open wide. The upper stems and calyxes, however, are warmly tinted pink to bronzy red. This plant is not for those gardeners who must have a great display, but many gardeners still love it! A variation with somewhat different leaf form and a freely branching inflorescence has been called *Geum ciliatum.*

*Geum triflorum* ranges over the North American continent and is mainly northern. It is frequent in the Black Hills and common on the prairie in Montana, North Dakota, and Canada. It flowers in May and June in its more southern reaches and displays plumed seed heads for many weeks.

## *Gilia (Giliastrum, Leptodactylon).* Gilia

Gilias comprise a very large genus, mainly of the mountains and farther west. Great Plains members often follow the trend of being inconspicuous and short-lived. There are a few to be considered.

The closely set, bright medium green, needle leaves of *Gilia rigidula* v. *acerosa (Gilia acerosa, Giliastrum acerosum)* are readily mistaken for those of a phlox until it is noticed that some are not simple but pinnatifid. The species has, as well, the appearance of some low phloxes and the phlox habit of propagating by rhizomes. The flowers are an intense, bright purplish blue, five-lobed, and produced at various levels of two to six inches on the foliage tuft. The species is native to southwestern Kansas, southern Colorado, the Oklahoma and Texas Panhandles, and to New Mexico and farther west. If a recently acquired plant proves adaptable and free-flowering, it will be valuable, bringing to the garden a true and brilliant gemlike blue which no phlox approaches.

Quite different is *Gilia (Ipomopsis) congesta* with a tight tuft of densely hairy, greenish leaves, divided into several narrow segments. One to several leafy stems, four to six inches long, terminate in dense knobs of small, dusky white flowers, the knobs an inch or more wide. One might wish for a clear or sparkling white. Although this insignificant and not uncommon plant of dry, stony ridges lasts for a remarkable number of years in the garden, brilliance is denied it. Its range is from Saskatchewan to South Dakota, Wyoming, and Montana, and possibly farther west.

By some botanical legerdemain, certain authorities join *Gilia iberidifolia* and *G. congesta*. This union is incomprehensible to the layperson, since there are no apparent resemblances. Twice I have brought home plants of *G. iberidifolia* from the limy sandstone cliffs of the Pine Ridge in Nebraska; and, though the species seemed an ideally beautiful subject, it failed as certainly as any biennial. *G. iberidifolia*, according to Rydberg, ranges from North Dakota to Nebraska, Colorado, and Utah. Several stems, lightly furnished with graceful pinnatifid leaves, ascend from the crown to seven or eight inches and branch into airy panicles of many small, white flowers in as charming a pattern as one could ask for. If further tests should prove it amenable to garden habitation, it would be a highly desirable rock garden subject.

Is there an admirable form of *Gilia (Leptodactylon) pungens*? In my bumbling, early gardening days I got a plant from Colorado; later, one from sandy, clayey, rough land in Wyoming. Both times it passed on and left only the faint regret that one feels in failing with a plant of slight interest. A prickly shrublet, picturesque in its irregular shape, more often six or eight inches tall than the 30 inches it is reported to attain, *G. pungens* spends the day in anonymity and toward night opens a scattering of remotely phloxlike flowers of the color of faded newspaper. Booth, writing for Montana, says the color may be "white, yellow, lilac, or pink, often sordid with a brownish purple pigment on the back of the lobes." Someone with a taste for knicknacks might like *G. pungens*.

## *Gutierrezia.* Broom weed, golden dome    plate 57

A plant with numerous tough, branching, slender stems, *Gutierrezia sarothrae* was found to be a convenient material for fashioning brooms by the Indians. Its name, "golden dome," popularized by Oscar H. Will & Co., nurserymen of Bismark, North Dakota, refers to the form of the mature plant and its September display of effulgent color. Frequent from Saskatchewan to New Mexico and in a few states westward, the plant is always attractive; it has small, narrow, vivid green leaves, and even when young and with only a few stems, it flowers well. In full development, countless stems from the base and from repeated branching—the outer branches resting on the ground—form a symmetrical half-dome, which is hidden by tiny, sparkling blossoms in September. The domed habit, accomplished by the many stems of equal length, characterizes the plant when no more than seven or eight inches tall, but the most perfect specimens are developed at 10 to 12 inches or occasionally taller.

*Gutierrezia* has been broken into several species, distinguished with difficulty by minor characters. These are generally passed over by present authorities who regard them as varieties of *G. sarothrae*. The ardent gardener doubtless will not disagree. As a perennial, it is one of those with deciduous leaves and partly deciduous stems; some of the lower stems remain alive over the winter and put forth leaves again. This gives it the proper rating of subshrub; that is, of shrubby habit but not truly woody.

## *Haplopappus (Oonopsis, Sideranthus, Stenotus).* Mountain-gold, goldenweed    plate 58

*Haplopappus* is an intriguing name—it used to be *Aplopappus*. A revision harking back to the Greek a-aspirate brought in the "haitch" sound and elevated the backwoods pronunciation to the current one.

The genus *Haplopappus* comprises yellow-flowered composites from a dozen or so genera that have lately been brought together. Many of the discarded names applied to species of no interest to gardeners. As with most large genera, *Haplopappus* contains some weeds, some shrubs, and some highly desirable garden material. A number of the choicest species inhabit the Great Plains and are also known westward into the mountains; yet not one of them was included by Gabrielson in his *Western American Alpines*, written fifty years ago.

It has been my fortune to know *Haplopappus (Stenotus) acaulis* only in pictures and descriptions. It produces great masses of flowers in a low cushion-mound, each head on its own tiny four-inch stem, from a wide-branching crown above a stiff taproot, which is common among dry-country plants. Individual heads may lack a few ray flowers, but so closely crowded are they and so festive with their long fluff of stamens that the effect is one of happy fulfillment. Out of flower there is the mass of stiff, little leaves, slightly rough, linear to spatulate, less than two inches long. The species is chiefly of Montana and Wyoming, near or in the mountains, as in Yellowstone National Park. The flowering season is from May to July, with plants at lower altitudes blooming first.

*Haplopappus (Stenotus) armerioides* is taller than the preceding species, rising to an occasional six inches, but often lower. Some of the little stems branch and carry an extra flower or two, aiding the delightful close-company pattern of blossoming. A plant of *H. armerioides* in my garden has grown 18 inches wide. The range is from the southern border of Canada through western Nebraska. The species is not readily seen along roads; its favorite haunts are high ridges and shaly slopes, which one must climb to find it. There it is occasionally plentiful. The blooming season is mainly June.

Two other species of *Haplopappus* are appealing, as checked from herbarium specimens. My notes for *H. fremontii*: "like a taller, leafy-stemmed *H. armerioides*"; and Pesman wrote in *Meet the Natives*, "low bushy plant of warm alkaline plains, [4,000 to 6,000 feet,] having entire stiff leaves and wide composite flowers with rigid bracts; decorative." My notes on *H. lanceolatus*: "branching stems to 10 or 12 inches, inch-wide flowers; a nice thing." It apparently prefers saline flats, from southern Saskatchewan to Colorado.

In my one fair trial, *Haplopappus (Oonopsis) multicaulis*, among the most diminutive and jewellike of the race, proved intractable. Did it lack selenium, the element its sometime neighbor, the woody aster, is said to require? Surely its loss was not due to low alkalinity. Nevertheless, in another trial I should offer it a heavier proportion of limestone chip. On a certain gentle slope along a roadside in northeastern Wyoming, and again on a hardpan-looking flat, *H. multicaulis* grows by the acre. It is a dominant rather than an exclusive occupant, though in those happy areas one has eyes for little else than these bright scatterings of clustered gems. The plant has the expected widely branched crown, much of it underground, above an indivisible taproot, and innumerable stiff, little leaves in tiny rosettes. From every rosette arises a slender stem up to three inches high, simple or carrying two or three flowers with small disks and wide, round-tipped rays so closely assembled as to conceal the lower parts—this in mid-June. The species belongs chiefly to the Wyoming Plains but has been found in north-western Nebraska, in southeastern Montana, and in bordering South Dakota, near the little quadrangle north of Belle Fourche, where stands the tall pole carrying the stars and stripes that marks the geographical center of the United States.

Its wide distribution marks *Haplopappus (Sideranthus) spinulosus* as a readily adaptable species; it does, however, keep to hot upland locations of silty clay, often mixed with ancient stream-bed gravel. The range covers the Plains from central Saskatchewan to Oklahoma, Texas, New Mexico, and beyond. The plant holds to the taproot pattern but has a small crown and depends on repeated branching of the three to six decumbent main stems for spread, attaining a close mat of five to 15 inches. Pinnately divided leaves, an inch or so in length, are bristle-tipped. The pleasing all-summer effect of fine-textured, gray-green does not change until September when gray-green buds burst into a mass of golden blossoms, asterlike rather than daisylike. The neat appearance continues even as the silvery pappus tufts fluff out in October.

There is, surely, variation from this typical form; but given the tendency of some botanists to lump forms that are similar in a num-ber of characters, one cannot tell by mere names what the plant may be like. The form *H. glaberrimus* is not even acknowledged in some current references, though gardeners would find it a distinctive form. Found in sandy areas and others where *H. spinulosus* never grows, *H. glaberriumus* has one to three, quite erect stems displaying larger, pinnatifid leaves that are green, not gray. The upper inch or two of the stem is a compact raceme of the golden aster heads, which open in July or early August. These differences continue under cultivation.

## *Hedeoma*. Pennyroyal

The perennials of the Plains that were once listed as *H. camporum* and *H. drummondii* are now considered to be *Hedeoma drummondii*. This hardy and delightfully fragrant little plant of the Mint family is likely to be found on any limy outcrop from Montana and North

Dakota southward. Its best development is seen in the garden, where it is a rounded, many-branched, bushlet of small, narrow leaves and slender, bilabiate, lavender flowers, less than an inch long, over a long season. It is pleasant to have about and, though individual plants may not last long, **H. *drummondii*** is always around somewhere in the garden.

## *Hedysarum*. Sweetvetch, sweetbroom

In late June, along the roadside on rounded knolls and well-drained flats in southern Saskatchewan and western North Dakota, may be seen an astragaluslike plant, its spreading branches well covered with pinnate leaves and numerous racemes of fresh and clear pink pea blossoms. The peculiar longish pods, or legumes, with constrictions betwcen the several rounded and flattened seeds, distinguish this beautiful plant as *Hedysarum alpinum*, sometimes called **H. *alpinum* v. *americanum***. The species is credited to the plateau of the Cypress Hills in Alberta and as far south as Wyoming and South Dakota, and far to the north and northeast of the Plains region. Its pleasant habit of outspread branching, usual height below a foot, and ample flowering recommend it for choice garden sites.

*Hedysarum boreale* has quite a different character and distribution. It puts up an erect and arching stem or two, about 16 inches long, with simple racemes of narrow, reddish purple peas about July. It occurs in the Cypress Hills and southwestern Alberta, in the higher Black Hills, along the foothills in Colorado and into western Oklahoma.

Occasionally found in meadowlands throughout the Canadian Plains and farther north, *Hedysarum mackenzii* has erect stems eight to 16 inches long and larger purple-rose peas.

## *Helianthus*. Sunflower

The perennial *Helianthus rigidus* qualifies as a beautiful subject when it presents freely in midsummer its deep yellow, cosmoslike suns on a 30-inch or taller growth clothed in rough, entire, dark green foliage. To be guarded against are the reaching rhizomes with plump and active tips. The annual *H. petiolaris* has similar proportions but produces golden flowers of finer grace and more uniform perfection, on long stems desirable for cut flowers over a longer season.

In the Nebraska Sandhills, a chance rancher acquaintance took me a half-mile along a fence line to see one of his favorites: the spectacular *Helianthus maximiliani*. Common throughout the Plains from south central Saskatchewan to Texas and the bordering areas from Manitoba to Missouri, here it grew well above the level of a marshy meadow. In August and September the flowers, two to three inches wide, appear sessile on the strictly upright main stem but actually are borne on short branches that lie close against the stalk; they face outward in a solid, golden column. The color is unusually rich; disks and rays are exquisitely patterned; and the display is long-lasting. The plant is bold, with long, narrow, rough leaves, but not ungainly, and may rise from a few inches to several feet, commonly four or more. Short rhizomes build colonies when provided with ordinary garden moisture.

### *Heuchera*. Alum-root

From northwestern Nebraska well into Canada, plant hunters will find occasional thick clusters of heavy-textured leaves suggesting those of pelargoniums. These belong to *Heuchera richardsonii*, a remarkably long-lived plant that is virtually evergreen. Its only value is to provide a dependable contribution of greenery, for its tall, slender scapes carry just odd green knobs of calyxes; petals there are, if you insist, tiny, purplish petals for which you will have to hunt.

### *Houstonia (Hedyotis)*. Narrow-leaf houstonia, bluet

Houstonias are commonly called bluets, and having known and loved the very blue, little, annual *H. minima* in my early years, I was astonished to learn that a pure white flower of the family had no other popular name than bluet. Fortunately, someone had invented the name "narrow-leafed houstonia," accurate if not inspired—a simple translation of the now obsolete specific *angustifolia*. The plant is now named *H. nigricans*. Would that the botanical errors of our forebears were all that remained to be corrected!

*Houstonia nigricans* is a well-established member of the flora of the Great Plains, occupying a portion of Nebraska and practically the whole state of Kansas and extending into the high and dry Oklahoma and Texas Panhandles; it also has been reported in portions of Arkansas, Missouri, Iowa, Illinois, and Indiana. This species forms clumps of several to many stems from the ground, seven to eight inches or more high, with plentiful leafage. The leaves are short as well as narrow. The stems break upward into many fine branches, each carrying a cluster of the sparkling, four-petaled, little flowers. As the early flowers fade, they are replaced by developing buds or by new clusters. *H. nigricans* blooms from May well into summer. It decorates many soils from sand to shales to rocky outcrops, readily populating roadside banks.

In rich, sandy soil in a shallow ravine in Saskatchewan, well to the east of Regina, I found the dainty, purplish, terminal clusters of *Houstonia longifolia* in late June. They were borne six inches high, or lower, with a sparse accompaniment of small, linear to linear-oblong leaves. A companion plant was the orange puccoon, *Lithospermum canescens*, a certain indicator of moister environment than is common to the Plains. In the North the bluet has been found even farther west than has the orange puccoon, in soils of good humus content.

## *Hymenoxys (Actinea, Actinella, Tetraneuris).*
## Hymenoxys plates 59, 60

This charming group of species, which has gathered many names in botanical treatments as indicated in the heading, is known as "little yellow daisies" in familiar language. Now called *Hymenoxys*, these little yellow daisies have amply wide rays with two notches at the tip, giving the rays three short lobes like those of *Gaillardia* and *Helenium*.

Typically, *Hymenoxys acaulis* begins as a single rosette of narrow, silvery leaves an inch or two long, with a leafless stem or scape supporting a single head at four to six inches above the foliage, sometimes taller on the Plains, sometimes lower in dwarf forms in the Rockies. With below-ground branching of the crown, the original rosette soon becomes two, then four, in a geometric progression; eventually a wide mat may be formed. Each rosette produces its own flower, so the total number of flowers for well-developed plants may be 30 or 40. And there is ample space for each flower above the leafage. The result is delightful and enthralling. *H. acaulis* (stemless) belies its epithet; there are in fact short stems which are hidden by the foliage.

In the wild, *Hymenoxys acaulis* is to be seen sparingly in the southwestern portions of the Canadian Plains, much more frequently in rugged places in lime-coated gravel and on limy outcrops across Montana and western North Dakota, and southward to the Oklahoma Panhandle and into Texas. Its adaptability and free-flowering in June, with scattered flowers later, make it an ideal rock plant. It is relatively long-lived. The crowns of *H. acaulis* do not remain simple, as from a single taproot; new rosettes put down roots of their own to obtain sustenance. This habit makes the older plants readily divisible.

The description of *Hymenoxys simplex*, the more frequent form on the Plains, indicates greener leaves, but all are somewhat silvery, some as much as the most silvery of the mountain plants. In a few areas the leafage is greener, but this often appears to be local or seasonal variation. *H. torreyana*, to be seen west of Cheyenne where the prairie stretches toward the Laramie Range, is notable for having less of the silvery silkiness and for its very handsome heads, as much as an inch and three-fourths wide.

A very different species is *Hymenoxys richardsonii*. The stems are much-branched and eight to 12 inches long. Inch-wide flower heads cover the upper half or more of the plant. The green and abundant leaves are pinnatifid, with narrowly linear divisions. The crown does not widen much. Long life is not to be expected. Northern Wyoming seems to be the southern limit of the species. Montana has much of *H. richardsonii*, also western North Dakota; in Saskatchewan and Alberta, it is common throughout the dry areas.

Southern in range, *Hymenoxys scaposa* is found in the narrow strip below the Republican River in Nebraska, in most of western Kansas and some of Colorado, becoming more frequent as it crosses western Oklahoma and the High Plains of Texas and New Mexico. The epithet *scaposa*, superseding such older names as *fastigiata*, *stenophylla*, and *linearis*, will be new to most readers. The plant is relatively low and carries its yellow daisies of tooth-tipped rays on slender scapes; otherwise, it bears no casual resemblance to *H. acaulis*. There are two principal types or varieties. The old (Coulter and Nelson) *New Manual of Rocky Mountain Botany* describes in closest detail one of them under the heading *Actinella fastigiata*. It has somewhat woody, rather coarse stems as much as eight inches long, more or less reclining, branching from the ground and again above. It is densely leafy with very narrow, or linear, green leaves that tend to grow upward. The general effect is that of a compact tuft. Each branchlet lifts its scape to about six inches and contributes its flower head to the mass effect of deep yellow. The stems are entirely winter-hardy, with a bit of green showing at the tip; the whole stem leafs out again in spring. The oldest plant at Prairie Gem Ranch is 30 years old. It has extended into a loose colony, two by three feet, and is a valued plant.

Plate 1. Claude Barr at his garden gate (1976

Plate 2. Part of Barr's cactus collection

Plate 3. The shade house Barr built for plants requiring protection from the sun

Plate 4. Badlands of South Dakota, near Barr's ranch

Plate 5. Limestone butte with yucca in foreground

Plate 6. Typical Great Plains vista, sagebrush in foreground

Plate 7. *Opuntia polyacantha* growing in pastureland near Barr's ranch

Plate 8. *Anemone caroliniana*, blue form

Plate 9. *Antennaria rosea* (ladies'-tobacco), red form

Plate 10. *Arenaria hookeri* (sandwort)
and *Eriogonum flavum*
(sulphur flower)

Plate 11. *Argemone polyanthemos* (sand poppy)

Plate 12. *Artemisia filifolia* (sage)

Plate 13. *Asclepias pumila* (milkweed), pink form

Plate 14. *Aster batesii*

Plate 15. *Aster fendleri*

Plate 16. *Aster kumleinii* 'Dream of Beauty'

Plate 17. *Astragalus barrii* (Barr's milkvetch)

Plate 18. *Astragalus bisculcatus* (two-grooved milkvetch)

Plate 19. *Astragalus ceramicus* (bird egg pea)

Plate 20. *Astragalus gilviflorus*

Plate 21. *Astragalus missouriensis* (sheep pod)

Plate 22. *Astragalus sericoleucus*

Plate 23. *Astragalus spatulatus*
(tufted milkvetch)

Plate 24. *Astragalus spatulatus*

Plate 25. *Balsamorrhiza sagittata* (balsamroot)

Plate 26. *Coryphantha vivipara*

Plate 27. *Echinocereus baileyi*

Plate 28. *Echinocereus reichenbachii*

Plate 29. *Echinocereus triglochidiatus*

Plate 30. *Echinocereus viridiflorus*

Plate 31. *Opuntia imbricata*

Plate 32. *Opuntia polyacantha* 'Giant'

Plate 33. *Opuntia polyacantha* with red center

Plate 34. *Opuntia polyacantha*, orange form

Plate 35. *Opuntia polyacantha*, pink form

Plate 36. *Opuntia* 'Super-rutila',
an *O. aurea* × *rutila* hybrid

Plate 37. *Callirhoë involucrata*
(poppy mallow, wine cups)

Plate 38. *Calochortus nuttallii* (mariposa tulip, sego lily)

Plate 39. *Calochortus nuttallii*

Plate 40. *Castilleja sessiliflora*
(Indian paintbrush)

Plate 41. *Chrysothamnus nauseosus* v.
*glabratus* (rabbit brush)

Plate 42. *Clematis fremontii*

Plate 43. *Clematis occidentalis*

Plate 44. *Clematis scottii*, pink form

Plate 45. *Coreopsis tinctoria* (tickseed)

Plate 46. *Cryptantha bradburyana* (butte candle)

Plate 47. *Delphinium bicolor* (larkspur)

Plate 48. *Delphinium virescens*

Plate 50. *Echinacea angustifolia* (coneflower)

Plate 49. *Dodecatheon pulchellus*
(shooting star)

Plate 51. *Erigeron pumilus*

Plate 52. *Erigeron subtrinervis*

Plate 53. *Erigeron trifidus*

Plate 54. *Eriogonum flavum* (sulphur flower)

Plate 55. *Eritrichium howardii*

Plate 56. *Erythronium mesochorium*

Plate 57. *Gutierrezia sarothrae* (broom weed)

Plate 58. *Haplopappus multicaulis*

Plate 59. *Hymenoxys acaulis*

Plate 60. *Hymenoxys scaposa*

Plate 61. *Ipomoea leptophylla* (bigroot bush morning-glory)

Plate 62. *Iris missouriensis*

Plate 63. *Lathyrus polymorphus*

Plate 64. *Lesquerella alpina*

Plate 65. *Leucocrinum montanum* (sand-lily)

Plate 66. *Liatris punctata* (blazing-star)

Plate 67. *Lilium umbellatum* (wild red lily)

Plate 68. *Lithophragma parviflora*
(woodland star)

Plate 69. *Lithospermum caroliniense* (puccoon)

Plate 70. *Lupinus argenteus* (lupine)

Plate 71. *Lygodesmia juncea*
(prairie-pink, skeleton weed)

Plate 72. *Machaeranthera glabriuscula*
(woody aster)

Plate 73. *Melampodium leucanthum*

Plate 74. *Mentzelia decapetala* (stickleaf)

Plate 75. *Mertensia lanceolata* (bluebell),
blue and white forms

Plate 76. *Microseris cuspidata*

Plate 77. *Mirabilis multiflora* (four-o'clock)

Plate 78. *Oenothera brachycarpa*
(Evening-primrose)

Plate 79. *Oenothera caespitosa* (Evening-primrose)

Plate 80. *Oenothera lavandulaefolia*

Plate 81. *Oenothera serrulata*
(*Calylophus serrulatus*)

Plate 82. *Oenothera speciosa*, pink form

Plate 83. *Oxytropis multiceps*

Plate 84. *Oxytropis sericea*

Plate 85. *Penstemon ambiguus*

Plate 86. *Penstemon angustifolius*, albino

Plate 87. *Penstemon angustifolius*

Plate 88. *Penstemon glaber*

Plate 89. *Penstemon haydeni*

Plate 91. *Penstemon nitidus*

Plate 90. *Penstemon haydeni* in a Sandhills blowout

Plate 92. *Petalostemon oligophyllus*
(prairie clover)

Plate 93. *Phlox alyssifolia* 'Pale Moon'

Plate 94. *Phlox andicola* near
Persian yellow rose

Plate 95. *Phlox hoodii*

Plate 96. *Polygala alba* (milkwort)

Plate 97. *Potentilla concinna* (cinquefoil)

Plate 98. *Prunus besseya* (sand cherry)

Plate 99. *Pulsatilla patens* (pasque flower)

Plate 100. *Rosa arkansana* 'J. W. Fargo'
(wild rose)

Plate 101. *Rudbeckia laciniata*

Plate 102. *Scutellaria resinosa* (skullcap)

Plate 103. *Sedum lanceolatum* (stonecrop)

Plate 104. *Senecio fendleri* (groundsel, ragwort)

Plate 105. *Solidago missouriensis* (goldenrod)

Plate 106. *Sphaeralcea coccinea* (scarlet mallow)

Plate 107. *Stanleya pinnata* (prince's plume)

Plate 108. *Talinum parviflorum* (sunbright)

Plate 109. *Thermopsis rhombifolia* (golden pea)

Plate 110. *Townsendia exscapa* (Easter-daisy)

Plate 111. *Townsendia hookeri*

Plate 112. *Tradescantia bracteata* (spiderwort), blue, pink, and white forms

Plate 113. *Viola vallicola* 'Gold Nugget' (violet)

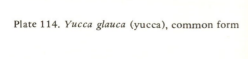

Plate 114. *Yucca glauca* (yucca), common form

Plate 115. *Yucca glauca*, red sepal form

Plate 116. *Zigadenus venenosus* (false camas)

Plate 117. *Zinnia grandiflora*

Plate 118. *Juniperus scopulorum*
with Badlands in background

Plate 119. *Yucca glauca* in the Black Hills. View toward Claude Barr's home

The description in Coulter and Nelson under the heading ***Actinella linearis*** is less detailed; it does not mention that the stems are shorter and slenderer, that the scapes are tall and slender, the leaves very slender, almost linear. Density of the green leafage and its upright stance and the especially neat arrangement of the mellow golden rays on scapes, which may be five to 10 inches tall, are left for the investigator to discover. This variant was the favorite little yellow daisy of Mrs. C. I. DeBevoise, one of the founders of the American Rock Garden Society. My two early importations met with misfortune after a brief life; whether the variety is capable of long life is yet to be learned. Years later, I visited the former place of Mrs. Neva Belew in western Oklahoma and dug up my own plants, and again more recently. The last lot, given a footing of sand, clay, limestone chip, and peat moss, has persisted through two winters. These plants were dug from hard, gravelly, silty clay as rather small individuals. They were not in close colonies, and their simple root systems gave no sign of colony-forming capacity.

## *Hypoxis*. Yellow star-grass

For a species with no reputation as a weed, the gentle and unobtrusive ***Hypoxis hirsuta***, known over much of the eastern half of the North American continent, has bravely faced the prevailing westerly winds and established itself as far as the center of Kansas, much farther in the Sandhills portion of Nebraska, almost to the Missouri River in its southerly course through the Dakotas and farther north, into Saskatchewan. Wise little plant that it is, it has sought out habitats where it can maintain its foothold, such as the often moist hay meadows in the Nebraska Sandhills. There, growing only four to six inches, it puts up its miniature reflections of the sun, singly or in clusters, over a long season beginning in spring. In the garden, several plants may be set close together for a pleasing effect.

## *Ipomoea*. Bigroot bush morning-glory     plate 61

One of the most spectacular individual plants of the Plains, ***Ipomoea leptophylla*** can be seen in sandy, silty, and gravelly places from Texas to central Montana. It appears as a bold, loose mound of arching, tapering stems with lance-linear leaves as much as six inches long. From June to August come ample trumpets of subdued rose-purple, about two inches wide—a welcome sight. The stems commonly grow 30 inches long, but since they are arching and drooping, they do not usually extend the spread of the plant beyond four feet or the height beyond two. The root of this bush morning-glory grows to an astonishing size. There is usually a foot of neck the thickness of a thumb or larger, a wide enlargement or tuber two feet long, and a simple or branching root that goes to a great depth. The tuber, obviously for water storage, serves to maintain life through long years of drought, yet often does not provide for maximum flowering. A peculiarity of the plant is that all green parts are frost-tender. In fall all is killed back by the first frost; the problem of spring frost is sidestepped by very late germination. The large, velvety, brown seeds should be planted so that they receive a good soaking and freezing before warm weather comes, though they will not germinate until days and nights are definitely warm. They are readily started by cutting or filing a small hole in the seed coat and soaking the seeds overnight in warm water. Transplanting may be done only when the plant is dormant.

## *Iris*. Wild iris, Missouri iris    plate 62

One of the major wild flowers of the Black Hills, **Iris missouriensis** appears nowhere else on the Great Plains, though it does occur in the outlying ranges of the western mountains. Near the 4,000-foot level, it is most often found in valleys, but at greater elevations it takes to rocky slopes and ridges. The species must be provided with abundant moisture early in the season if flowering, which occurs in June, is to take place. Late in the season, the plant's endurance of drought is remarkable. In my garden, self-sown seedlings have matured into flowering plants in almost full sun in unmodified tough gumbo, with only the natural rainfall.

The Black Hills strains of **Iris missouriensis** are, perhaps, somewhat dwarfed, for they never reach the two feet sometimes reported in other locations; a common height for the narrow, stiff leaves is 12 to 14 inches, even with much shade, with the flags just above. The color of the rather narrow segments is generally a silvery light blue, with darker linings on the falls and a touch of yellow along the midrib. Specimens may be seen with heavier linings, or with the lines arranged in a noticeable pattern, or with the yellow patch increased to a splotch. There are occasional albinos, some with a fair-sized patch of gold.

*Juniperus.* Red cedar, creeping juniper, common juniper

Variation should be expected in any species of plant that crosses a continent or circles a hemisphere, and in the juniper especially there appears a tendency to endless variation. Numerous cultivars have been named and propagated by commercial growers. A cultivar name, indicated by single quotes, provides a ready means of identifying a plant that is in the nursery trade and is propagated vegetatively. Unfortunately, it does not, even when registered, prevent renaming.

Almost equally vulnerable is the botanical name, *Juniperus communis*, which has borne a number of varietal names. On the Plains, this wide-ranging species closely resembles *J. communis* v. *depressa*, which forms a very beautiful spread of 10 to even 15 feet, grows 24 to 30 inches tall, and has wide twigs of partly silvered needles as long as one-half inch. In the Black Hills, it often accepts much shade as it climbs above 7,000 feet, or much sun at levels as low as 3,000 feet. At the latter level, at least, it can be rated as weatherproof. In my garden, a 40-year-old specimen is a prized possession. It is in full sun for most of the day and exposed to the strong, westerly prairie winds.

On the Plains *Juniperus communis* is found only as far south as the rugged portion of western Nebraska, and the Plains of Wyoming. Northward it occurs in the Badlands of North Dakota, in rugged parts of Montana, and through most of the Canadian Plains.

Generally northern and ocurring across the North American continent, *Juniperus horizontalis* has adapted to the Great Plains and in particular locations shows remarkable variation. It ranges from Wyoming and South Dakota through Montana and North Dakota, and becomes common throughout the drier parts of Alberta and Saskatchewan. Its favorite habitat is on sloping stony ground, often steeply sloping and away from the sun. In places it ventures over a limy summit to a southern exposure. There one may find remarkable varieties that are compact, silver to green, and as low as two inches above the ground. In contrast, I observed a specimen in the wild with a spread of 30 feet and a height of three to five inches; the ground was completely carpeted. The leaves of *J. horizontalis* are tiny and imbricated, diminutively shaggy, fine-textured. Its branches root as they advance. Where a root of suitable size for digging is found, the extremity of the branch may be trimmed back and a transplant obtained.

The range of the western cedar, **Juniperus scopulorum**, is limited on the north and east by the Missouri River in Montana and the Dakotas, and to certain rough portions of Nebraska, Colorado, and other southern Plains states. The species is scattered far westward in the mountains. It is slow growing and remains a small tree, except in favored locations. Its ability to endure drought largely determines the extent of its Plains range and its frequent occurrence in pure stands. Its typical outline is pyramidal, with graceful branching from the ground. Its leaves are mere overlapping scales. Its "cones" ripen in the second year to a blue-black berry with a heavy bluish bloom and are much sought for Christmas decorations. These fruits are borne only on pistillate trees. As a tree, *J. scopulorum* is especially valuable for dry and exposed places. As a garden ornament, it may be trimmed to any desired form and held to size for many years. In certain areas, the foliage tends to be silvery, varying from a striking blue-silver on the new growth to a more permanent silveriness on older leaves. In a local area of the Little Missouri Badlands in North Dakota, the tree assumes a narrow columnar form and remains quite small.

## *Kuhnia*. Kuhnia

It is difficult to attach a scientific name to the plant under this heading, which is of interest to gardeners. It is a prairie plant with many spreading stems from a stout taproot. Its many leaves are rough-textured, ovate-lanceolate, long-tapering, and prominently toothed toward the tip. Numerous fluffy cream-white corymbs appear in the summer. The plant is a low mound, the stems of 12 inches or less reaching outward, then upward to present the flower clusters upright—altogether a pleasing habit. It is not especially noticeable, except in flower or when decked with its even more conspicuous, luminous, gray-white, seed pompons or pappus. Its chief charm is this long-lasting, after-frost show from September to December, when the winds slowly disperse the seeds with their flaring tassels. It is presently classified as **Kuhnia eupatorioides v. corymbosa** (which now includes the former **glutinosa** and **suaveolens**). Other varieties are also presently included in the group species; they are upright and tall, obtrusively weedy, and lack the well-clustered flowers and seed tufts. We can ignore them and call our chosen type simply kuhnia. It is often seen along roadsides and in pastures from Montana and North Dakota to Texas.

## *Lathyrus*. Wild sweet pea, sand pea      plate 63

Almost exclusively of the Plains from North Dakota and Wyoming to Oklahoma, especially in sand or sandy soils, the sand pea spreads patches of magnetic color on flats, road banks, and steep slopes, built by the wind in the lea of blowouts, in April or May. The individual flower in a cluster of two to five is almost an inch long and of ample width, from light to strong purplish pink in the banner—never "blue" except in the withered state—and white to pink in the wing petals. The stem and leaves, without tendrils, are a waxy, glaucous, green. Often a colony completely covers the ground with more flowers than leafage, but a lone flowering stem or two attracts and charms. This is *Lathyrus polymorphus*, formerly known as *L. ornatus (L. stipulaceus, L. incanus)*. There are two forms, not distinguishable at a glance; *ornatus*, quite glabrous, and *incanus*, softly velvety. Both are frequently found in the same area.

A colony is established by deep-seated, rhizome-bearing roots; since the roots and shoots are slender and brittle, they are difficult to move. The plant should not be placed in the garden, where its dense growth, four to six inches tall, will overrun more delicate plants. It is not rampant, however. Relieved of strong competition, it thrives even in heavy soils.

*Lathyrus hapemanii* A. Nels., listed by Rydberg in *Flora of the Prairies and Plains*, is also *L. polymorphus*. It was discovered by Dr. H. Hapeman in southern Nebraska and described by Dr. A. Nelson as "yellow or ochroleucous" from a discolored, dried specimen, according to Dr. Hapeman, who gave me plants from his garden. Seedlings from this pure white-flowered strain reverted to purplish pink; hence the white form must have been an albino. The plant pictured in plate 63 was growing near Carpenter, Wyoming.

*Lathyrus ochroleucus*, a green-foliaged, tendriled, pale yellow to white, smaller-flowered species, grows 30 or more inches tall and frequents shady places from the Black Hills northward, especially throughout the Canadian area. It has mildly aggressive roots and is easily grown in shade—if anyone likes its color.

## *Lesquerella*. Bladder-pod, lesquerella      plate 64

From the vast and weedy Mustard family, a few species of *Lesquerella* and *Physaria* can be considered appealing rock garden prospects, because of their novel and distinctive form and fine color. The most compact and diminutive is **Lesquerella alpina**. In full flower it is a startling solid gold tuft or bun, dropped by chance on solid, gray or brown rock. At times it appears as the sole occupant of the almost invisible fissures in which the roots find anchorage. Plants with a four-inch spread are to be seen in their native footings. Around the flower mass a slight fringe of narrow, gray leaves may show. The crowded, cruciform florets seem to have pushed and shoved in their exuberant effort to be all upstage at the same moment. Their manners are the same, whether south in the Nebraska Panhandle or along the Pine Ridge in Wyoming in May, or far up in North Dakota and Montana in June. *L. alpina* has been reported in Utah and Colorado and has been given its name because it is found at high altitudes, though Pesman did not list it for his state of Colorado in *Meet The Natives*. Is this species normally short-lived, or did I give it too strong a ration of limestone chips? Small plants, which I brought in, wintered and flowered, then failed to survive the summer.

Over wide stretches of the Pierre clay pastures of western South Dakota appears an insignificant and puzzling bladder-pod which I have been told is **Lesquerella arenosa**. It is frequent around Prairie Gem Ranch and even comes uninvited into my garden to display some indifferent bits of bright color briefly in May. In the manuals the closest specific description is that of *L. arenosa*, but I suspect that the plant has no name and remains a case for a qualified taxonomist. The epithet *arenosa*, meaning "sand loving," is here inappropriate. On other soils, including sandy but not dune sand, other bladder-pods, which are similar in stem and leaf and pod characters, carry splendid racemes two and a half inches long and well filled with golden blossoms—a delightful effect—and to these the same name, *L. arenosa*, has been applied. Any gardener would at once take into his or her heart this lovely flower and the name *L. arenosa*, and leave the unworthy variant of the gumbo to the botanists. The indicated range for the species is from southern South Dakota northward. In *Wild Plants of the Canadian Prairies*, Budd and Best write, "Not necessarily on sandy ground, for it has been collected on the Regina plains." But I know of no gumbo in Saskatchewan.

A regular denizen of the sands, **Lesquerella ludoviciana**, lanky, narrow-petaled, and lacking color, has no desirable forms. Other lesquerellas, intermediate between the tiny, crowded *L. alpina* and the much larger *L. spatulata*, are often found throughout the Plains. Their smooth-edged, lanceolate, gray leaves in rosettes readily place them in the genus, but identifying them by any technical description is difficult. None that I have seen offers outstanding performance.

It is a happier moment when one finds *Lesquerella ovalifolia*, handsome in its distinctive leaf pattern and abundant racemes of relatively large, wide-petaled, brilliant golden flowers. This species has a wide range from mid-Nebraska to Oklahoma, Texas, and New Mexico. It grows readily from seed and has a reasonable life span. The leaves, orbicular to oval, an inch or so long, are in basal rosettes; they are smooth-edged, rather stiff, and gray with a thick texture of stellate hairs which appear, under a hand lens, to be star-shaped clusters. Does this description appeal to a busy gardener? The stellate hairs do give the foliage a microscopic sparkle; moreover, such a coating enables the leaf to resist the stresses of summer and winter and to maintain a useful degree of evergreenness. In addition, hairiness indicates that the plant is well suited to endure heat and dry air and that it requires drainage.

*Lesquerella spatulata* occurs from Manitoba to Montana, to Nebraska and Utah, according to Rydberg. This fine species varies with the locality. On a butte of the rawest of badland clays, well-supplied with limestone fragments, its habit and flowering reach perfection; in seemingly identical footing on a butte a dozen miles away, where I have observed it for many years, the flower never glows with quite the effulgence of the other. This probably represents only a drifting apart in types, an evolutionary movement. There can have been no interchange between these habitats, since the intervening badland clays and sands were long ago eroded to uncover the gumbo on which *L. spatulata* does not appear. In the gumbo of my garden it self-sows moderately, but plainly prefers the scree beds. Its leaves are broadly spatulate with a short, sharp tip; it survives the winter as a beautiful symmetrical rosette which is formed in the fall.

Most of these species have stiff, little-branched, deep-reaching roots. Small plants are moved readily. The name "bladder-pod" refers to the oval, inflated capsules, about a fourth of an inch long, which yield an ample quantity of reddish brown, disklike seeds.

## *Leucocrinum*. Sand-lily    plate 65

Several thick, moisture-storing roots, spreading from a tiny crown two inches underground, mark the precocious little sand-lily, *Leucocrinum montanum*, in place of the expected bulb. All growth arises from this buried crown: channeled leaves of light glaucous green, four to eight inches long; and six-segmented, white corollas diffusing a gentle breath of spring, where dozens or hundreds sparkle on a warming slope on which a snowbank has lately lain. Flowering of any one plant lasts for many days and the colonies, according to exposure, from early April to the end of May. Many flowers in a close cluster may open at one time, and a mature plant, with multiple crowns, may produce as many as 40 flowers in a season. Since the long tube of the blossom comes from underground, the large, angular, black seeds are formed deep down. One digs for them. The flower may be little more than an inch or all of two inches wide, the lobes, or petals, often straplike. The finest forms, however, have quite wide petals. The plants are dormant by midsummer and reappear in the spring. They can be safely transplanted, even with much of the long roots lost, but may skip a years's flowering while becoming adjusted.

The sand-lily prefers a firm clay or sandy clay loam or gravelly clay to pure sand. This lone species of the genus is especially abundant in western South Dakota and Nebraska. Elsewhere its distribution follows a peculiar pattern; it takes to the foothills in Colorado and goes down to New Mexico; it also occurs in extreme southwestern North Dakota and in the Plains and mountains of Montana and Wyoming, as well as in scattered stations as far as California and Oregon.

## *Lewisia*. Bitter-root

As it is the nature of species to extend their range, *Lewisia rediviva*, chiefly at home in the mountains from Montana to Arizona and to California and British Columbia, has slipped away from the paternal roof in the latitude of the Bighorn Mountains in northern Wyoming and by its unique facility for seed dispersal has spread a wide salient on the Great Plains. It is one of the loveliest flowes of the West and Montana's floral emblem. Wide, many-petaled, glowing rose-pink, close to the ground, singly or in cluster, hiding such wisps of leaf as remain, the flower gives the prairies a rare complexion in favored expanses, beginning in mid-June. A thick, curiously branching, shallow red root, with a single or many crowns, produces from a few to more than 50 flowers. Soon many shining black seeds ripen in a thin-cased ovary, while the showy flower parts bleach and fold over, building a sort of chambered nautilus by which means **L. *rediviva*** has happily taken advantage of the urgent winds and voyaged eastward. The footing in this extended range, where the bitter-root has met with success, is a uniform silty loam with an increment of volcanic ash and usually free from gravel; sands, shales, and low spots are passed over. The infrequent heavy rains during the summer, when the dormant plant is fitted to endure a long drought, may penetrate well below the depth of the root without detriment in the well-drained sites the species chooses. In September or later, new leaves come directly from the crown, half an inch below the ground; dark green, awl-shaped, succulent, in a tuft or small rosette, they remain through winter and in spring spread into a flat rosette about four inches wide, a cradle for the incipient buds.

Doubtless this exquisite immigrant has fully adjusted to the new Plains habitat and will extend its ground as far as agreeable footing permits. Good land lies ahead. Some day a whirling air current will waft a cargo of seeds across the narrow Belle Fourche River, and the final 45 miles of Wyoming will have been entered.

Seeds germinate readily when moisture and temperature are suitable, and they are known to sprout at temperatures just above freezing. During first and even second dormancies, the shallow roots may be too undeveloped to withstand the stresses of heat and drought; they simply burn out. In the garden a light mulch or a lath half-shade takes the place of shielding, sparse, and low prairie grasses in the wild.

## *Liatris*. Blazing-star, gay-feather, liatris      plate 66

The blazing-stars lavishly contribute strong purple or rose-purple to late summer landscapes or the garden. The color, clear and beautiful, is accentuated by transmitted and reflected light. Two general types of inflorescence are common; the one with long, slender spikes of solid color, the heads of few florets closely set; the other with spaced, large heads, sessile or on short peduncles.

Following the latter pattern is *Liatris aspera*—now the correct name of a species that borders or extends sparingly on to the Plains from the East. It is listed in older works and often grown in gardens under the name **L. *scariosa***, which properly applies to a related species of the East. *L. aspera* attains a height of a yard or more, and the long raceme is composed of wide flower heads, each with as many as 40 florets. It flowers in September.

In my garden *Liatris lancifolia*, whether obtained from the valley of the Platte River or from moist meadows in the Sandhills, dons its Tyrian raiment and commands attention in August. The plants may exceed a yard in height, and the rodlike, empurpled inflorescence, in full flower midway through the blooming cycle, fills much of its length. Habitats of this lovely species range from the southeastern tip of South Dakota through Nebraska to just across the Wyoming line; through much of the High Plains of Kansas, to Denver in Colorado, and to the New Mexico mountains.

If the case of *Liatris lancifolia* is not one of closely parallel evolution, it may be a western element cut off by the continental ice sheets of the glacial age from *L. spicata* of the eastern states. It is essentially *L. spicata* "gone western." Gaiser, the monographer of *Liatris*, points out no differences between *L. lancifolia* and *L. spicata* other than the wider basal leaves in *L. lancifolia*. The original *L. lancifolia* came from wet places in the New Mexico mountains. The same gay-feather when late discovered in the Great Plains was referred to as *L. kansana* in some manuals, but Gaiser did not think these two could be distinguished. To be botanically correct we must refer to our "spicata west" as *L. lancifolia*.

With the widest portion of its range from Alberta to Manitoba, *Liatris ligulistylis* occupies the western sections of the Dakotas, the prairies of Montana and Wyoming, and in Colorado withdraws to the foothills and lower mountains. As do most members of the genus, it grows from a shallow, flattish, cormlike rootstock, with a rosette of long, oblanceolate leaves on each stem. The height is commonly 18 to 20 inches with the heads sessile, or taller and with some branching. The heads are extra wide masses of luminous purple fluff, and the uppermost, which opens first, may have many more than the average of 70 florets. This color and texture provide an intriguing contrast for the adjacent bract-enclosed buds of glossy maroon. Flowering occurs throughout July. After the seeds ripen and disperse, the ample circles of bracts spread widely and simulate flower forms, valued for winter arrangements.

Rydberg gave the name *Liatris haywardii* to a species of the Black Hills and elsewhere. From a gardener's viewpoint it is simply

*L. ligulistylis* with green bud-bracts instead of the highly colored ones.

*Liatris mucronata*, a segregate from *L. punctata*, is frequent in eastern Kansas; its full range is not yet known. Its close arrangement of small heads of fine purple is patterned like that of *L. punctata*, but its spires of bloom are longer and held less erect, and its similar narrow leaves have fewer dots. Its less obvious but critical differentiating feature is the globular corm, in contrast to the elongated rootstock of the other. The flowering time of *L. mucronata*, late August and September, in part overlaps that of *L. punctata*.

A true product of the Great Plains environment, *Liatris punctata* has a thick, deep-reaching, moisture-storing taproot. So it is sure to develop its many spires of fine clear purple, even in a dry year, above the ample tuft of mainly basal, long and narrow, dotted, and harshly rough leaves. A common height is 10 inches, rarely 14 inches; even in the far South, where much vegetation grows taller, only a few stems reach 20 inches. Some of these southern plants have been given specific or varietal names — but there is little to distinguish them. In moist climates, *L. punctata* often seems to need lime or potash to stiffen its stems, which grow erect in its native soils. This liatris occupies the entire Plains region as far north as Edmonton, Alberta, and Prince Albert, Saskatchewan, and a wide border to the east from Manitoba to Texas. Its flowering season is mainly August.

*Liatris pycnostachya* is a large and showy gay-feather with a somewhat club-shaped inflorescence, its principal range extends over the moister midwestern prairies; it comes briefly on to the Plains from North Dakota to Oklahoma, and in Kansas reaches to about the 1,800-foot contour. This species also has the elongated rootstock. Its flowering season is August-September.

Three varieties of the mainly eastern *Liatris squarrosa* are Great Plains dwellers. *L. squarrosa* v. *glabrata* ranges from sandy areas of extreme southern South Dakota through all the Sandhills portion of Nebraska, into the sands of Yuma County in northeastern Colorado, across Kansas from northeast to southwest, and beyond to the sandy Canadian River country of Texas. Novel rather than showy, it has long slender dark leaves, long prickly-appearing bracts, and deeple purple floret tufts which are eye-catching and ornamental in the garden. In very sterile sand the plant may reach a height of eight to 10 inches and bear a single head; elsewhere it may grow 18 to 30 inches tall and carry 10 or 20 heads. *L. squarrosa* v. *compacta*, distinctive for having a very leafy stem but otherwise a close approximation of v. *glabrata*, is reported to begin its blooming in June in central Kansas. The characteristic feature of *L. squarrosa* v. *hirsuta* is the hairiness of its green parts, at least when the plant is young. These three varieties grow from small, globular corms. All are among the earlier-flowering kinds.

The Great Plains region marks the westward extension of the genus *Liatris*, which is mostly concentrated in the eastern United States. The species *L. ligulistylis* and *L. punctata* are thought to have originated on the Plains, and only these two and the New Mexico member of the *L. spicata*-*L. lancifolia* complex reach the western mountains.

## *Lilium*. Wild red lily      plate 67

*Lilium umbellatum*, or *L. philadelphicum* v. *andinum*? Both names have their adherents. As distinguished from the eastern *L. philadelphicum*, our western plant is lower; has narrower, lanceolate leaves scattered on the stem, except for a whorl at the summit; bears its flowers singly or in an umbel of no more than three; and is adaptable to alkaline soils. The flower color is a rich burnt orange-red with blackish spots low on the segments; blooming occurs about July 1. Whether growing on grassy hummocks in moist meadows of the Nebraska Sandhills or better-drained meadows in North Dakota, Saskatchewan, and Alberta, the wild red lily lifts its stems and flowers into the sun. In its Black Hills habitat and in mountains to the west, it seeks coolness in the shade of thin forest or other vegetation. It is important that the somewhat fleshy roots be kept fresh, as well as the small, rough-scaly bulb. In the garden this lily does not survive prolonged drying out; otherwise, its culture is simple in half-shade and in a soil well supplied with humus to the depth of the bulb or deeper. A four-inch depth is suitable.

## *Linnaea*. Twin-flower

A dainty and ingratiating member of the Honeysuckle family is *Linnaea borealis* v. *americana*. In the more delicate and typical European form, the great Linnaeus chose to have this plant commemorate his name. As one of the most untypical of Great Plains habitants, the twin-flower maintains a footing, doubtless as a relict of moister times, in many northern sites. Requirements are coolness and freedom from alkalinity, if not a degree of acidity; but as to moisture—the twin-flower must face some rough times during the long Plains droughts. It has retreats in the Black Hills, in the Killdeers of North Dakota, in southeastern Montana, and in the wooded spots of Canada. Slender stems, which lie upon the ground, are often reddish tinted, many inches long, and branching little. Hardly mat-forming, the stems carry paired, dark green leaves of thumbnail size; from them arise dainty upright stems, to four inches, which bear in summer the couplets of the nodding, funnelform, pink flowers of amazing fragrance.

## *Linum*. Wild blue flax

Covering the Plains from Texas into southern Canada, though by no means to be seen everywhere, **Linum lewisii** in the morning opens alluring light true blue, inch-wide blossoms which, like bubbles in the wind, are gone by noon. These are borne, at 12 to 20 inches, from May well into summer. Never becoming clumpy or overbearing, the plant puts up only a few slender stems, clothed with a complement of narrow, inch-long, light glaucous green leaves, and retains an admirable airy quality. Wild blue flax grows readily from seed.

## *Lithophragma*. Woodland star, prairie star    plate 68

Very common in the Black Hills in valleys or on high slopes, wooded or sunny, is the dainty **Lithophragma parviflora**. Because it is so unobtrusive when not in flower and so early dormant, the plant makes its presence known only for a brief period in the spring. But the gardener who has brought it home cherishes the few weeks of slash-tipped, sparkling white stars and plans for their certain return another spring. In Wyoming, in favorable soil, **L. parviflora** thrives under the open sky. The species is also found in Montana and a narrow strip of Canada, both of which places, along with Wyoming, are reported to have a somewhat similar species, **L. bulbifera**—this I have never seen, or recognized. These members of the Saxifrage clan come from tiny, multiplying, pink tubers, an inch or so deep, and form small clusters of much-divided, velvety dark leaves, or mats when many plants lie close together. Soon upright stems with diminished leaves begin to show the novel stars at four inches. For a few weeks the stems lengthen with four or five flowers out at one time, until at 12 inches a lone star closes the act. The tubers have remarkable stamina and, with good drainage, need only a small reserve of undisturbed space.

## *Lithospermum*. Puccoon (an Indian name), lithosperm plate 69

The showy puccoons of the Great Plains belong also to the midland states and provinces. In our region, a few to several stems rise in the spring from an underground crown, grow to a height of 12 inches or less, and bear yellow or orange flowers. The leaves are relatively small and narrow, more or less grayish. The roots are brown to black, thick tapering, seldom branching. Pencil-thin or smaller roots are easily transplanted to well-drained locations, preferably when plants are dormant or show little growth, for mature foliage quickly smothers and blackens. These species are propagated by seed.

*Lithospermum canescens*, the hoary puccoon, blooms in a soft deep orange. The five petals have smooth edges; the leaves grow two inches long and are hairy but rather green. The species avoids the drier Plains, northward from Texas, then reaches much farther west in the sands of Nebraska and southern South Dakota and in North Dakota and Saskatchewan, again extends westward where richer, moisture-retentive soils cater to its preferences.

Bearing the largest flowers of the Plains trio, *Lithospermum caroliniense (L. gmelinii)*, the Carolina puccoon, accepts drier footing and is at home where its favored sandy soils prevail, from southern South Dakota to Texas. Its rich deep yellow flowers, up to three-fourths of an inch wide, are freely borne, mainly in June, over the rounded, domelike bush. Of this I have had only damaged roots, which failed.

With lightly slashed and ruffled petals, the fringed puccoon, *Lithospermum incisum (L. linearifolium)*, glows delightfully in medium yellow, mainly in May. This kind, not unknown on heavy soils, is far more frequent in loose sand and flowers there in gay abundance. Many stonelike, polished, whitish seeds are produced later, cleistogamously, from colorless flowers. *L. incisum* covers the Plains region from Canada to Texas and Mexico, and extends somewhat westward as well as into the midland from the Plains.

## *Lobelia*. Cardinal flower, lobelia

Not commonly known and not readily seen, *Lobelia cardinalis* v. *phyllostachya (L. splendens)* dwells mostly above the 1,800-foot contour in Kansas and across into Colorado. It makes its presence known unfailingly by tallish spires of a deeper crimson than that of the more eastern **L. cardinalis**. Also different are the leaves, linear to linear-lanceolate. Its need for moisture restricts this lobelia to secluded hideouts. It flowers in July and later.

Especially abundant in sandhill swales and wet meadows in Nebraska and extending into neighboring states, **Lobelia siphilitica v. ludoviciana** bears, from August on, slender, bright deep blue spikes 10 to 20 inches long. This variety is less hairy and lower.

## *Lomatium (Cogswellia)*. Wild parsley

Many are the wild parsleys, and many names have been bandied about, until it has become a task for the uninitiated to determine, by consulting a manual, what plant he or she has found and so say what is the correct name. Few of the parsleys are worth the checking, however. An admirable one is **Lomatium foeniculaceum (L. villosum)** of April and May. Pleasing soft green-gray, ferny leaf masses, a few inches tall, and many wide compound umbels of mellow gold are to its credit; the plant's chief demerit is that it is completely dormant by June. This parsley might bear the name "wild celery" because of its taste and fragrance. It comes from a thick pencillike root and is common, especially in heavy soils, from Nebraska to Canada. By contrast, a parsley with highly glossy parts can be found in the genus **Musineon**.

## *Lupinus*. Lupine   plate 70

In widely separated places over the Plains one comes upon lupines singly or in scattered colonies, or upon vast fields of thousands upon thousands which at a little distance merge into an unbroken, vibrant purple-blue sheet. This is the color of most of our lupines, though the hue varies from lighter to stronger purple, according to the species or perhaps according to locality and soil. Lupine leaf and flower patterns are neat, attractive, and intriguing. The leaves are composed of a few to many leaflets, all attached digitately to the leaf-stalk tip, and the plump, tapering racemes of pea florets are closely set. A plant with many branching stems and clusters of flowers may be a nice size for the garden. Try digging one, or a dozen. The soil may be hard and stony and, though the plant may be only 10 to 12 inches high, the root will be coarse and tough enough to turn a spade—and you will probably be unable to discover its depth. There seem to be no small plants, and, when blooming is at its best, ripe seed will not be available for some weeks. You will, however, when you are miles away, remember those acres of purple with a stipple or two of pink or of sparkling white.

Finding a name for your lupine, with the aid of descriptions or with the assistance of botanists, may be as frustrating as the attempt at collecting, so alike are the leaves and their silky vesture of hairs and so variable is the species in different habitats. And so often does the name *Lupinus argenteus* appear that you begin to rely on that name for any lupine, whether it be the compact, blue-purple plant of Montana; the laxer, more purplish one of Wyoming; or the immense, mounded, purplish pinks and whites of the Pine Ridge table in Nebraska. If the flattish, beanlike seed is available, it may be of a fine lupine or it may be of *L. parviflorus*, *L. alpestris*, or another of less impact, but there seem to be no weeds. *L. argenteus* is recorded for the Cypress Hills and elsewhere in southern Canada, extreme western portions of the Dakotas, and for the foothills of Colorado.

*Lupinus plattensis* is readily distinguished by its different coloring, a light purple with a vivid dark purple blotch at the center. The florets are borne in upright, broad spires 10 to 14 inches high. The dark leaves are of typical pattern, as is the deeply plunging root. This distinctive and desirable species inhabits rugged places in western Nebraska, southeastern Wyoming, and through Colorado into the western Oklahoma Panhandle.

Scattered through the general lupine range is the little annual *Lupinus pusillus*, bright blue with a white flash, seen briefly in June. It does not have quite the pure blue of the Texas blue-bonnet, which is not native to the high Plains, nor does it attempt a landscape effect, but it is eye-catching in its modest way. Hurriedly it ripens a quota of seeds and drops out of sight. In the garden, the plant is sure to bring forth welcome pairs of its broad seed-leaves in April.

## *Lygodesmia.* Prairie-pink, skeleton weed      plate 71

The slender, upright stems and their furnishing of long-attenuate, linear leaves, all in faintly glaucous green, are markedly inconspicuous in *Lygodesmia grandiflora*. But especially fitting is their setting for the May-July production of two-inch, chicory-type blooms in a glamorous soft, deep pink. The flowers were half-open and nodding when I first saw this plant, but their color was unforgettable. Roots judged ample to support the plants I brought into my garden seemed to fail almost at once and soon not a remnant remained. But with another spring up came leaves and stems, then flowers with their thrilling color. Early dormancy seems to be the species' order. A small colony remains with me under average care. This species is said to be plentiful on low gravelly hills along the mountains of Wyoming and Colorado and somewhat to the west. Its local distribution indicates some root spreading, without weediness. The general height is eight inches.

Almost all aspects of *Lygodesmia juncea* indicate a "shady character," including weediness. The remarks of M. Walter Pesman in his *Meet the Natives* (of Colorado) are amusing: "Looks like a poor grass, blooms like a puny pink, and belongs to the chicory family; light brown, hairy plumes after blooming; often full of galls." This 12-inch, wide-ranging, and common plant seldom carries enough color to attract interest.

## *Lysimachia (Steironema).* Loosestrife

Inch-wide, five-petaled, yellow flowers, which drop quickly, do not redeem the tall and leafy stem of *Lysimachia ciliata*, or its freely traveling rhizomes.

## *Machaeranthera.* Machaeranthera     plate 72

The machaeranthas, once included in *Aster*, have now been set apart, on the basis of their taproots, with others of like characteristic. *Machaeranthera canescens*, long known as *Aster canescens*, is typical. This profusely branched biennial is 18 inches to two feet tall and well covered from August to October with handsome rayed heads of purple-blue and gold, an inch or more wide. The leaves are plentiful in varying sizes as much as three inches long, oblanceolate, with small, spaced teeth. Fine effects result from mass planting.

Rydberg recognized four species for the Plains, including the pretty annual *Machaeranthera tanacetifolia*, similar in coloring to *M. canescens*, with much-divided leaves in tansy pattern; and many more species that occur farther west. But machaeranthas are among the most variable of groups and almost every colony the length and breadth of the Plains has its peculiar features. Fairly constant is the strong blue color. An outstanding one, which I once found along a road in sandhill country, is *M. sessiliflora (M. linearis)* with almost stalkless heads massed closely along the stems and the wide fringe of deep purple-blue rays glowing as if lit from within.

The woody aster, known to be dangerous to browsing animals because of the high content of selenium it absorbs, is now called *Machaeranthera (Xylorhiza) glabriuscula*. It is a low (eight-inch-high), branching subshrub with rather small, linear-oblanceolate leaves and a succession of heads, neatly fashioned and striking for so small a plant, of wide, white rays about a wide, golden disk. It is at home on the alkaline plains of Wyoming and a narrow reach in South Dakota. My plants from near the Wyoming line endured for a few years without thriving. I am told that the plant must have its habitual dose of the poison, which, by the way, affects only animals that consume quantities of the herbage.

## *Mahonia (Berberis)*. Oregon-grape, holly-grape

Highly valued on the Plains because of the scarcity of broad-leaved evergreens in this region, *Mahonia repens* combines a rich, compact, and low effect of stiff, hollylike foliage with plump clusters of light to medium yellow flowers in early spring and equal clusters of berries, black-purple with bloom, in late season. Its appearance at all times is pleasant. The fruit possesses a strong and distinctive flavor, but in its early stage of ripeness is far from edible. With October frosts, the bitterness disappears and the taste becomes agreeable. Combined with apple, it makes a delicious jelly.

In my prairie garden, *Mahonia repens* thrives in the heavy soil in half-shade, and in years of good moisture extends a network of roots for a dense ground cover, well under a foot high. It transplants readily from mature offsets taken in a small ball of earth. Where there is little or no snow cover, a light protection from dry air is needed to avoid winter burn. In the wild, the holly-grape prefers sheltered to densely shaded northern slopes. It is at home in the canyons of Pine Ridge in northwestern Nebraska, in the canyons of Little White River of southern South Dakota, in the Black Hills and Cave Hills of South Dakota and Wyoming, in the scattered rugged portions of Montana, and throughout the mountainous West.

## *Maianthemum*. Wild lily-of-the-valley

*Maianthemum canadense* is a low ground cover with its very wide, glossy, ribbed leaves resembling those of the lily-of-the-valley more than do its small, upright spikes of tiny, white flowers. It is common in the granites of the Black Hills, on partly shaded north slopes in the richest of soils, and in similar soils on the Canadian Plains and far to the north. It is a woodlander whose greater range lies to the east.

## *Melampodium*. White zinnia, rock daisy    plate 73

The wide, densely branched, low-bushlet habit, which various genera have adopted to meet the challenge of the intense, day-long Plains sun, has been refined into a veritable rock garden jewel by *Melampodium leucanthum*. (Some authorities prefer the name *M. cinereum* to *M. leucanthum*.) From June to frost, upon the fine-textured, subdued dark green leafage closely sits a bounty of glowing white, full-faced daisies, convexed, cameolike, the wide rays notched at the tip. There are seemingly endless variations in leaf pattern, pubescence, and other minor characters. A frequent roadside plant, *Melampodium leucanthum* inhabits gravelly and sandy clays or dune sands, over the southwestern fourth of Kansas, adjacent Colorado, western Oklahoma, and the Texas Panhandle, and south and west beyond the Plains region. At Prairie Gem Ranch this zinnia relative is fully hardy and thrives in a sandy, limy scree, where it self-sows moderately. Here, it starts blooming when four inches tall and hardly reaches ten.

## *Mentzelia (Nuttallia)*. Evening star, stickleaf    plate 74

Large-flowered and showy, even spectacular in its late afternoon opening and in the cool of early morning, *Mentzelia decapetala* bears four-inch or wider, 10-petaled, creamy flowers, with prominent brush of light gold stamens. It fulfills its destiny in making one great display, usually in its second year, rarely delayed another year when weather or injury has held back production. The species is exacting about drainage and often chooses steep slopes of shale or gravelly soil; prolonged wetness may cause failure at any stage of growth. Still it is worth growing. The wide-branching plant attains a height of 24, rarely 36 inches. The flowering season, July to late fall; the range, southern Canada to Texas.

The perennial or biennial *Mentzelia multiflora* is a 10-petaled, golden yellow star, an inch and a half to two inches wide, which opens at sundown. Its shining white stems branch widely and reach a height of 12 to 24 inches. It is mainly western—but its Plains range in southern Wyoming extends almost to the eastern line.

Widely branching below the middle of the main stem and producing masses of creamy yellow or straw-colored flowers, two inches wide, *Mentzelia nuda* belongs to extreme western Nebraska, southern Wyoming, and Oklahoma. The species has been reported at various places in this area, but what I have seen there instead, flowering from July to late fall, is *M. stricta*. This has cream-colored flowers, two or two and a half inches wide, the diverging stamens also creamy. The plant develops one to three stems, stiffly erect, branching little. In the garden, northern stock usually attains a height of 24 to 30 inches; but in the south, e.g., in Oklahoma and Texas, it reaches an ungainly five feet. *M. stricta* will live for several years, if too much wetness can be avoided. The stars are beautiful—where they are not eclipsed by *M. decapetala*.

The long-lived perennial of the genus, *M. oligosperma*, wide, dense, and low, has no admirers; its inch-wide stars are the color of spoiled oranges.

The common name "stickleaf" refers to the stiff, hooked hairs, which cover the leaves and enable them to cling to clothing.

## *Mertensia*. Bluebell, mertensia    plate 75

Reaching a height of four inches more often than its maximum height of eight, *Mertensia humilis* takes full advantage of its territory in southeastern Wyoming, studding the ground with such frequency that in May and June the low, truncated Laramie Hills are literally blue, a picture worth a journey to see. From this favorite haunt, *M. humilis* ranges westward across the Laramie Plains, eastward toward Cheyenne, and north-eastward many miles beyond the irrigated country around Wheatland to the North Platte River. The stems and broad little leaves are light glaucous green and the close little clusters of bells are an intense cerulean. The thick, semituberous root, with crown well underground, indicates permanence.

Flowering along with and aiding *M. humilis* in its grand display is *Mertensia lanceolata*. Elsewhere it seeks far horizons, covering the Plains portions of Wyoming, Montana, southern Saskatcehwan, and North and South Dakota to beyond the Missouri River. It continues in the heavy clays and limestones of western Nebraska, and in Colorado follows the foothills and the adjacent Plains and montane zones down to New Mexico. In mild springs *M. lanceolata* will show color by early May, at not more than two inches from the ground; then, with good moisture it will stretch up, branching widely into ample panicles and carry on until late June. Many arching stems from the simple or branching, thick, deep root form a wide bushlet 10 inches high. Dormancy comes in early summer. With good space the plant lives for many years.

Its flower color is much like that of the well-known *M. virginica*, a soft but intense blue. The charm of its daintily modeled, wide-flaring bells and lavish flowering over a long season give it a high rating among the mertensias of the world. The occasional albino is also a treasure. A certain area in the Black Hills is populated by a green-leaved form, the corolla tube of which is a glossy, deep sapphire. Nowhere does *M. lanceolata* provide a spectacle, but in good years mile after pasture mile will be lightly sprinkled with this gem.

*Mertensia paniculata* has wide leaves and graceful small, blue flowers, borne high on the tall, upright plant. This species ranges over the North American continent and is found across the Canadian Plains in and bordering the bush and northern forests.

## *Microseris (Nothocalais, Ptilocalais, Agoseris)*    plate 76

Under these names quite a number of attractive low, yellow flowers have been switched from genus to genus, while specifics have remained constant.

*Microseris (Nothocalais) cuspidata* is a brilliant early spring visitant in golden yellow, the rather flat, two-inch-wide head fashioned entirely of narrow ray flowers. Scape after scape from the ground maintains a succession of blossoms, first at two inches, later at six or eight inches, for about three weeks. Thick moisture-storing roots support a group of crowns, each with its loose rosette of narrow, tapering leaves, wavy-edged and white-margined. *M. cuspidata* is typical of the Plains from southern Canada to Oklahoma in loamy to heavy soils. Dormant early in the season, it is readily transplanted to well-drained sites. Multiple crowns may be divided; root cuttings strike easily.

*Microseris (Ptilocalais) nutans* has a similar flower, though smaller, a glowing lighter yellow, and in season some weeks later. Nodding buds on branching stems turn lightly, gracefully erect to open at six to 10 inches. The stems carry a few small leaves above the basal tufts of narrow, light green leaves. The root is spindle-shaped, spongy and soft. On the Plains *M. nutans* is found across Montana and Wyoming, rarely in the Pine Ridge corner of Nebraska, then far to the west. It is delightful in the garden; dormant during the summer, and should be propagated from seeds.

There are, indeed, species properly called *Agoseris*—many occur farther west. The remarkable and variable *A. glauca* is found from plains to timberline in Colorado, in the Black Hills in South Dakota, and on the prairies northward into lower Saskatchewan. Patterned somewhat like *Microseris* species, it lacks their refinement and appeal. It is dormant in late summer. In a trial in my garden, it proved transient.

### *Mirabilis (Allionia).* Four-o'clock     plate 77

The outstanding member of this genus is *Mirabilis multiflora*. The flower closely follows the pattern of the common garden annual and the color of the familiar purplish rose form, but is often of a brighter or deeper hue. The leaf also is similar, but more ovoid and of heavier texture. The plant is long-lived and hardy. It is widely branching, the outer branches lying on the ground; the general outline is that of a dense mound four feet wide and 20 inches high. Four to six flowers cluster in a deep involucre at branch tips and, opening in succession, fairly envelop the mound in color. This performance is unbroken from July to frost. A late afternoon and morning showpiece, it elicits exclamations of delight. *M. multiflora* is native to southern Colorado, except the extreme east, and to other states south and west.

Two of the former allionias are *Mirabilis hirsuta* and *M. linearis*, which have a wide distribution over the Plains. These put up one to several upright stems that are sometimes purplish, have inconspicuous leafage, and grow to 16 inches or higher. In a rather long season they deck themselves with a pretty bouquet of small ruffled, white or pale pink trumpets late in the day, and until mid-morning. Then there is *M. nyctaginea* with larger, reddish flowers, a few at the top of a taller plant. None of the three species are admissable to the garden, because of spreading roots and relatively little beauty.

### *Monarda.* Horsemint, bergamot, beebalm

A significant feature of the *Monarda fistulosa* of the Plains is its low stature, a natural response to altitude, low humidity, and little moisture. A stock I selected, however, in a dry year for apparent dwarfness has stretched up readily to 30 inches under conditions of better rainfall. Variable characters, such as leaf shape and length of leaf stalk, that have been used, botanically, to distinguish such varieties as *mollis* and *menthaefolia*, have little significance in the garden. Of greater import are the wide, full pompon flower heads which selected strains, such as the astonishingly fine one of the Killdeer Mountains of North Dakota, are capable of bearing. When the short rhizomatous roots have established a good clump of stems, each with one to three heads in medium to deeper lavender, the mass effect is thrilling. The flowers have a gentle fragrance, and a crushed leaf has a distinctive and pungent odor — dear to those who have long known it. The finest flower production results from keeping a plant to small proportions. *M. fistulosa* occurs in favored spots across most of the Great Plains and most of North America.

## *Musineon (Daucophyllum)*. Wild parsley

Sparkling with reflected light from lacquered, dark green stems, leaves, and golden compound umbels, *Musineon tenuifolius* is as elegantly attired as a buttercup. This charming plant lifts numerous wide clusters six or seven inches high in May and June. Rather than having the usual protective armaments of dry-country plants, such as waxy or hairy coating, this wild parsley depends on throwing strong light away from its sensitive parts. The leaves are divided into mere airy ribs, then enough are crowded into its eight-inch space to shade its bit of ground. In the Black Hills, *M. tenuifolius* often takes advantage of light upper shade and seems to like some richness of soil. Elsewhere in its range in eastern Wyoming and western South Dakota and Nebraska it is often found, surprisingly, on soils as raw as badlands.

Musineon divaricatus is an early-flowering prairie plant, very abundant on heavier soils from southern Canada to Nebraska and Colorado. Although the plant's foliage is rather glossy and its umbels are bright yellow, it has a weedy appearance and is soon dormant.

## *Nemastylis*. Prairie irid

The prairie of southeastern Kansas, where *Nemastylis acuta (N. geminflora)* grows, lies below the 1,900-foot contour, the technical border level of the Great Plains; yet in this westernmost reach of the species, its has acquired drought-resistance and temperature-hardiness adequate for its permanent occupancy of my Dakota garden. My first bulbs of *N. acuta*, one of the most precious of all bulbous plants, were the gift of Alberta Magers of Sterling, Kansas, 30 years ago. Stiff, pleated leaves rise six inches or more from a many-coated, brown bulb at a four-inch depth. As many as five flowers open, one or two at a time, at about the height of the leaves, on the upward-branching scape. Two inches wide, with broad segments of a rare luminous light blue, they are like a glorified *Sisyrinchium*, now commonly called blue-eyed-grass. At this latitude, the flowering season is June. Propagation is by seed; though the bulb has been known to offset at the base, such increase occurs very infrequently. A rather hard soil is preferred.

## *Oenothera*. Evening-primrose, oenothera    plates 78-82

Years back, botanists split up some of the large genera, such as *Oenothera*, and gave groups of similar species separate generic names. The system had its advantages, especially if one learned the oenotheras that way, for generic names like *Pachylophus*, *Galpinsia*, *Meriolix*, and others, bring to mind particular types of flower and often the type of the plant. Such names are used in present-day classification, chiefly as subgenus designations; in more popular usage the name *Oenothera* is applied to all. It is my intent to consider here species of beauty and value in the garden. Weedy kinds will not be mentioned, while others, "beautiful but dumb," will be pointed out as a warning.

A very long season of bloom (steady flowering from spring to frost) distinguishes many of the evening-primroses. To maintain such a schedule of production, some plants reduce the size of the flower during dry periods.

*Oenothera (Anogra) albicaulis* often whitens an entire uncropped field in sandy areas. As a winter annual it produces its low flowers by May; these fine, symmetrical, wide-lobed saucers hold their beauty through many daylight hours.

Perhaps the largest-flowered of the Great Plains species is *Oenothera (Lavauxia) brachycarpa*. The very long and slender hypanthium— tubular extension of the flower receptacle—lifts the magnificent soft yellow flower from short stems near the ground to just above the mass of long, gray leaves, as the dusk of evening is settling down. Unfortunately, the flowers wither with the warmth of early morning, but it is an unequaled treasure for the night garden. This oenothera has deep-reaching, fleshy roots that travel about, not unduly, and form a loose colony. It is native from western Kansas through central Colorado, and west and south.

Setting the pattern for many of the larger-flowered evening-primroses, the great white *O. (Pachylophus) caespitosa*, locally called "gumbo-lily," has four wide, heart-shaped petals, like an open parachute landing upside down. These flowers, two and a half to four inches wide, open so rapidly in late afternoon that the movement of their unfolding may be watched. If the following day is cool and moist, they may remain fresh all day; some may turn pink, but some strains keep their pure white until the flowers wither. Flowers usually close before noon, the hour determined by the strength of the sun. They are delightfully fragrant. The flowering season extends from early May to August. Rosettes of irregularly margined, oblanceolate leaves form at the ground from a fleshy, branching, deep-reaching root which may branch upward to add more crowns; but the true *O. caespitosa* has no faculty for colonizing except by seed, and rarely can a plant be divided. In nature, though, the species takes to the stickiest and slimiest of clays. It lives the longest on steep, badland buttes where drainage is immediate and the rooting zone contains much limestone fragment and grit. For best results in the garden, one-third of the rooting medium should be sand. *O. caespitosa* does not conform to a type even on the Plains, where it is frequent from southern Saskatchewan to western Nebraska and northern Colorado. There it takes to the foothills and higher mountains, and spreads westward and southward, breaking into a bewildering array of subspecies, varieties, and forms.

A tendency to sport has occurred in my garden where an occasional plant puts up a coarse stem up to four inches long, otherwise not differing from the type. Similar stemming up to as much as 12 inches distinguishes *O. caespitosa* ssp. *eximia*, which occurs from about the latitude of Colorado Springs to New Mexico. Another variant is *O. caespitosa* ssp. *montana*, native from South Dakota through western Nebraska and south, and west to Oregon. On the Plains it is smaller in plant and flower, the green parts often having red tints, gray leaf margins and veins, and the flowers aging to pink.

*Oenothera (Anogra) coronopifolia* spreads its thickets of low stems and finely incised leaves along roadways and occasionally in lightly wooded places. Through summer heat it holds its flat, white saucers wide open to the sun, even when individual flowers are reduced to less than an inch. Although delicate and beautiful, the plant has rapidly wandering roots, which make it one of the nuisance species. Western portions of South Dakota, Nebraska, and Kansas, and New Mexico and west represent its range.

The galpinsia group (calylophus) displays a different flower: yellow, squarish, and crinkled. Flowers of *O. fendleri*, light yellow, about two inches wide, are continuously produced over the summer and fall months on ascending stems eight to 14 inches tall, according to the strain. The leaves are small, lanceolate, bright green. The species has a taproot; propagation is by seed. *O. greggii* and *O. hartwegii* are similar in plant, in flower, and in southern Plains range from southern Kansas and Colorado, south and west. The former is darker green, quite hairy, somewhat shrubby; the latter less erect, velvety in stem and leaf. The withering flowers of the galpinsias turn to reddish orange, an identifying feature.

*Oenothera lavandulaefolia* wear a galpinsia flower of richer yellow, upon a diffusely branching, matlike, shrubby, taprooted plant. Each of the daily bounty of four-square flowers faces directly upright. This oenothera opens in lessening afternoon light and holds well into the next day. It is a gem of the first water, long-lived, and a perfect subject for the limy rock garden. Its small, lavenderlike leaves are dark and faintly gray. The species' range starts in Texas and Oklahoma and more western reaches, comes up through westernmost Kansas and Nebraska, and Colorado and Wyoming; then in this favored corner of South Dakota follows, for a few miles, the Greenhorn Limestone bordering the Black Hills.

An endemic of northwestern Kansas and a neighboring strip of Nebraska is *Oenothera (Megapterium) fremontii*, a low kind with lanceolate, entire leaves, silvery with a fine pubescence, two or three inches long, and relatively enormous, primrose-yellow saucers. The many-stemmed plant with deep taproot forms a five-inch mound. Belonging to the group with smooth, winged capsules, *O. fremontii* has pods an inch or less and small, grayish seeds. In its scale, it is a suitable companion for *O. caespitosa*.

The type species of the megapterium group is *O. missouriensis* (now *O. macrocarpa*), larger in leaf and flower and with much longer, trailing stems than *O. fremontii*. Its conspicuous and ornamental, oval seed capsules are as much as two inches wide, three inches long. Its range extends from the more moist, eastern two-thirds of Kansas, to adjacent Missouri, and south to Texas. It has been much grown in gardens, yet in two trials here it did not survive the long droughts. Rated as a variety, *O. missouriensis* v. *incana* neignbors the type in a broad, more western zone from Nebraska to Oklahoma and Texas.

It has the to-be-expected different aspect of an adapted High Plains plant, and it is perfectly content at Prairie Gem Ranch where it self-sows. The glorious flowers and great winged pods are practically the same as the type, but the eight-inch stems are stiffly erect or ascending and the leaves broadly lanceolate, sometimes quite silvery or green in the same colony.

Traditionally—to me, incomprehensibly—*O. missouriensis* v. *oklahomensis* is awarded only varietal rating. This grows in a separate environment as an endemic in the red gypsum soils and in crevices of the white gypsum rock in northcentral Oklahoma and in like footing for a brief distance across the Kansas line. From the large root, dozens of slender stems form a complete half-dome 18 to 20 inches high, which during peak periods produces more than a hundred large, brilliant yellow flowers a day. *O. missouriensis* v. *oklahomensis* is completely glabrous. Leaves are green, stems glossy, leaf-stalks and pedicels red, the sepals of the unopened buds conspicuously dotted with red. The winged seed capsules are only a little over an inch long, the seeds medium in size and brown. Singularly, *O. missouriensis* v. *oklahomensis* crosses freely with *O. fremontii*, which is held to be distinct from *O. missouriensis*, while over many years there has been no evident crossing with *O. missouriensis* v. *incana*.

In the Texas Panhandle an apparent form of *O. missouriensis* v. *incana* grows five to eight inches tall, has broad, white-silvery leaves with short, appressed hairs, and narrow, winged pods an inch long. This also is hardy in the North, and its general character qualifies it for a smaller, limy rock garden nook. It might well bear an old synonymic name, *O. argophylla*—without reference to aunt or cousin *O. missouriensis*—so distinct is it!

Bearing the name *Oenothera (Anogra) pallida* v. *latifolia*, a medium-sized, white flower grows in thickets along sandy roadsides from Wyoming and South Dakota to Oklahoma and New Mexico. It has gray to green, pinnatifid leaves and reaches a foot or more. In heavy clay at Prairie Gem Ranch, it quickly demonstrated its rapid spreading and was discarded.

Strongly shrubby *Oenothera (Meriolix) serrulata*, now known as *Calylophus serrulatus* and commonly called tooth-leaved evening primrose, is frequent over the entire Plains, somewhat eastward as well, and south into lower Texas. Diffusely low-branched and well filled with small, glossy, minutely toothed leaves, it presents a bright covering of yellow sundrops from May through August. They remain open through most of the day. *O. serrulata* is well behaved in the garden. In its northern reaches its common height is 10 inches, and its flower an inch or a little more in width. In the better forms its petals are wide and overlapping, forming a full, round saucer. A remarkably fine form, known from the vicinity of Oklahoma City to the broken and sandy upper Texas Panhandle, bears two-inch-wide saucers on a larger plant. Most often seen in sandy soils in the wild, *O. serrulata* is not at all exacting in the garden.

"So beautiful that one is tolerant of its colonizing," wrote Louise Beebe Wilder of *Oenothera speciosa*, truly but incautiously. If the marvel must be grown, let it be with an awareness of the hazards. The long-season masses of pristine white or, in a rare form, mellow pink are well worth the space allotted. They are morning flowers, opening upright or nearly so from nodding buds, two and a half to three inches wide. If the available space imposes restrictions, however, it is better at the start to enclose the incipient colony with a metal or concrete band to a depth of eight inches. The alternative is repeated weeding, while adventive sprouts are small, to thwart the buildup of strength in in the new roots. *O. speciosa* is not one of the indestructibles; extreme drought will kill it, so will excess wetness. The species is at home in southeastern Nebraska, portions of Missouri, Kansas westward to well up on the High Plains, then to Texas and down to lower ground again.

## Orchids

The yellow lady's-slipper has been noted under the heading *Cypripedium*; the Venus's-slipper, *Calypso bulbosa*, dainty and fancifully colored, occurs in the Black Hills, the Cypress Hills, and to the north and east in Saskatchewan. Several species of *Habenaria* and other genera appear frequently enough to be recorded from the Black Hills to the Canadian bush borders. Relicts of an earlier, moister climate, they are now restricted to their narrow hideouts, as totally unsuited to the general habitat of the Great Plains as to the unspecialized garden. The few I have seen have hardly sufficient appeal to merit the listing.

## *Oxytropis*. Locoweed, point-vetch, oxytropis      plates 83, 84

One of the finest examples of Great Plains flora, *Oxytropis* of the pea family consists of many showy species and varieties. One kind or several are to be seen in every section of the Plains in May and June. Although closely related to **Astragalus** with its many different types of growth, **Oxytropis**, with an exception or two, holds to a habit and flowering pattern much desired in the garden, and a scale made to order for the rock garden. There is the diminutive treasure *O. multiceps* and several comparatively dwarf ones that lift their spires of bloom five to seven inches, and larger kinds that reach 12 inches or so. The all-season appearance of an oxytropis is that of a rosette, or a number of rosettes.

*Oxytropis campestris* was described and named by Linnaeus from European material; the species is widespread in Europe and Asia. Careful comparison has disclosed that many American forms once rated as species have the essential character of *O. campestris*. Under this heading Barneby placed seven varietal groups; only two, v. *gracilis* and v. *dispar*, concern us on the Great Plains.

The type of *O. campestris* v. *gracilis* of the Black Hills is hardly of garden interest. Farrer, who could praise to the skies a plant he admired and with equal facility demolish another, rated the *O. campestris* that had favored Britain "in alighting on one or two lone rocks," as "a fat and dowdyish long head of large dim-yellow blossoms." Our near relative, *O. campestris* v. *gracilis*, to voice a well-considered opinion, is a pauperish, slender spike of weather-worn cream. It was finally banished from my garden. In the *O. campestris* v. *gracilis* complex, however, two especially choice forms, the one-time *Oxytropis villosus* and *O. macounii*, should not be overlooked. The former, the lovely yellow-cream, large-flowered, very gray-leaved plant flowering in May, dwells along the Minnekahta Limestone, a belt formation more or less encircling the Black Hills, and perhaps elsewhere. In my garden it developed into a handsome, wide plant and survived for several years. *O. macounii*, which carries specific status in Budd and Best, *Wild Plants of the Canadian Prairies*, occurs from southwestern Manitoba as far north as Saskatoon and west to the mountains, plentifully on prairies and hills in southwestern Saskatchewan and southern Alberta. Occurrence farther south is uncertain. This I have twice grown from seed; the plant flowered and was enjoyed briefly, a very lovely thing with many crowded clusters in soft light yellow, held at six or eight inches. This kind often flowers in May and is gone by mid-June. My seed came from Calgary, but I still seek the "really yellow" form I am told grows in that vicinity.

*Oxytropis campestris* v. *dispar*, as presently reported, is confined to North Dakota. Its flower color is said to run from white to cream and to dark blue and purple—with as many as 15 shades all in the same colony. This I may have seen in green seed, just as *O. lambertii* was coming into full bloom in late June.

To borrow the apt description from Barneby's "Revision of North American Species of Oxytropis," *Oxytropis lagopus* is "low and densely caepitose, the several crowns clustered on the summit of a simple or forking taproot, the herbage everywhere silky-pilose with long, silvery, spreading hairs." The two (of three) technical varieties I have seen unfortunately were not in fresh flower. *V. atro-purpurea* is confined mainly to the Wyoming plains, from Cheyenne in the south into the rugged northwestern portion of Nebraska and a short way into Montana; v. *lagopus* mainly to Montana, in the mountains and out on the Plains at least as far as Great Falls. Both varieties grow on sandy bluffs, grassy hillsides, and gravelly knolls, flowering very early in spring in short racemes of relatively large florets, brilliant pink to purple in the one, pink-purple to bluish purple in the other. They are little fellows, five inches high or somewhat taller.

Widespread and widely known as purple loco, *Oxytropis lambertii* is often in evidence along roadsides, in sandy areas, or on any partly barren ground. Where the environment is right, vast fields of this loco are seen. It is common in all the Plains states and extends into Iowa and Minnesota, but thins out as it crosses into Canada; in Colorado, as expected, it climbs into the foothills. In the average colony, there is much variation in color, from light purple toward the standard red-purple; darker tones tend toward a purer purple rather than toward blue. Not often is a pink or bluish or white flower found, but with good fortune one now and then sees a loco with color as fine as that of the American Beauty rose. In middle latitudes the flowering season is June, well apart from the May-flowering kinds. The mats of long, pinnate, silver-green leaves are ornamental throughout the warm months.

An outstanding variant from typical *O. lambertii* has been known as *Oxytropis plattensis*; it is now held as not distinct. On limy bluffs of the North Platte River in Nebraska, among a hundred or so of *O. lambertii* on which the last flowers were fading, there appeared, one June, smaller, bright new racemes in a hue close to cherry-red. These were found to be on separate plants which were not distinguishable except by corolla color and size. The scapes were only five or six inches tall. A thrilling find. Perhaps it deserves specific distinction?

Outdoing other dwarfs, **Oxytropis multiceps** reduces loco character to gemlike scale. A dense bun of silery silky, pinnate leaves hardly over an inch long supports short scapes of relatively enormous rotund, purple-tinted pink pea flowers. One, two, or four blossoms to the scape, which may fail to lift them upright, they loll in the sun for a few days or a week, content upon their silken cushion. On a scree in my garden, after some early losses, several plants doubled in diameter and flowered beautifully in their third spring. In the wild, some of the tightly foliaged mats of *O. multiceps* spread to four or five inches and carry blooms that almost hide the foliage. This oxytropis ranges the southeastern quarter of Wyoming, touches Nebraska, and reaches halfway down Colorado, on plain and mountain in stony ground.

Because of misidentifications, the little-known **Oxytropis nana** has as vague an individuality in the descriptions given in most references as in the name. Thomas Nuttall, who had a diminutive specimen at hand, gave it this name before the wide vaiability of the species was known. The most distinguishing feature of *O. nana* is a general shaggy-hairiness. Otherwise it can be depauperate or luxuriant, variable in size of flower, and, in separated colonies, white, pink-tinted, or purple. It is known on the Plains in eastern Wyoming and following up the North Platte River into the mountains.

At Crow Butte, a detached portion of the Pine Ridge in Nebraska— named for the Crow Indian tribe that was brought in by the government to fight the Sioux, and which the hard-fighting Sioux drove on to the butte—**Oxytropis sericea** flowers in a beautiful rose-pink. This is readily distinguished from *O. lambertii* by the larger florets, shorter scapes, wider, more uniformly gray leaflets, and a flowering period in May rather than June. For many miles to the west along the Ridge, beyond Fort Robinson, *O. sericea* appears only in light lavender, pale blue, and oyster-white.

One May, in the vicinity of a limestone-capped badland butte near home, I spotted a small patch of reddish loco, manifestly *O. sericea*. A marvel, for this was in *O. lambertii* country; *O. lambertii* everywhere, and still tight in the bud, was waiting for June. Moreover, this loco had a distinctly strong wine-red cast rather than the purple-red of the other. Years later, on May 20, I found the same red *O. sericea* was found in extensive, intermittent patches, 40 miles from home in

Nebraska, well to the north of the Pine Ridge. It was traced west in that state, then into Dakota for twenty-five miles, then into Nebraska again, and into Wyoming for as many more miles. The red carpet widened as it unrolled westward, often visible for a mile or more until the color grayed out in the distance. This was at all points within sight of the Pine Ridge escarpment, on low, clayey ridges and rolling slopes with coarse, rounded gravels indicating ancient stream deposits. The flower color deepened or lightened in individual plants—no pink, though a tinge of red-salmon marked a few. Deeper tones were of an intensified red without hint of purple. There were no albinos. No other species was present.

Now, however, several former species have been found to carry the essential characters of **Oxytropis sericea** and have been gathered under this name. Of chief interest to Great Plains dwellers are the fomer *O. albiflora*, the fine large-flowered white with purple-tipped keel, covering extensive fields in Colorado, and *O. pinetorum* with the usual silvery leaf, scapes of five to 12 inches, and an all-white flower often tinged green.

How blue is the "blue" of *Oxytropis splendens*? Dr. O. A. Stevens, of North Dakota, uses only blue in his description. The late W. R. Reader, Superintendent of Parks at Calgary, Alberta, described it as "a truly lovely plant with its densely hairy and silvery pinnate leaves, from which rise scapes of deep purple, pea-shaped blossoms, contrasting so delightfully with the gray foliage." The splendid loco is a Plains species across northern Montana and North Dakota and from southern Manitoba to the Rockies; a mountain habitant to Alaska, and southward to New Mexico. More eastern-ranging representatives are referred to as blue, those of the West as purple. A variation in type of hairiness is noted in the western plants; these are called v. *richardsonii* by some authorities. The species is set apart from others by four rows of leaflets arranged in whorls in contrast to the two rows in a simple pinnate leaf. I have attempted to raise this from seeds; but the few little seedlings were destroyed by one of our worst droughts.

## *Paronychia*. Whitlow-wort

The whitlow-worts are related to the pinks (*Dianthus*), but they have tiny and inconspicuous, yellow flowers. One questions their purpose in the floral scheme. On gravelly roadsides, *Paronychia jamesii* appears as a fine-stemmed subshrub, much-branched above, especially noticeable in late fall when the eight-inch high bushlets turn a bright reddish brown. Its range is from southern Wyoming and western Nebraska to Oklahoma and New Mexico. *P. sessiliflora* forms small mats, hardly an inch high, of tiny, glossy green or gray leaves, which are sometimes mistaken for those of a creeping phlox. It occurs from southern Canada to Texas and somewhat westward from the Plains. Hardly worth space in the garden, except as a novelty.

### *Penstemon*. Penstemon, beard-tongue      plates 85-91

Throughout the many species of **Penstemon**, all North American but perhaps one or two, climate is the principal determining factor in distribution. All the eastern and southern kinds, herbaceous and with upright stem, accustomed to greater rainfall and humidity, stop short of the Great Plains border in their westward extensions. In the varied climates farther west, type-groups of species have developed: moisture-loving "shrubbies" in the northwestern states and adjacent Canada; a few tall shrubs in California; very low stem-rooting, and very flat creeping kinds in the dry Southwest; large-flowered, tender species in Mexico; and scattered everywhere, almost uncounted herbaceous ones with upright stems. Of this assemblage only *Penstemon procerus*, dark blue, cluster-flowered, slender, and wide-ranging, has ventured into the Plains sectors of Northern Montana, Alberta, and Saskatchewan, even crossing to Manitoba. Two others have entered Alberta sufficiently to be recorded.

The twenty or so penstemons of the Great Plains hold well to their own domain in distribution. A few, such as *P. grandiflorus*, advance into new ground in some northcentral states, while others have climbed to foothill elevations in southern Wyoming, Colorado, and New Mexico. There are some endemics. All are herbaceous and tend to grow upright; prominent basal, overwintering leaf clusters are the rule and the promise of good flowering. Adapted to the vagaries of the climate, the thick leaves of many kinds are protected by a glaucous, waxy coating or are more or less hairy. Others are green, glossy, and light-reflecting. Thin-leaved ones, such as *P. procerus* and *P. gracilis*, seek better soils or cool areas. In a series of favorable seasons a life of five years is usual, but *P. glaber* and *P. nitidus* are known to double that span. A shortened life is often the result of unendurable drought, while the plant is carrying its habitual burden of slow-maturing seeds. Removing some or all the seed stalks conserves the strength of the plant and induces new crown offsets, which will bear the next year's flowers. The rooting medium is not so important to most kinds as are thorough drainage and ample space; one part of sand in three is desirable.

*Penstemon albidus* is one of the most widespread, from well up in Canada down to Texas and New Mexico, and both east and west from this principal region. It grows eight to 12 inches tall and has broad, rough, green leaves and in June large flowers in a packed spike. The flowers are a fine white at best; sometimes with dark lines in the throat with reddish calyxes and stems to mar its purity. *P. albidus* is of the Aurator Group, along with *P. auriberbis*, *P. cobaea*, *P. eriantherus*, and others which are rather exacting in moisture and soil requirements and not among the easiest to accommodate in the garden. In the wild *P. albidus* selects a firm footing in sandy clay or silt loam with gravel, always with the best drainage. There it will develop four to six stalks in hardly as many years. The entire corolla of this normally white flower is sometimes purple-tinted, especially in the far South.

In general appearance *Penstemon alpinus*, *P. brandegei*, and *P. glaber* are much alike, yet are readily recognized when one has become familiar with their differences. And they are set apart in their ranges. South of the North Platte River in Wyoming and in Colorado, close to the mountains and climbing 1,000 feet or so, a large and brilliant dark blue flower in showy masses or single spires above dark green, lanceolate leaves may be assumed to be *P. alpinus*. It is lower than the others, an average of 16 inches or so; its flowering season is mainly July. In southern Colorado and northeastern New Mexico, *P. brandegei* (or *P. alpinus* ssp. *brandegei*) takes over and lifts practically the same enticing blue to as much as 24 inches. Gladys T. Nisbet, authority on penstemons in New Mexico, states that it blooms in the last half of June and through July "in the lower mountains and on the high plains close to the mountains." She tells of garden-grown plants living five to eight years and of older plants with as many as 30 stalks. She reports also many intermediate forms, where *P. alpinus* and *P. brandegei* meet in southern Colorado.

North from the North Platte River, *Penstemon glaber* carries the dark blue banner into southern Montana and a corner of North Dakota and into western South Dakota and northwestern Nebraska. *P. glaber* is a name that has often been misapplied. The true plant is of the Great Plains and enters the mountains little or not at all. Stems and foliage are glossy, dark green, neither glaucous nor hairy, and appear dull only in a dried specimen. Leaves are broadly to narrowly lanceolate. The species exhibits variability and reacts strongly to seasonal vagaries of sunshine and rain; it grows 18 to 20 inches tall on the average, and may reach 24 or even 30 inches. A wide-crowned plant may produce, along with tall stems, a few stems of only eight to 12 inches, all bearing nice clusters of the wide trumpets. During wet periods the color may be pale, so that the novice will question the species. After a wet June one may expect to find the color of early flowers disappointing; then, with July turning hot and dry, the upper portion of the spike will come out in an intensity of lustrous blue that is a marvel of nature's magic.

A usual life-span for *P. glaber* is a half-dozen years. It has been known to last a dozen years, and, in an exposed position in much sun and no excess of moisture, to form a wide crown with many flowering stems. In this native climate the growth is upright, no doubt because of the dry atmosphere and stiffening soil nutrients, such as lime and potash. In the wild it proves itself adaptable to such sites as limestone or granite crevices, old mine dumps, shale banks, river bluffs, and loamy slopes; the hottest of exposures or to half-shade.

In my garden at Prairie Gem Ranch, *P. alpinus* has been about equal in color value to *P. glaber*, never approaching the depth and purity of those seen along a creek near Pueblo or in the exciting panoramic effect of a roadside stretch on the Laramie Plains. At the ranch, mostly seeding itself and often in the raw gumbo, *P. alpinus* has almost disappeared after many years, while *P. glaber* seems as content as in any wild habitat. The comparison is possibly unfair. *P. alpinus* might respond to a scree or almost any improved footing. This unkindly gumbo, which in nature's hand would be supporting a light growth of pasture grasses and an adapted praire flower or two, has forced upon me endless excuses.

A flowery stretch of sandhills in northeastern Colorado, between Holyoke and Wray, marks the northern limit of *Penstemon ambiguus*, a fine-stemmed, densely branched bush about 18 inches high. Its day-to-day, high-fashion attire of flat-limbed blossoms, often described as phloxlike, makes it a prized possession in its flowering season, June to late August. The flower is a glistening white or near white, with the purple-pink of slender throats and petal reverses showing through. The ample leafage is linear-filiform. My old plants, grown from seed, have survived for many years and have widened their crowns slowly; but it is the nature of the species to spread more widely by rhizomes where space and moisture are available. The range of *P. ambiguus* stretches to the sands of southwestern Kansas and down to western Texas and in New Mexico as far as Albuquerque.

Plump columns of wide trumpets, more intensely brilliant than any sky, above long and narrow, channeled, glaucous blue-green leaves are an exciting introduction to *Penstemon angustifolius* when grouped on an expanse of yellow sand. The northern sector of its range borders the Montana-North Dakota line and extends eastward; southward the range widens, including the Laramie Plains and a portion of Colorado; and in South Dakota and especially in the Nebraska Sandhills runs far eastward. Soils in which it is found, other than loose sand, include light loams and even fine-textured shales. With freedom from crowding and overshading, which all penstemons need, *P. angustifolius* will thrive even in clay with garden care, good drainage, and apparently a degree of alkalinity. A common height is ten or 12 inches. The flowering season is late May and June. The finest display of this species I have seen was in Nebraska, on a two-mile stretch of powdery and little-used back road, leading down to the Niobrara River. A few pink ones were among them. Elsewhere, fine albinos are sometimes found.

In western Kansas, southern Colorado, and northeastern New mexico, *Penstemon caudatus* replaces *P. angustifolus* and is sometimes rated a subspecies of the latter. It is generally taller, with wider leaves, and paler flowers. Its epithet, *caudatus*, refers to a taillike ending of the bracts subtending the flower clusters.

*Penstemon auriberbis* is a fuzzy little plant, more often six inches in height than its possible maximum of 14. Its large, lavender or bluish purple, pouched trumpets are headlighted by a great golden-bearded staminode. In my garden this penstemon flowered well, then dwindled steadily, and disappeared. It may have met too high a pH here, since it comes from sagebrush slopes, on plains and foothills from midway in Colorado into northeastern New Mexico. This rare jewel should be tried by anyone who can hope to accommodate this group of penstemons.

A staminode or so-called sterile fifth stamen, from which *Penstemon auriberbis* gets its name, is a slender, curving "tongue" thrusting forward from the tube of the corolla, ostensibly to "make the flower pretty." More scientifically, it is a flamboyant traffic signal for aerial visitors seeking nectar, which may, quite incidentally, transport pollen from flower to flower.

A native of western portions of Kansas and Oklahoma, western Texas, and southeastern New Mexico is *Penstemon buckleyi*. It has been described as a "small grandiflorus," because of its stiff, glaucous gray stems and leaves and lavender trumpets. But the comparison does no honor to *P. grandiflorus*, nor does it lift from its lowly state this 16-inch, mostly single-stemmed, poor relation with its narrow, pale trumpets.

The flower of the wild foxglove, *Penstemon cobaea*, is so large and wide in the throat as to be more a bell than a trumpet. This species holds sway from southeastern Nebraska through most of Kansas and to lowland Texas. In northerly areas it lifts its wide panicles 15 to 20 inches; in the far South, as much as 24 inches. Purplish lines mark the lower throat of the white corolla and sometimes tint the whole flower. My plants did not last long; doubtless they might live longer in the right footing of sandy and rocky soil or with a less erratic ration of moisture than my garden affords.

In this continent-wide genus, it is comforting to have one penstemon that is content with the tough and difficult prairie gumbo, uncertain rainfall, and shifty temperature to be found all across and about Prairie Gem Ranch. This is *Penstemon eriantherus*. In the garden where the soil is basically the plant's native clay, it maintains itself readily, grateful for relief from the strenuous competition of native grasses. But with equal intent it marks roadsides and pastures and, at its most spectacular, paints a half-mile of sparse grassland with lovely warm lavender. It has a wide lanceolate leaf, rough-hairy, often purplish underneath; hairy stems eight to 12 inches tall; and closely packed spires illuminated by prominent golden tongues. The plant may live five or six years. If replacement is needed, seeds are always awaiting that spingtime of ample rain when their protective coating can be dissolved and the plantlets enabled to send roots deep down to more lasting moisture. Although a mature *P. eriantherus* may survive extreme drought with no green showing, its normal dormant state in propitious seasons is a nice rosette, or several, of evergreen leaves, ready to advance with the first warming days of March toward flowering in June.

*Penstemon eriantherus* covers the northern Plains from a narrow border in Canada to northwestern Nebraska, southeastern Wyoming including the Laramie Plains, and the northern edge of Colorado.

In western Montana there is variation to a larger-flowered form, readily recognizable, called *P. eriantherus v. saliens*. This and, perhaps, other variants go into the mountains and on to Washington and British Columbia.

Of *Penstemon fendleri*, I have found no enthusiastic description, though its flowers are fairly large and violet to blue, somewhat scattered on the stiff and erect stem, which is often solitary and, like the rather broad leaves, smooth and somewhat grayish. Its range extends from southwestern Oklahoma, to the Staked Plains of Texas and eastern New Mexico, and west into the mountains. It flowers in May and June.

A somewhat lonely wanderer from the vicinity of Oklahoma City to northern New Mexico, *Penstemon gracilis* makes a narrow trail near the base of the mountains up through Colorado and into Wyoming; spreads into rugged northwestern Nebraska, through the Dakotas and eastern Montana and far into Saskatchewan; then into Manitoba, Minnesota, and to Wisconsin. Despite its wide range, *P. gracilis* is a rather frail plant, not long-lived. Commonly 10 to 12 inches or taller, its has a simple or rarely branched stem and quite small, dark green leaves. Inconspicuous even where frequent, the small, pale lacrimataries which serve as flowers stir little interest.

The distribution of *Penstemon grandiflorus* seems largely determined by the availability of sand, soft loams, and gritty mixtures. In the garden, however, it is not exacting. Nebraska with its vast reaches of sand is the population center of the species. All neighboring states are included, corners of Oklahoma, Missouri, and of North Dakota, Minnesota, and Wisconsin. The stately and well-attired *P. grandiflorus*, with long spikes of very large, lavender trumpets and broad, spoon-shaped, glaucous-gray, basal and stem leaves, is a favorite in June gardens, as are the albino, pink, and purple forms that nature occasionally provides. Good moisture is a requisite for germination, even after seeds have been frozen. Cuttings are readily rooted. The occasional plant that lives beyond the usual three or four years and forms a multiple crown may be divided.

In recent years *P. grandiflorus* has been crossed, apparently by chance, with another tall, glaucous species, the scarlet-flowered *P. murrayanus*, native of Texas. The results have been amazing. The hybrid offspring regularly sport to a great variety of colors. These are known as Seeba Hybrids, commemorating the name of Lena Seeba, who discovered the first hybrid in her Nebraska garden. They are distinguishable from *P. grandiflorus* only by corolla color, and not even then in the seedlings that revert to nature's wild product. With industrious bees winging pollen here and there, it is no longer possible to maintain pure *P. grandiflorus*, where the hybrids are close neighbors. There are also the sporting Fate Hybrids, with the narrower trumpets and more of the scarlet of *P. murrayanus*, and the Avalon Hybrids with some nice broader-trumpeted reds.

The greatest of the sand areas, which are geographical marks of all the states and provinces of the Great Plains, are the Sandhills of Nebraska, extending over some millions of acres. Here dwells the distinguished endemic **Penstemon haydeni**, the blowout penstemon. Blowouts are those peculiar pits bored in the deep sand by the swirling action of prevailing westerly and northwesterly storm winds. The adapted penstemon is often the first plant to take advantage of the cleared and barren ground, both within the excavation and beyond where the wind-load is dropped. *P. haydeni* has very long and narrow, channeled, waxy, glaucous green leaves, not basal but low on a heavy stalk that rises stiffly to 10 to 24 inches. Subtending the closely set and ample clusters of large, milky blue flowers are bracts of astonishing width, broadly spoon-shaped and sharp-tipped. They give the plant a distinctive effect. Enticing to bees and pleasing to the human sense, the flower has a strong and carrying fragrance. Branches put out from the lower leaf axils dip to the ground and turn up at the tip; these, when partly covered by drifting sand, strike root. Colonizing, however, is usually accomplished by seedlings. In the plant's natural abode in deep sand, there is never an excess of moisture. In the garden, where moisture is moderate and prolonged drought is avoided, *P. haydenii* lives for several years—one of the most distinctive, intriguing, and beautiful of penstemon species.

A rather striking member of the hairy clan, **Penstemon jamesii**, related to *P. auriberbis*, *P. eriantherus*, and such, lives in southeastern Colorado, the plains and mountains of New Mexico, and farther south. Variable in many characters, it lines a low to tall, one-sided raceme with large, pouched, light to deep lavender trumpets through June in its southern haunts where, with good winter and spring moisture, it colors roadsides and pastures.

Closely resembling *P. angustifolius*, **Penstemon nitidus** flowers from early to late May, much ahead of any other penstemon at Prairie

Gem Ranch. The former flowers mainly in June. Both are strongly glaucous, reach a height of 10 to 12 inches, and have brilliant light blue florets of good size, those of *P. nitidus* often a shade deeper. Seasonal temperature and rainfall, however, somewhat affect the hue of these two. In *P. nitidus* the leaves are shorter and broader, less channeled, distinctly four-ranked in early season; and in most strains, there are prominent wide bracts among the lower flower clusters. The range begins well down in Nebraska, covers all the Plains of Wyoming and Montana and western portions of the Dakotas, and the southwestern and southcentral Plains in Canada as far as Saskatoon. *P. nitidus* is a favorite because of its low stature, early flowering, and intensity of blue, and it has the reputation of coming truer to color in varying environments than some other penstemons. It has a relatively long life-span, where moisture is never excessive, and forms a wide crown with many flowering stems. The so-called *P. nitidus* v. *polyphyllus* grows taller, and the stretched-out inflorescence greatly lessens its color impact.

In northern Montana and through Alberta and Saskatchewan, as far as Saskatoon at least, the wandering western *Penstemon procerus* finds its favored cooler habitats. With slender stem and dark, daintily toothed foliage, it reaches a height of four to 14 inches there and bears tiers of small, closely clustered, dark blue blossoms. I grew this penstemon for some years and thought little of it; then came a flowering period with much moisture and coolness, and *P. procerus* responded with an intense, clear color. In *Wild Plants of the Canadian Prairies*, Budd and Best report that it usually blooms from the end of May to August in large colonies around slough margins, in shelter of shrubs, and in openings in woodlands.

Native from southeastern Wyoming to northern New Mexico, *Penstemon secundiflorus* has proven a stalwart at Prairie Gem Ranch over many years, caring for itself by reseeding, never weedy. The only attention required is to keep it reasonably free from close crowding. The plant is smooth, light glaucous green; the leaves are broadly lanceolate, long-tapering; the height is 10 to 18 inches. The flowers are clean-looking, large, close together on one side of the stem, opening upward through several weeks in June and July. The flower of the more northern stock from sandy plains in central Colorado and northward is accurately described as reddish lavender. Mrs. Nisbet describes that of the southern range as "dark blue or strongly shaded with violet, often appearing red-violet in the field."

Closely related to **P. secundiflorus** is **Penstemon lavendulus** of like appearance, though dwarfer, the flowers nearly the same but less secundly disposed on the stem. It ranges more into the mountains, except that it occurs also along the bluffs of the Arkansas River below Pueblo. There it has been known as **P. versicolor**. Harrington, in *Manual of the Plants of Colorado*, describes the color as "light to pinkish purple, often darker, calyx lobes often pink, the staminode densely golden hairy." In contrast, the staminode of **P. secundiflorus** has the tongue "glabrous or with few short hairs at the apex" – in other words, with a less showy headlight. In two trials in my garden, **P. lavendulus** has remained only briefly, failing after one flowering. It may have needed more constant moisture; perhaps this was another instance of heavy seed-setting resulting in too great a strain on the plant when steady drought ensued.

**Penstemon unilateralis** and **P. virens** occur sparsely on the Plains. The former grows 20 to 24 inches tall with a tapering effect. There is a long spike of medium blue to light purple flowers which vary in color in the same corolla. The leaves are deep green, slender, and tapering. The plant is especially susceptible to late-season drying-out so that a crowded field of one year may show very few plants the next. It is an attractive subject for the garden. **P. unilateralis** appears on the Plains border at Granite, west of Cheyenne, and doubtless elsewhere near the foothills.

**Penstemon virens**, a companion of **P. unilateralis** at Granite, has a quite different character. It forms a widening mat with short, branching, horizontal stems putting down new roots to establish additional crowns. It is long-lived in the garden and valued for that feature as well as for its masses of small, lively deep purple-blue blossoms that rise nine to 12 inches. The leafage is of neat texture, small, glossy, dark green. Both species are found in Wyoming, Colorado, and indefinitely west.

## *Petalostemon.* Prairie clover     plate 92

Most prairie clovers bear their numerous small, crowded, pealike flowers on long cones rather than in cloverlike heads. About the base of the cone a circlet of several rows of florets opens in red-purple, white or ochroleucous, or silvery rose, and progresses slowly to the tip. According to the species, the flowering season runs from early June to August. All send up slender, branching, airily foliaged stems from the ground, several or many, eight to 18 inches or more, arching or spreading, and developing their flowering heads for successive blooming. Sandy soil is preferred; but some fine colonies are seen on heavier soils. All species have fleshy deep taproots which branch little and require good drainage.

*Petalostemon candidus* is a long-coned, white-flowered species of the midland states and the Plains. Until the stems stretch taller and the long inflorescences (two inches or more) are formed, it is not distinguishable from *P. oligophyllus*, which attains half the height, disposes its stems at lower angles, and restricts its flowering cones to an inch or so. These two retain their distinct characters in the garden. Their flowers are a rather dull white, somewhat relieved by an aura of light yellow anthers. *P. compactus*, native from southern Wyoming to New Mexico, also extends a short way into Nebraska and Kansas. Its heads are especially dense, one to four inches long, and yellowish white. *P. multiflorus*, ranging from southern Nebraska to Texas, grows 12 to 24 inches tall and branches profusely to display a multitude of white heads, with the very short cone in flower along its full length. In his *Kansas Wild Flowers*, William Chase Stevens wonders "why we have not made more use of it in our gardens, and why *Hortus* gives it but two barren lines."

At an early stage *Petalostemon purpureus* can hardly be distinguished from the white-flowered kinds. The habit is much the same; the small, short, pinnate leaves are, perhaps, narrower in their division and darker green. The thick cones, which attain a length of two inches, are dark green, a bit silvery hairy, and the circlets of flowers are a beautiful purple-red from light to deep in hue. A gay atmosphere is added by many long-filamented anthers of gold, orange, or burnt orange. A delightful fragrance surrounds the plant. *P. mollis* is virtually another *P. purpureus* with an all-over coating, sparse or heavy, of silky hairs.

A regular denizen of loose sands, from eastern Saskatchewan to Texas, *Petalostemon villosus* is silvery gray-green throughout, rather densely leafy. The arching stems of 20 inches or less spread widely to poise the clustered, plump cones horizontally. The petals of lovely silvery rose, advance slowly the three inches to the upturned tip.

The flowering season is July and August. The overall height of the plant remains under 12 inches.

## *Phacelia.*

As a rather rare plant, **Phacelia leucophylla** haunts the Badlands of North Dakota and other rough places, including northwestern Nebraska, adjacent Wyoming, and parts west. Often considered a variety of **P. hastata**, it has a conspicuous silver-white rosette of broad, elliptic, ribbed leaves; a stiff stem with smaller leaves, to 15 inches or so; and neat, uncoiling racemes of narrow-tubed florets of a hue as indefinable in its neutral lavender as the shadow of a vanished hope.

The only other mentionable species of the Plains is the 10-inch annual **Phacelia linearis** which, with its light purple-blue, half-inch saucers, freely borne, provides a pleasant foil for the rich golden suns of **Arnica fulgens** under the pines at Upton, Wyoming, in June.

## *Phlox*. Phlox      plates 93-95

The phlox species, which are widespread over the Great Plains, are typical western plants that form a distinctive element of the region's flora. They are low-growing and form wide or close colonies, mats, cushions, and buns. The hard foliage is suited to the rigorous climate; the leaves are narrow or small, often needlelike or prickly tipped, in some species so diminutive and closely crowded as to hide the stems. Except in **P. longifolia** and **P. oklahomensis**, the stems are remarkably short and display the multitudinous blossoms in masses or sheets, small or wide, as the suitability of the ground or the age of the colony determines. Flower sizes vary from about one-quarter inch wide among the smallest, as in **P. muscoides**, to more than an inch wide in **P. alyssifolia**, and flower colors from flat-white to fine blued-white, softly glowing pearl-gray, delicate to strong lavender, powder-blue to, rarely, deeper blue, and from the faintest tint of pink to a full-bodied pink, perhaps with a tint of lavender or, rarely, of salmon—again in **P. alyssifolia**. Fragrance is variable with the species or with the strain; in some kinds, when the air is filled with the scent of many flowers, it is reminiscent of wild sweet william, the name I once knew for **P. divaricata**.

Over the vast expanses of the Plains, the phloxes have little choice of habitat; all are inured to open sun and have become dependent on intense light to a greater degree than most genera. They frequent limestone exposures, limy gravel deposits of ancient streams or terminal moraines, where strong competition is restricted. They put down roots to remarkable depths and grow into colonies by means of deep-seated rhizomes as well as by seeds. They often live to a great age. The widely adapted *P. andicola* also inhabits areas of sparsely grassed, heavy alkaline clays and loose sands.

The adaptation of these phloxes to soils of high pH is uniform. Only one small colony, that of **Phlox hoodii**, has been found in a granite region in the Black Hills. A start from that particular clone thrived in the high alkalinity of my garden for a number of years—until the drought of 1964, with less than nine inches of rainfall, did away with it.

Among dwellers of rugged portions of the Plains, **Phlox alyssifolia** is outstanding in character quality and color. This admirable plant became known to me back in 1916, when I drove with team and wagon over the 18 miles of open prairie from my new homestead to the Cheyenne River and across, to dig ponderosa pines to plant for windbreaks. It was early May. *P. alyssifolia* was everywhere, with **Dodecatheon pulchellus, Mertensia lanceolata, Phlox andicola,** and **Viola nuttalli.** The prize was the low, wide, fragrant pink phlox. It was only natural to bring home a chosen specimen in a good spadeful of its native loam and set it into my raw gumbo—not where it was in danger of invading grass roots but where cultivation would give it the fairest chance. It deserved the choicest of rock garden sites, but at the time I had not heard of rock gardens. That was fifty years ago. The plant was never moved. Today its self-propagated, ground-hiding mat covers, perhaps, two square yards, though over the years young offset plants have been freely marketed.

The leaves of **Phlox alyssifolia** are approximately an eighth of an inch wide and about an inch long in the larger forms. When mature, they have a noticeable whitish margin. They remain throughout the season but die with the coming of winter, leaving only a tiny bit of green at the tip of the stem. This will break into new leaves with the first warmth of spring and then almost immediately into a cluster of flower buds which will open through late April and May. The stems are hardy to winter cold, and the newer shoots renew their foliage with spring; procumbent in habit, the tips reach upward commonly to four inches.

Classifying this or any other Plains phlox as a shrub is inaccurate and misleading. The Plains phloxes do not have true woodiness; but there is no better term for this type of overwintering plant than shrubby or subshrub. In the center of any wide mat of **P. alyssifolia** can be found an old root that remains for years, becoming coarse and woody but continuing to function as a source of new sprouts and of long, slender, horizontal rhizomes, at a depth of six inches or so, from which new plants arise within the mat or close around its margins. The new plants are prime for transplanting by their second or third spring. This habit holds for all the regional species except, possibly, **P. scleranthifolia** and some forms of **P. hoodii**, which put down new roots freely from stems lying upon the soil.

**Phlox alyssifolia** ranges south to the North Platte River in southeastern Wyoming, takes in a bit of Nebraska, most of the Black Hills and some rugged prairie to the east; almost all the Plains northward through Wyoming and Montana and small portions of Alberta, Saskatchewan, and North Dakota. In northwestern Montana it extends into the lower mountains. As a species it first received botanical recognition in Saskatchewan, near Wood Mountain, on June 7, 1895. Budd and Best, in *Wild Plants of the Canadian Prairies*, describe the color as purplish or bluish—possibly from a pressed specimen. In western Montana, where a highway crosses a formation of slabby limestone for a mile or two, the species makes a great show in white. It reaches its finest development in the Black Hills region where, keeping to the recurrent limestone formations, it rises from prairie levels to 6,500 feet. Most extensive panoramas lie along the Greenhorn limestone bordering the prairie. There, at the season's height, the crest of the escarpment takes on a glow of pink, often lavender-tinted, occasionally purplish, rarely salmon. Rare whites are regarded as albinos in this locality. The corollas measure from five-eighths to more than an inch wide—and all in the same population.

The widespread, fine white species of the Great Plains is **Phlox andicola** (**P. planitiarum** in some references). This has needle leaves and mostly upright stems, and in favored spots grows so densely as to present a mat of flowers. Older plants branch widely in ample space and of their own weight become procumbent, filling a few inches of ground with flowers averaging three-fourths of an inch wide. Blossoming begins in May to late April and lasts well toward the end of June. Some flowers are a glowing pure white, with a speck of golden anther showing; others a faintly blued-white; on rare occasions one will open in lavender, usually to fade in the intense sun. Some definite blues have been found. The corolla lobes are well rounded at the tip, the flower usually starry in effect. Withered flowers are neatly disposed of, making way for the next to open. *P. andicola* propagates by seed and by rhizomes which distribute the offsets widely. It is found throughout the Sandhills region of Nebraska, including a salient reaching the eastern border of the Plains. It covers with equal thoroughness the western half of South Dakota, including sandhills, badlands, vast reaches of gumbo clay, and typical Great Plains lean loams. A good portion of western North Dakota, some of Wyoming and Colorado, and a corner of Kansas are in its territory.

The subspecies, *Phlox andicola* ssp. *parvula*, was first recognized as distinct at Cedar Butte, a badlands eminence to the southeast of the Black Hills. Later, it was found farther south on badland loam and occupying a hillside exclusively, many miles to the northeast, near Badlands National Monument. Dr. Edgar T. Wherry found it over much of western North Dakota and took his type specimen in that state. He then recognized it as the larger needle-leaved prairie phlox, which stretches across Montana to the mountains, and he recorded a stand in Wyoming. This is, briefly, a *Phlox andicola* of smaller proportions in stem, foliage, and flower, the corolla measuring over a half-inch; it is intermediate in size between *P. andicola* and *P. hoodii*. But in its habit, including the prolonged flowering period, it is plainly close to *P. andicola*. At Cedar Butte the three grow in close proximity. One compares the neighboring plants and decides to try the odd one in the garden. Very well. Its stamina is equal to that of *P. andicola*, and there is an indefinable quality about its flower that gains a special niche in one's affections. Finally, on the Greenhorn, south of the Black Hills, I found the form to which I gave the name 'Dr. Wherry,' in his honor: a *P. andicola* ssp. *parvula* with wide and overlapping petals, daintily cupped, the most wonderful gem in the genus *Phlox* I have ever seen. Dr. Wherry was very appreciative.

Notwithstanding the distinctive leaf arrangement in the square-shoot phlox, *Phlox bryoides*, which provides instant identification, casual observers, and some professionals as well, continue to confuse this species with one or another form of *P. hoodii*. The leaves of *Phlox bryoides* are so short and wide, though narrowing to a needlelike tip, and so closely overlap one another that the exposed portion appears wider than long. They are set in such regular rows on the four sides of the stem that the shoots appear "square." *P. bryoides* flowers later in May than do most other kinds of phlox, the mats whitened with bloom.

The habit of **Phlox bryoides** in forming humpy mounds is most evident on the limestone at Morton Pass in the Laramie Hills; but all growth, even in the garden, is so patterned as a plant attains maturity and demonstrates its unique beauty and charm. This species spreads across the sothern Wyoming plains into Nebraska, into adjoining Colorado, along the mountains well toward their southern limit, and northward into the Montana mountains.

Rather long, needle-shaped, but flexible leaves, long, trailing stems, and white flowers above medium size mark **Phlox diffusa** ssp. *scleranthifolia*. In its Great Plains range it is restricted to a few miles in the southern Black Hills; its relatives are far away in the western mountains. This phlox does best on steep, north-facing slopes, as in Hot Brook Canyon above Hot Springs. There in as much as half-shade it drapes over a convenient rock, spreading festoons to 18 inches and covering them with white in May. This habit qualifies it as a wall plant, for in a wall the lengthening stems may find the accustomed dryness. Somewhat wide mats may be encouraged on nearly flat sites, with the growth kept relatively dry on a slab of stone or a stone chip surface. Where the stems touch soil, they root readily; stolonizing has not been observed. This phlox also belongs to limestone areas. Despite its preference for cooler sites, it is remarkably drought-resistant even in much sun, and there it tends to form buns and cushions.

Well-known and highly valued, dwarf and densely foliaged **Phlox hoodii** ranges the High Plains, bypassing Kansas, from near the southern border of Colorado, as between Trinidad and Trinchera, well into Alberta and Saskatchewan and western Manitoba. The species first received botanical recognition at Carlton House, some forty miles north of Saskatoon. Budd and Best, in *Wild Plants of the Canadian Prairies*, do not segregate types, though all across the provinces *P. hoodii* is found quite green in one place, silvery gray and more dwaf in another; not infrequently the variants grow side by side. In his monograph *The Genus Phlox*, Wherry described five subspecies found on the Plains: **P. hoodii** ssp. *hoodii*, **P. hoodii** ssp. *glabrata*, and **P. hoodii** ssp. *muscoides*. The last possibly reaches its ultimate compactness and silvery fuzziness on the summit of Crow Butte in Nebaska, where it grows in minute cracks in the massive rock. There it is subject to all the winds that blow; to intense direct and reflected light, and to all the heat the rock can absorb; to whatever winter cold may come; to the naked situation with snow cover removed by wind; and to a moisture supply measured by the capacity of the narrow crevices. Chiseled from the rock and brought into a milder environment, plants develop longer nodes and the leaves diverge more widely from the stem. As for hairiness, **P. hoodii** ssp. *muscoides* soon loses the woolliness that is its strongest point of distinction. Still, these very dwarf plants maintain in the garden an especially low and compact habit: they have short leaves for which Wherry's monograph sets the maximum at about one-tenth of an inch, with the pubescence conspicuous or absent. For typical **P. hoodii**, the leaf measurement runs from one-tenth to one-fifth of an inch; for **P. hoodii** ssp. *glabrata* somewhat longer.

To repeat, the plant with the most inviting display of blooms is not to be dug; rather, it is the small offsets of new growth, whether from rooted stems or rhizomes, which are suitable for transplanting. A well-rooted young plant may be moved in full flower, even bare-rooted. Success in the garden hinges on retaining the level of moisture in green parts and roots, before replanting and afterward—the hard-leaved phloxes do not wilt in the ordinary sense, and in the withered stage, difficult to detect, are beyond recovery. To meet this need for moisture, an airtight covering for humidity should be used. These phloxes have another peculiar need, that of light. They fade quickly in poor light, so they must be exposed to sun, or its equivalent, during the cooler portion of each 24 hours. ("Under-bench" treatment has been found as fatal as drying out). These methods are in common use at Prairie Gem Ranch. They should be employed when plants are at or near dormancy, in early spring or late fall.

Equipped with measuring stick and hand lens, the explorer finds miles of **P. hoodii** coming under the specifications for **P. hoodii** ssp. *muscoides*, including the extensive spreads in southern Wyoming and western Nebraska of the dark green and nearly glabrate forms. **P. hoodii** ssp. *muscoides* keeps very close to the ground. On the long, loamy slopes down from Crow Butte, typical **Phlox hoodii** takes over the short-grass pastures and, to reach its share of light, stretches upward to two inches. The crowning attraction is the finely modeled flower. Northerly, in the states and provinces along the international boundary, ecological factors bring about denser populations of this phlox on rocky flats and hilly pastures, where it conspicuously whitens portions of the landscape in early spring. It is so low-growing that it survives under the close mowing of golf courses. (When British visitors were playing golf in Calgary, someone noticed numerous phlox plants in the turf with ripe seeds. Soon the game was neglected, while eager player-gardeners dropped to their knees to gather seeds of *Phlox hoodii*.)

From one of the highest points on the Plains, a few miles from Colorado Springs, Kathleen Marriage sent me a deep-colored *Phlox longifolia*. As a rule, the upright-flowering stems of this species reach five to seven inches, with green leaves in proportion, and they bear clusters of many flowers of good size, the petals either rounded or with a shallow notch. I received the somewhat grayed-red phlox many years ago, when lath house management was new to me. I set it close to the wall where it might spread into the open. But winds always carried away winter's snows and the phlox found the place to be unbearably dry. The natural range of *P. longifolia* includes mountains and valleys from central Colorado far to the west and northwest. But it is well adapted to the Plains, and I have since grown it for many years, first in a fine clear pink from seed sent by D. M. Andrews of Boulder, Colorado; then in a pure white from Clara Regan of Butte, Montana. For plants established in locations providing good snow cover, the annual low precipitation poses no problem. In drought and heat the plant loses its leaves; then, with a good rain, it grows new ones from the same nodes. Close colonies are formed and offer a fine show of flowers in May and June. Planted in scree or other media containing much sand, the deep, long-reaching rhizomes find their way into nearby gumbo and seem more suited there. With six to eight inches of root that mostly has few branches, this phlox transplants easily.

In northwestern Oklahoma, excluding the Panhandle, grows the somewhat sprawly *Phlox oklahomensis*. This species has partly upright stems about four inches tall, linear-lanceolate leaves two inches and more in length, and small clusters of notch-petaled stars of lilac, lavender, or pink to white. In Oklahoma, above the 1,800-foot level, it extends over at least three counties and is hardy, though its general range extends eastward and southward into Kansas, Arkansas, and Texas. *P. oklahomensis*, which blooms in early spring, diffuses a delicate fragrance.

By the Teton River in northwestern Montana, I found a handsome large-flowered, especially pure white phlox growing in gravel. It was reminiscent of *P. andicola*, but quite distinctive. I had no opportunity to collect plants. Dried specimens were identified by Dr. Wherry as *Phlox variabilis*. It seems probable that this beautiful species will be found to have a wide range on the Plains, though its known haunts are principally in the mountains.

In the heart of the Black Hills stands a lonely peak, Flag Mountain, with the pinnacle supporting a National Forest lookout tower. It looks down over the few miles of Reynolds Prairie and an expanse of the higher Hills. The main bulk of the mountain is granite, the upper two or three hundred feet a remnant of the great limestone, the Pahasapa, which is here based directly on the granite. Covering the narrow and more or less crumbling summit, and all the lower extent of the limestone, is a marvelous little phlox, whose niche in the genus *Phlox* has yet to be determined. It differs from possible close relatives in its diminutive size, in the absence of a whitish margin to the leaf, and in its exclusive occupancy of this habitat, which has been traced for some miles northwesterly. In clay and humus in narrow crevices on the height, where it is open to all the vagaries of weather, the tiny plant holds so closely to the rock that it stands scarcely half an inch high; in sheltered places, perhaps, an inch. The tiny leaves are remarkably broad; a large percentage of the flowers, of many hues running to a vivid pink, have full, rounded petals. Plants brought to my garden have survived in half-shade and have proved capable of increasing by rhizomes.

Dr. Dale M. Smith has visited Flag Mountain and is engaged in a scientific study of this novel phlox.

## *Physalis (Quincula)*. Ground-cherry

A certain root-running ground-cherry native to my local soil type is such a persistent pest in my garden that I distrust anything with the name *Physalis*. There are numerous species with small, pendant, yellowish flowers quite lacking in garden interest. *Physalis lobata* is so different it was once given a generic name of its own, *Quincula*. The plant is low, with velvety, sinuately margined ovate leaves that are two inches long. Its five-sided, nearly round, flattish flowers open to more than an inch across and are posed nicely upward; their soft, mauvish red-purple lends great distinction. The corolla has a woolly, white star at the center and dull gold anthers. The blooming season is long. The husk-protected cherries have a mild flavor and are suitable for pies and preserves. The species ranges the Plains from central Kansas and Colorado to Texas and southwestward. A small colony of seven or eight feet graced a sunny, limy knoll in Kansas; unfortunately, there was no opportunity for collecting them. I should be pleased to test the species in my garden.

## *Physaria*. Bladder-pod

Two species, *Physaria brassicoides* and *P. didymocarpa*, are recorded as inhabitants of the Plains, although they must be rare. In eroding shale below a cap of sandstone on a butte in Wyoming, I discovered a few young plants of one of these species. Sparse rosettes of broadly spatulate, cupped leaves with a single projection on either side like the upper points of a shield were all covered with a fine density of glinting starry hairs. The plants I brought home lived over the winter, flowered in spring freely enough, but with stingy, narrow-armed, yellow crosses, then departed with mystifying haste. Once I grew a bed of one of the species from seed. After the indifferent flowers came a profusion of their somewhat remarkable pale green pods, which were wrinkly, double, and inflated. Not one plant lived, and nothing came again from seed.

## *Physocarpus*. Ninebark

The ninebarks are low shrubs bearing rounded corymbs of small, white flowers; the heads of blooms, the foliage, and the growth habit somewhat resemble those of some spiraeas. Their common name derives from their shreddy bark. *Physocarpus intermedius* is a more western plant and differs in a number of details from *P. opulifolius*, but there is no consensus as to the native range of either. Of much significance to gardeners is the much lower growth, usually five feet or less, of *P. intermedius*, a very graceful and beautiful plant in June, when covered and somewhat weighted down with its white, umbellike clusters. It does not spread by root. It is probably safe to assign its range to a section of the Niobrara River in northern Nebraska, to the Black Hills, and to the lower foothills of the mountains of Wyoming and Colorado.

Whole hillsides of the upper elevations of the Black Hills are abloom in June with *Physocarpus monogynus*. It is also credited to the foothills of Wyoming, Colorado, and New Mexico, ranging taller in the southern parts of its range. This plant rarely reaches 30 inches, even in cultivation, and it thrives in half-shade, with the normal low rainfall at Prairie Gem Ranch. Its growth is more upright than arching, and its dense flower clusters cover pleasingly all the upper branches. It spreads by root to a moderate degree.

## *Polygala*. Milkwort, lady-fingers     plate 96

From Texas to Montana one may find *Polygala alba*, on a firm or gravelly soil. Low clusters of linear, dark leaves and delicate, sparingly leafy stems lift long tapering fingers of small butterflylike white flowers, toward the end of June. Hardly showy, but where a close group lifts many stems six to eight inches, carrying the best white of which the species is capable, the effect is airy and charming.

## *Potentilla*. Cinquefoil, silver weed     plate 97

Among the many species in this genus, 30 and more on the Plains, are some that look like weeds and some, brought on trust into my garden, that act like weeds and which ultimately must be banished. Such is *Potentilla anserina*, with little, five-petaled, brilliant yellow roses, a dense cover of pinnate leaves, and leafy, flowering runners that spread into a colony much too rapidly. "Silver weed" is a common name, though in some forms the upper leaf surface is a rich, deep green.

From the latitude of the Black Hills far into Canada, and far southward along the mountains, is a veritable gem, *Potentilla concinna*. The plant pictured in plate 97 was growing in the Laramie Hills. With one to many rosettes of five-fingered, toothed leaves close to the ground and short flowering stems that lie quite low and bear numerous yellow blossoms, it is well behaved and a welcome early spring possession in the garden. *P. concinna* varies widely. From place to place, variant to variant, the leaf may measure an inch to two inches or more, and it may be very gray or rather green with only a light silvering of hairs. An extra dwarf form has a few teeth near the tip of the three inner leaflets (the two outer ones are tiny), and all leaflets are deep velvety green above, and white below.

Rydberg's *Potentilla divisa*, now regarded as a variety, appears in early spring in abundant silver fur and retains a conspicuous grayness throughout the season. At flowering in April or early May, the plant is a close mat of leaves, which is studded with a double handful of pirate's gold. This type is frequent on limestone in the Black Hills and has been noted in the Cypress Hills, usually in sun. Somewhat similar is a form that has not been given a name; its longer petioled leaves compose a looser, gray-green mat, and the slender, prostrate stems carry the flowers beyond the leaf mass. It is a valley plant and flowers later. Late in the season these two develop leaves up to three inches long. In all forms the petal tips are slightly notched, and the bases of the golden petals carry an accent dot of orange. They are long-lived plants.

Above dense clusters of ruffly pinnate basal leaves, *Potentilla (Drymocallis) fissa* lifts several ten-inch stems and a continual show of butter-yellow roses in May and June. It spreads moderately by underground offsets into a dense colony. Common in the Black Hills in light shade, and from Alberta to Colorado and Utah.

Somewhat of a rarity over the northern Plains, including Alberta and Saskatchewan, is *Potentilla plattensis*. The entire plant—pinnate leaves of dark green at the crown and along the slender stems, and the flowers—lies so flat as to rise only an inch or so. Even a small plant carries a generous sprinkling of half-inch, rounded flowerlets of the most brilliant yellow imaginable. A plant with a maximum spread of 16 inches disposes its leaves as mere background for the scintillating blossoms which appear as if dropped in scattering handfuls. *P. plattensis* is content in the half-shade of my lath house in a good loam, though its native ground may be moist, rich soil along a brook or a gravelly ridge in full prairie sun.

Certainly not weedy in the garden is *Potentilla pensylvanica*, which stays gray throughout the season, produces pinnate leaves and few stems, and grows 10 to 12 inches tall. Year after year without special care, it occupies an allotted spot and presents its bits of light yellow over a long period without affording much show. Similarly unimpressive are *P. effusa*, *P. gracilis*, *P. hippiana*, and *P. pulcherrima*, of varying leaf pattern. These might respond with better flowering under encouraging treatment.

*Potentilla fruticosa* is an attractive shrub preferring the high limestone exposures of the Black Hills, the frequent buttes of Montana and North Dakota, and still lower ground over the Canadian prairies. Its average appearance is a densely branched bush 20 to 24 inches tall, well covered with grayish, short, pinnate leaves and recurrent, bright yellow saucers, an inch wide or less. It is practically drought-proof and not exacting as to soil.

## *Prunus*. Sand cherry, western choke cherry    plate 98

The typical sand cherry of the Plains, *Prunus besseya*, is a rarely erect shrublet, less than a foot in branch length, and lightly foliaged. Indeed, it may go unnoticed when not bearing its early spring, dainty, white, five-petaled flowers, two to four in a cluster, or along in summer its surprisingly large, brownish to purple, green-fleshed fruits which are juicy and pleasantly edible when fully ripe. The sand cherry requires space to itself to ensure its moisture supply. In the wild it frequents rocky places where little else can grow or stretches of barren sand. It is at home from north central Kansas through the Sandhills of Nebraska and northeastern Colorado, the White River Badlands of South Dakota, the Badlands of the Little Missouri River in North Dakota, the foothills of the Black Hills, and westward to the foothills of the Rockies.

A quite different type is *Prunus melanocarpa*, rather distantly related to the trees of the eastern half of the continent, *P. serotina*, wild black cherry, and *P. virginiana*, choke cherry. Our choke cherry of the Plains displays a thicket-forming habit, where favored by moisture and some shade. There it may grow only five to eight feet tall; where its roots reach a drainage course, it may attain a height of 12 feet or more. Its clean, wide, glossy leaves and abundance of fragrant bloom in finger lengths of small, white flowers, crowded on the branches, are delightfully ornamental. When fully ripe, the shining black cherries, as much as half an inch in diameter but usually less, are sweet and delicious. They are sought for jelly or jam, preferably with other fruit for mildness and added pectin. One of the finest of all unfermented drinks is made from this fruit, the seeds included for their almondlike flavor: put a cup of fruit and a cup of sugar into a quart jar, fill with boiling water, and set away for six weeks.

In its choice sites along streams or in breaks, *Prunus melanocarpa* appear frequently from Saskatchewan to New Mexico on the open plains, into the Black hills to above 5,000 feet, and into the Rockies and far to the west.

## *Psilostrophe*. Paperflower

From shady soil by a cattle trail, well south in Oklahoma, I brought home on October a few roots with almost dormant green parts of *Psilostrophe villosa* but failed to establish it. I had found it in full flower in early July. At neither date were seeds available. Those first-observed plants were low, smoothly rounded bushlets, plated in intricate pattern with softly glowing, golden, half-inch composite flowers. Small disks and wide rays were of the same hue; in each flower head three wide rays completed a fully rounded, daintily cupped circle, each ray with three neatly rounded lobes of equal measure, a novel and lovely design. The plant is rated perennial; ranging from the southern border of Kansas into the Panhandle of Texas, it should be hardy. The leaves are irregularly shaped, from lanceolate to spatulate, occasionally somwhat lobed, coated loosely with white wool which rubs off and discloses a dark green underlayer. The finest development of the rounded, diversely branching bushlet, which reaches a height of 10 to 12 inches, occurs in full sun.

In a second trial from a different locality, **P.** *villosa* has proved hardy through a difficult winter; but that, an unknown stock, dug when flowers were not present, may fall far short of the expected perfection in flower form and in the pattern of the inflorescence.

## *Psoralea (Pediomelum)*. Indian-turnip, pomme blanche, breadroot

This genus of the Pea family, with somewhat lupinelike leaves, includes the low, June-blooming **Psoralea esculenta** whose starchy, tuberous root is still highly prized by the Indians in stews and soups. It was also a staple article of food, either raw or cooked, of early explorers; the French called it *pomme blanche*, others "breadroot." The short, wide spikes of dull purple flowers, to eight inches or taller, are borne abundantly and last for many days; the lower florets turn a contrasting light buff before withering. This effect is eye-catching, though hardly showy. The plant soon ripens its small, beanlike seeds and dries up. It is frequent from southern Canada to Texas.

**Psoralea hypogaea**, a smaller, short-stemmed, densely leafy member of the genus with short clusters of dull, dark purple, is usually found on sandy ground. A mere novelty.

## *Pulsatilla*. Pasque flower, crocus     plate 99

"Pasque flower" at first thought seems a borrowed, foreign name; yet the species, **Pulsatilla patens**, is both North American and European. In our region it was first named **P.** *ludoviciana* as a presumed new species. "Crocus" is a name dear to many old-timers and persists in common usage. *P. patens*, the floral emblem of both Saskatchewan and South Dakota, is at home over most of the province in rugged places, whereas in the state it stretches sparingly throughout and in the Black Hills is fantastically abundant. It appears in Oklahoma and Texas, also in favored places across Iowa to northern Illinois and Wisconsin, northward to the Yukon and Alaska, and in the western mountains.

Blooming is foretold by the appearance in late fall of plump buds at ground level, on crowns a little below. In earliest spring the buds rapidly enlarge and push tentatively upward, warm-robed in silver fur, preferring to dodge severe weather. They open into lavender satin beauties, with gold-centers and deeper lavender to blue and deep purple outer wraps. Under optimal growing conditions, their six-pointed stars may luxuriate to a magnificent, full four inches of spread. When after several days the sepals have fallen, the leaves, finely divided and handsome, will come from the ground, and showy, glossy seed plumes will form and sway in the breeze which pasque flowers love.

In my nearby hunting ground I have often seen clear pink pasque flowers; pure white ones are extremely rare. Even more infrequent is a striking full pompon of narrow segments, seen only in lavender. Such a flower is borne with frustrating infrequency, and the plant will likely revert to the normal, six-segmented flower the following year.

Fresh seeds germinate readily, but the plantlets are not moved easily. At any age of the pasque flower, successful transplanting depends on lifting it with enough soil to avoid disturbing the roots. An early spring heat wave forces the blossoms to open prematurely, but a steady supply of moisture at that time will provide a retarding coolness to the plant. Drainage is imperative, and rich soil in the upper couple of inches is welcome. In my garden, shade through the heat of the day or permanent half-shade is necessary. However, in gardens with less extreme conditions full sun is advisable. By planting pasque flowers in different exposures, blooming may extend over a month.

## *Ranunculus*. Buttercup

How many species bear tbe name *Ranunculus* and how few are entitled to the honored name "buttercup"! In wet ground or partly submerged in still water, a scrawny plant sometimes discloses an identifying leaf and a wisp of color. If one has known buttercups in all the happy connotations of the name, one looks quickly elsewhere.

High on the rich, black-soil summit of the Cypress Hills in late June, I found a scattered dozen or two of *Ranunculus cardiophyllus*; erect, foot-high, stems with some wide leaves at the base, a few much-divided leaves upward, and two or three flowers with the petallike sepals wide and gracefully cupped, and with all the longed-for gloss and brilliant color a buttercup should have. Somehow I drew satisfaction from its ground being dusty dry, though it had not long been so, for deep blue, little *Viola adunca* and many others were beautiful and fresh a few steps away. Some days later I found *R. cardiophyllus* again, this time on the sunny side of a ravine leading down to the Missouri River, southwest of Williston, in North Dakota. Dr. O. A. Stevens of that state made the identification. It had not been previously reported for the state; though it is said to range farther south and far to the west, it seems to be rare on the Plains.

Not so *Ranunculus glaberrimus*, which covers much of Wyoming, Montana, and southern Alberta and areas farther west. The Dakotas, however, have little of it. As a garden plant it is, perhaps, transient everywhere and possibly short-lived in the wild, depending on new seedling stock in favorable seasons to spread a golden carpet over a sagebrush flat or a small valley nook. The early spring show is soon past; the withered and brown plant parts soon disappear.

## *Ratibida (Lepachys).* Coneflower

This is justly called "prairie coneflower," because of its abundance almost everywhere on the Plains, though its range is much wider. Commonly 20 to 24 inches tall, *Ratibida columnifera* branches freely above the base; remains airy and open, though rather narrowly upright, with pinnatifid foliage deeply cut; and bears a profusion of distinctively patterned composites. A tall cone, at first gray-green, turns brown as its disk flowers open beginning at the base, where a few wide and long, often gracefully twisted, rich yellow rays are attached. In local areas, the rays of an occasional plant are splashed or centered with crimson or maroon, or are entirely of that color, rich and velvety. D. M. Andrews was the authority who said that in southwestern Colorado maroon is the common color and yellow-rayed plants are rare. In most references, this handsome deep red is termed "purplish brown" and the species "perennial." At Prairie Gem Ranch, whether in the pastures or in the garden, it is often biennial. *R. columnifera* provides a bright note for early July and is richly fragrant.

## *Rhus.* Smooth sumac, three-leaf sumac, poison oak, poison ivy, poison sumac

The smooth sumac of the Plains and other portions of the West, and extending eastward to below typical Plains elevations, has been known as **Rhus cismontana.** It may be considered a dwarf form of **R. glabra,** if morphology, geography, and certain minor characteristics, which may be ecological effects, are discounted. The dwarfness of the western form continues under cultivation, reflecting an inborn habit. Through much of its range it hardly reaches five feet; whereas the eastern, taller form imported to the Plains or mountains tends to strive toward its accustomed maximum of double that height or more. Both forms carry their mass of glossy pinnate leaves well up from the ground, and with adequate moisture change to thrilling tones of crimson in October. Their flowers are small, indifferent, yellow, resulting in large, pointed clusters of bright red fruits late in the season. A root-spreading tendency is easily controlled.

**Rhus trilobata** is more definitely a species of the Plains and areas farther west. It is typically a low, dense bush or clump, well furnished with deep green, three-parted leaves an inch or so in length and irregular in outline. It frequently grows in exposed and dry places to which it is especially adapted, being able to hold its excellent depth of green through trying droughts. This faculty and its dense leafiness to ground level make it a valuable hedge plant for dry locations. Its small, yellow flowers in early spring result in tight clusters of rich red berries, which remain for some time after the leaves have fallen. The autumn display of leaf color runs through every hue from yellow through orange and copper to deep maroon.

**R. trilobata** has been given many familiar names, such as "lemonade sumac" for the lemonlike acid of its fruits which can be used for a refreshing drink. A commoner name is "skunk-bush"—a plain libel, for while the bruised wood has a strong and unpleasant odor, it is clearly not that of skunk. There is little occasion to smell the wood or the leaves which are less offensive. Some spreading by stolons presents no problem where a mower is used.

Since the poison oaks, and ivies, belong to the genus **Rhus** (though they are sometimes found under the generic **Toxicodendron**), I bring up the name **Rhus radicans v. rydbergii,** the poison oak of the Plains and portions of the farther West, as well as parts of the eastern half of the continent, to warn readers that this plant differs from the beautiful and harmless red-berried sumacs by readily recognized features with which everyone should be familiar. Its shrubby, erect stems, usually unbranched, reach from a few to 12 inches or occasionally taller and carry, especially upward, prominent, pinnately three-parted leaves of bright green, the leaflets usually three or more inches long. A critically dangerous time is late autumn, when the stems are tipped by close panicles of interesting whitish berries and the leaves take on brilliant colors. No parts of the plant should be touched. Even spatters of sap from the roots when the plant is dormant, broken in an effort at eradication or, incidentally, in digging other plants, can cause serious poisoning. In the absence of water and soap, gasoline is thoroughly effective for cleansing. The plant is more often chanced upon where other vegetation is not dense, as in rough ground.

## *Ribes*. Wild currant

*Ribes cereum*? *Ribes inebrians*? Rydberg preferred the latter for the Plains, with the former as a synonym, but his descriptions are confused. The handsome and well-mannered currant of South Dakota, the canyon country of western Nebraska, Colorado, New Mexico and states adjoining, grows to six feet—often much lower—but has the "usually pink or pinkish" flowers, the flower color in the Black Hills whence came my garden plants. Here a fine old specimen finds the environment to its liking; a dense, slender-stemmed bush, it requires no special care. A few seedlings appear, but the old plant keeps its place. The flowers are not as large as those of the golden currant, nor as showy, but a compensation comes in August when a good crop of light scarlet, quarter-inch or larger currants ripens to charm the eye rather than the tastebuds. In the wild, this shrub seeks the light shelter of scattered pines.

A worthy ornamental and fruiting shrub, **Ribes odoratum** is known as the golden currant, though a similar and smaller species residing farther west bears the technical name **R. aureum**, the golden. The names are confused in general usage; but it is the former that bears in early spring the abundant short racemes of larger, golden flowers delightfully fragrant of clove. It also bears the larger fruits and, importantly, will grow and perform well in drier and more difficult gardening situations than perhaps any other fruit bearer.

In the cluster the fruits vary in size, the larger reaching half an inch. They are fully ripe when the pedicel takes on the color of the currant and are then mildly acid and very pleasant eating. The connoisseur may discover that some strains produce fruits of faintly brown-tinted black, and others, somewhat elongated, have a bluish tinge and have an edge in enticing flavor. There are yellow-fruited strains of similar delight.

*Ribes odoratum* sends up many slender, arching stems from the ground, branching above, to a common height of some 40 inches. The plant is not densely leafy. The leaves are two inches long or less, deeply lobed and dentate. Long, searching roots at a shallow depth send up suckers—to no detriment where a thicket may be permitted, otherwise to be trimmed to ground level or below in June.

## *Rosa*. Rose, wild rose     plate 100

All the native roses of the Plains make free use of their deep-seated rhizomes to enlarge their territories, but in the competition of the wild they usually do not travel far. Just down the road from my garden a colony of *Rosa arkansana*, aided by the disturbed soil of the dirt grade, after many years has spread its domain to 30 feet or so. But such "weediness" serves not to dissuade those who love the beauty and fragrance of these endearing flowers from bringing them into the garden.

The name *Rosa arkansana* has been taken to cover a number of closely related forms of the low roses which once were named as species. A prominent characteristic, however, written into the technical outline of *R. arkansana*, that of dying back to the ground annually, does not serve as an identification mark elsewhere than in the relatively small type locality in Colorado. Over the length and breadth of its range, other members of this species complex will be found as shrubs reliable in hardiness, leafing out to the tip in spring, and flowering from old wood as well as, occasionally, in corymbs at the apex of new shoots from the ground in true *R. arkansana* fashion. The plant may be lower or taller than the type's 12 inches; the leaflets five to seven; the two-inch flowers coming, mainly in June, in lovely pink of varying tone; and the crimson hips, from round to pear-shaped, remaining long upon the plant. The group species has a wide distribution from southern Canada to Texas, to the east as far as Wisconsin and Illinois, and far to the west.

The provincial floral emblem of Alberta is the wild rose. In North Dakota the legislative act of making the wild rose the state flower designated the technically named **R. suffulta**, now regarded a constituent of **R. arkansana**.

A kindly old gentleman, the late J. W. Fargo, led me across a secret ridge crest on his property in the southern tip of the Black Hills, where grew a double wild rose in a colony of perhaps 50 plants. I was told I might dig freely, on condition that I distributed the rare gem under his, the discoverer's name. Sent to the late F. L. Skinner, the noted originator of lilies, roses, and other hardy plants in Dropmore, Manitoba, they were pronounced the best double wild rose he had seen. The flower is larger than the normal single form, having about 40 petals, more than two rows of them large, with inner petals grading to tiny, all opening to show the golden center. The free-flowering peak is reached in early July. The Fargo rose uses the *Rosa arkansana* trick of sending up a strong shoot from the ground to prolong its season with a wide corymb opening gradually over many days. The fragrance of this rose is mild and fine.

There is good evidence that *Rosa blanda* comes to the eastern border of the Plains, as reported by a number of local authorities. But if the white, five-petaled rose I have met with in the rugged canyons of northwestern Nebraska and in the Black Hills be *R. blanda*, it has taken on manners befitting the environment, shortening its lengthy stems to about 20 inches and reducing its traditional pinkness to practically zero. Only the freshest flowers on a dewy morning have a hint of blush, and in high sun and low humidity they become white. In the local plants, root traveling is fairly restrained.

With small and neatly fashioned leaflets of deep green, textured like metal with a medium gloss; upright stems of dark red; inch and a half wide, five-petaled flowers of purest white; and, finally, small, round, deep crimson hips, *Rosa foliolosa* must be accorded high rank in the jewellike workmanship of nature. Yet its only known common name is "prairie rose." Its native ground is northern Texas, and Oklahoma eastward to Arkansas. Stock, which was sent me from Oklahoma 30 years ago, has weathered temperatures of $18°F$ below zero, with no snow at all, and then flowered. Although it does not rise above 10 inches in height, it seldom has the advantage of full snow protection. Each daintily modeled flower holds the eye for a moment of tribute; and flowers continue to come for several weeks in midseason. The plant is said to grow taller in the South.

The principal taller pink rose of the Plains is **Rosa woodsii**, which I have not attempted to grow in the garden. It is to be seen often in valley locations, where it may have the advantage of receiving more moisture. In full sun it forms dense thickets, rises to 40 inches or so and in late spring, with fine branching over the upper growth, completely covers itself with bloom and fills the buoyant air with fragrance. The closely massed hips, bright crimson to scarlet, also present a period of color. **R. woodsii** as a group species embraces a number of varieties that formerly bore specific names. It is listed by Canadian authorities for the southern one-sixth of the Canadian Plains and is found southward to Texas. Doubtless properly rated a variant of this is **R. acicularis**, though credited to the entire Canadian Plains area and southward through the Plains states by certain authors. It is described as lower than **R. woodsii**; other distinctions are difficult to recognize.

## *Rudbeckia*. Black-eyed susan, golden-glow    plate 101

A fine flower in any company of like proportions, black-eyed susan, **Rudbeckia hirta**, is a composite with broad rays of a yellow so deep it is almost orange and a dark brown, smooth, low cone. Through July and August the plant produces many flowers on stems 12 to 20 inches long; flowers last a long time and are neatly disposed of as they wither. Basal leaves are many, oblong-lanceolate or oblanceolate, rough, ribbed, and usually entire, six inches or more in length. The stem leaves are much reduced. Fortunately, or otherwise, the plant is biennial. It is frequent in the Black Hills; on the Plains generally it seeks better soils and moisture. Some botanists discern a varietal difference, principally in leaf form and stem length, separating our western form from those of eastern North America and calling ours **R. serotina**.

The name "golden-glow" brings to mind a very tall, very double-flowered garden plant of June to August. The double form is a sport from the wild **Rudbeckia laciniata**, which has a single but well-filled fringe of rays about a yellow center. To some tastes, this is more beautiful than the double; to others, it appears coarse and untidy. The leaves are much divided and bold in outline. **R. laciniata** is common near certain streams in the higher Black Hills and avoids the drier

Plains. With garden care it grows into a wide, close clump and is long-lived.

## *Ruellia*. Wild petunia, ruellia

Among the ruellias, which cover much of the eastern United States, two species reach the Plains, especially in Kansas. They are much-branched, leafy, deciduous perennials and provide a succession of blue-lavender petunias, about an inch and a half wide, from June to September. The root system delves wide and deep, enabling the plant to remain fresh and productive through much dry weather.

*Ruellia humilis* is adapted to open sun and is common over the eastern half of Kansas. It grows to a foot or more, with somewhat hairy stems and ovate to oblong, hairy margined leaves, not conspicuously grayish. Many seeds are borne cleistogamously in late season, by which means it may become weedy. This species has been called **R. ciliosa** and **R. caroliniana**.

*Ruellia strepens* is a taller, greener plant, somewhat smaller-flowered, drought-resistant, but adapted to woodsy shade. It is less frequent westward.

## *Rumex*. Dock, sour greens

Often in areas of loose sand may be seen a low and rather coarse plant, especially noticeable in early summer when its mature, winged fruits suggest two of its unscientific names: "wild begonia" and "wild hydrangea." During that season it puts on a fascinating show in deep pink or light and luscious crimson. It is, nonetheless, a dock, **Rumex venosus**, with most of the unwelcome habits of its relatives and outdoing some with its long-reaching rhizomes, which in my tough clay seem to search endlessly for sand. Sand, no doubt, and perhaps some alchemy are needed to concoct its enticing coloration. In my alkaline soil, it achieves only scanty raiment of indifferent green.

## *Salvia*. Blue sage

Valued for its exquisite blue flowers, produced in abundance during September-October, is **Salvia pitcheri** (**S. azurea v. grandiflora**). Wide panicles top the numerous 40-inch stems to provide fine color for some weeks in broad, lower-lipped flowers of mint family type. A white-flowered form is reported. The slender, sometimes branching stems are well furnished with faintly downy, linear to linear-lance-shaped leaves. From the crown many tough, slender roots descend to great depths for moisture unavailable to most plants, ensuring long life; the blooming, however, is dependent on good seasonal rainfall. *S. pitcheri* is native chiefly from southeastern Nebraska to south-eastern Colorado and south to Texas. (*S. azurea* is a smaller, less colorful plant of eastern Texas and eastward.)

## *Sambucus*. Elder, elderberry

The brilliant red-berried elder, entirely glabrous in stem and foliage, growing freely close to a north wall at Prairie Gem Ranch, should be, according to Rydberg's description, *Sambucus microbotrys*. The range of this form is given as South Dakota (Black Hills), Colorado, and south to Arizona and Utah. It is possibly a variation from *S. pubens* (*S. racemosa* ssp. *pubens*), which occurs throughout the North American continent, and to which the name *S. microbotrys* is often subordinated by authors. My plants stand about three feet tall, and their attractive small, elongated fruit clusters ripen in July, to be stripped by various birds shortly thereafter. In the Black Hills the fruiting plant is occasionally glimpsed from a roadway, high or low among the rocks. It has also been observed in cultivation, growing to about five feet, keeping erect and looking healthy from the time it bears its abundant elongate, creamy white flower clusters through fruiting, and holding its large, pinnate leaves well. A bright yellow-fruited form is less frequent. *S. pubens*, described as softly hairy in various parts, is also reported for this area, but I have not distinguished it.

## *Sanguinaria*. Bloodroot

In addition to its unexpected occurrence in the northern Black Hills, *Sanguinaria canadensis* frequents sheltered places some four hundred miles to the east, in the moist, rich soils along the eastern borders of North Dakota, South Dakota, Nebraska, and south, remote even there from High Plains elevations and climate. How, then, did these lone colonies develop far to the west within the Plains? It is to be assumed that during well-watered and forested times the bloodroot took a natural course in extending its range as far as the Black Hills. Then, with increased aridity resulting from the retreat of the glacial ice, this succulent and shelter-adapted plant died out, as doubtless did many others, except where it had found the only permanent ecological refuge in the northern Black Hills, which are to the present day favored with higher annual rainfall than other portions of the region.

In the watered and shaded garden of Mrs. Floyd Brown in Lead, I saw the bloodroot flourishing in the company of tall ferns. The lovely white, narrow-petaled flowers were as fine as the species produces anywhere in its range over the eastern half of this continent. In my garden on the prairie, however, bloodroot plants that she generously gave me did not fare as well; once their large, woodland-type leaves attained full size, brisk winds readily broke them down, and the thick, reddish rhizomes soon dried to extinction.

## *Sarcobatus*. Greasewood

For an exotic or desertlike effect, ***Sarcobatus vermiculatus*** excels in its range on the Plains from Saskatchewan to Texas. It also occurs farther west. Branching densely and angularly, it may grow to six feet. The light gray of the bark harmonizes with the faintly bluish light green of the slender, inch and a half, worm-shaped leaves. Its flowers are negligible. In fall wide-margined fruiting calyxes, closely lining the upper twigs, are conspicuous by their lightly crowded effect, though hardly differing in color tone from the foliage. The branches are somewhat spiny. With free seeding, ***S. vermiculatus*** tends to form thickets and crowd out other vegetation. It may need an alkaline soil.

## *Schrankia (Leptoglottis)*. Sensitive brier

Small, hooked prickles, strong and sharp enough to scratch or penetrate the skin, make the presence of ***Schrankia uncinata*** known on contact. One experiences this armament, which is borne on the long, low-postured stems and on leaf rachises and peduncles, and if unaware of the plant till then, looks down to see the disturbed leaflets of the rather skeletonlike, pinnate leaves quickly folding together in self-protection. If the flowers are present, they become the center of interest. In a lengthening raceme, small round knobs of green bud clusters develop into symmetrical, inch-wide balls of fluff of a lovely rose-pink. This unique flower appears to be composed entirely of long filaments, with petals hidden and anthers inconspicuous. The flowering season covers many weeks between June and September. Each of the several to many trailing or clambering, little-branched stems carries its complement of flowers. The stems, which may reach three feet, come from a deep root. *S. uncinata* ranges from central western South Dakota through Nebraska and Kansas to southeastern Colorado and Texas and into some bordering states to the east. Where space is available, this plant is a treasure of fragrance and beauty.

A smaller species of similar habit, *S. microphylla*, inhabits southeastern and southern states.

## *Scutellaria*. Scullcap     plate 102

An inconspicuous little plant, except when it bears its bright purple-blue flowers, *Scutellaria brittonii* is probably restricted to Wyoming and Colorado; to the foothills in the latter state, but in Wyoming it comes onto the prairie as far as Cheyenne. The upper lobe of the corolla of *S. brittonii* is crested in the form of a skullcap. The stems are mostly under five inches high, the leaves an inch or so long, entire, puberulent but green. The flowering season is long, since succeeding pairs of blossoms are borne in the axils of the lengthening stems. A member of the mint family, this little plant gains territory by putting out unexpectedly thick, pale yellow rhizomes; but in the many years in my garden it has never traveled far, and new plants are scattered rather than clumped. It has never overrun any neighbor, being content to find a bit of space of its own.

Quite different in habit is *Scutellaria resinosa*, a typical Great Plains densely branched bushlet, growing about 10 inches high from a taproot. The flowers follow the lengthening stems, keeping the plant conspicously blue for a long season. Small, puberulent gray leaves give the effect of a pleasing fine texture in harmony with the small, roundish blossoms. This species of great charm and perfect garden behavior is frequent in a large area of northcentral Kansas and extends to Texas and Arizona. It has been reported for Nebraska and Colorado.

## *Sedum*. Stonecrop     plate 103

The yellow-flowered stonecrop of the eastern slope of the central and southern Rockies and of portions of the Great Plains was originally named *Sedum lanceolatum*. Shortly after its official naming, *S. stenopetalum* was discovered and named farther to the west. Enter trouble; both species were then placed as *S. stenopetalum*, and thus has *S. lanceolatum* been known until recently.

The mature **Sedum lanceolatum** produces a number of inconspicuous stems of two to four inches, well furnished with short, succulent, green or bronzy leaves. In late June the stems erupt at the
apex into starforked cymes of starry, golden fires. Often they catch
the eye from woodsy shade, but the plant is in its glory in the open,
in a bit of loose rock material seasoned with humus. There it flowers
bravely, though drought may redden and wither the leafage. The leaves
of this species may drop as the flowers mature, whereas it is the mark
of **S. stenopetalum** to retain the leaves after anthesis and to grow a
number of short, well-leaved branchlets along the stem.

**Sedum lanceolatum** is the species of the Colorado foothills, of wide
expanses of the Laramie Hills, of rugged portions of northwestern
Nebraska, of the Black Hills, and of the Cypress Hills. Definite limits
of the two species are not at hand, but **S. stenopetalum** was noted
where the mountains meet the Plains in northwestern Montana.

## *Senecio.* Groundsel, ragwort, senecio      plate 104

The time-honored common names of some senecios are not very
descriptive of the finer species of the Great Plains; "ragwort" probably refers to a scantily rayed flower, whereas "groundsel," even
more conjectural, may have referred to ground-gaining habits. The
half-dozen species listed are of acceptable habit and excellent in flower
form and color.

A rich, all-yellow, daisy-form flower is borne freely enough by
**Senecio canus** on a smooth, light gray plant to make it highly desirable. It may come into flower at 10 to 20 inches; each head has an
especially neat setting of round-tipped rays about a small disk, and is
three-fourths of an inch wide. The leaves are flat, up to four inches
long, oblong or lanceolate, or pinnatifid on the upper stems. **S. canus**
accepts sun or partial shade and forms a moderate colony. According
to Rydberg, **S. canus** is known from Manitoba to Nebraska and Colorado, and far to the west.

A gray-white plant, and yellow-flowered also, is **Senecio purshianus**;
only in these two traits is it like **S. canus** with which it is currently
confused. This species inhabits sunny, limy places; forms a wide, compound crown; and lifts on its many stems a rounded or a flat-topped
display as much as eight to 10 inches wide. The flowers are somewhat
lighter in hue than those of **S. canus**. In selected forms they are

beautifully symmetrical. Especially different are the leaves, two inches long, with edges rolled under, and maintained in a dense basal tuft through the winter. The crown is readily divisible, but there is no spreading from the root. Rydberg gives the range as Saskatchewan, South Dakota, Texas, and the far West.

A somewhat rare species is *Senecio fendleri*. This grows in dense, leafy clumps with many stems and bears a flat-topped bouquet of neat small, deep yellow, orange-centered daisies. The leaves are gray-green, oblanceolate, much incised, and ruffly. On an extensive ancient sand and gravel deposit in western Nebraska, where I found numerous small colonies of *S. fendleri* in full sun, the flowers were borne at six inches. At Granite, Wyoming, in shade for much of the day, it grew about 10 inches high. In Colorado, it is found in the mountains at 8,000 feet and up.

A taller plant (16 to 18 inches), *Senecio plattensis* finds a home in much-scattered, small patches on dry prairie upland, just the opposite of the damp habitats sought by so many of the groundsels. Almost all its leaves are pinnatifid, with a prominent toothed lobe at the tip. The lower stem and undersides of the basal, clustered leaves are often a purplish maroon. Otherwise stems and foliage are green; they are apt to be hairy about the nodes early in the season, later to become glabrescent. The species tends to form colonies so dense as to become its own worst competitor; but in my garden, after many years, it covers a space of less then five feet. It wins an honored place by bearing at the apex of each stem an ample, flat-topped cluster of inch-wide heads of as perfect a pattern of many rays as nature could devise, all in deep, rich yellow and centered about a disk of intense, glowing orange. Its flowering season is June. *S. plattensis* is found in all the Plains states and the province of Saskatchewan, also over much of the United States to the east.

In *Senecio riddellii*, the light green leaves in pinnate arrangement are reduced to mere veins, so that however many leaves the stems put up from the indivisible, taprooted crown, the plant always has a light and airy effect. Twenty to 24 inches is a common height. In September or early October, the much-branched and widened upper portion becomes a mass of light yellow, inch-wide or larger flowers, with rays well separated, in keeping with the general airy appearance of the plant. Its pale yellow flowers are a welcome rarity among the deep yellow of other late-blooming prairie flowers.

**Senecio spartioides** is a lower plant, 10 to 20 inches high, very much on the pattern of **S. riddellii** except for its broadly linear leaves. It is plentiful in certain areas, over much of the same range, and extends far to the southwest. And there are other dry-land senecios whose attractive descriptions suggest they would be worth knowing.

**Senecio longilobus** (**S. douglasii** v. **longilobus**). In the rugged Cimarron Canyon pasture country of far western Oklahoma a shallow, rocky ravine neared the roadside and, deepening, curved away. Here were numerous plants of the tree cactus, **Opuntia imbricata**. To check the late-October stage of yellow ripeness of the showy fruits, I stepped from the car and at once was struck by the prospect of a natural rock garden, an acre or two in extent. I saw much bare or rocky ground, in keeping with the locality; much water-worn and weathered sandstone in smooth stretches and on ledges; impressive cactus, berried three-leaf sumac, rabbit brush showing fading yellow, minor shrubbery, and a patch of dwarf **Yucca harrimanae**, each in its carefully chosen site; many small herbaceous things—silver-green rosettes of hymenoxys, and small penstemons attired in bronzy green for the coming dormant season. It was a delight to wander down the dry waterway and observe nature's management of the novel plant materials.

On an upper terrace appeared filigrees of skeletonized leaves half hidden in sparkling crystalline hairs. Stems and leaves were gray to green; the leaves, up to two inches long, were mere veins in pinnate pattern, and their fanciful curving created a charming and refined effect. The plants were manifestly shrubby in the lower parts, many-stemmed, upright, with short side branches, and topped with the dry, seed-dispersing involucres of a composite. This was **Senecio longilobus**, as identified at the herbarium at Laramie, where pressed specimens carried medium yellow flower heads an inch wide. The species commonly grows a foot high and is said to attain greater height. Its range is southeastern Colorado, southward and westward. Two young plants, which I recently acquired, are off to a good start in my garden.

## *Shepherdia*. Buffalo-berry

A conspicuously gray-green, fine-leaved shrub of the northern Plains including Nebraska, **Shepherdia argentea** becomes highly attractive when carrying its dense and crowded load of small, scarlet berries in summer. The early color is only the promise of ripeness; not until frost has worked its alchemy on the excess of acid and bitterness does this fruit become edible, and even then, larger quantities should not be consumed. Its pectin content is high, and buffalo-berry jelly is delicious. The flowers of both staminate and pistillate plants, tiny and with little color, carry a faint breath of spring in early April. There is a yellow-fruited variety.

As an ornamental, *Shepherdia argentea* has several scores against it: widely traveling roots, spine-tipped branches, and weak wood which is readily broken by wind or weight of snow. In the wild the shrub protects itself by choosing sheltered ravines and by forming thickets. While there may be nonbearing years even when pollen is available, it seems that the sexes are often not well mixed; thus colonies of either sex are formed in which fruiting never occurs. The male plant is identified at flowering time by the blossom, which is about twice the size of the female blossom. An average height for the silver buffalo-berry is six to eight feet. Its range includes southern Canada, rare occurrences to the east of the Plains, and portions of the Rockies to New Mexico.

*Shepherdia canadensis* forms a neat, somewhat symmetrical bush seldom more than three feet high. Usually in protected positions, it prefers northern slopes and shelter in order to conserve moisture. It is desirable for its restrained habit, the dark green of its small, ovate to oval leaves, with young stems and underside of leaves brownish in season. The tiny flowers are negligible. The berries, a distinctive dark red in keeping with the foliage effect, have an astonishing bitterness acceptable only to certain wild life. Canadian buffalo-berry is principally northern and has a wide range beyond the Plains. In the United States it is confined to the more rugged portions; in Canada, to the outer fringes of the Plains region as well.

## *Sisyrinchium.* Blue-eyed grass

The genus *Sisyrinchium* has presented a fertile field of hardly significant morphological variations, and numbers of segregates have been described from material that botanists were once content to call *S. angustifolium*. Most of these have small tufts or dense clusters of narrow, upright, grasslike, and faintly glaucous leaves and stems of similar height and appearance, which bear mainly from May to July numerous six-petaled, flat, yellow-eyed and violet-blue blossoms, three-fourths of an inch wide. The chief grass flower of the Plains is now called *Sisyrinchium montanum*; it thrives in better soils in ravines or on northern slopes where part-time shade retards drying, though it is subject to extended drought even in these locations. In the environment of Prairie Gem Ranch, this familiar species often forms clumps the width of a hand and finds suitable nooks around the garden in which to display its free flowering at six to ten inches.

The white-flowered **Sisyrinchium campestre** is readily distinguished, likewise its much rarer form in delicate powder-blue. This species appears in the eastern portions of South Dakota and Nebraska and extends westward to Plains elevations in Kansas and Oklahoma. It is a greener plant than *S. montanum* and grows about eight inches high. The charm of its freely borne and graceful stars ensures its welcome.

## *Smilacina.* False solomon's seal

In a remarkable adaptive departure from the cool shade and moisture familiarly associated with **Smilacina**, *S. stellata* has become both sun- and drought-enduring in its course across the Plains. Probably birds have distributed its seeds to prairie ravines and sterile spots in badlands. There it spreads readily by roots in periods of good moisture into a dense, ground-shading colony and under stress maintains the pleasing texture of wide-oblanceolate foliage, a foot or less high. Still it retains a preference for moist, sandy soils in shade, and in such situations grows to 18 inches. Its very short, terminal racemes of small, white stars carry little impact, and its greenish, dark-striped berries are a minor attraction. Its persistence and determined colony-forming qualify it for certain spots remote from one's garden treasures. *S. stellata* occurs from about the middle of Kansas northward and over much of this continent eastward.

## *Solidago.* Goldenrod, solidago     plate 105

Goldenrods naturally separate themselves into two classes, those that are to be admired at a distance and those that may safely, or with minimum care, be enjoyed in the garden. Tall goldenrods and those with strong tendencies to form colonies are not considered here, since they are extremely difficult to eradicate. Among lower-growing kinds, 30 inches or less in the average environment, are a number which by very short processes build a moderately wide crown and provide masses of handsome flowers. A few dwarf species especially characteristic of the Great Plains form colonies to a limited degree, and at

Prairie Gem Ranch are worth the trouble taken to control their spreading.

High on the great Gray Limestone of the Black Hills I came upon a small colony of *Solidago missouriensis*, flowering at six to eight inches. I took slight notice of the goldenrod. But it was so dwarf in a year not especially dry, that its image remained in my mind; by the time I had descended the precipitous slope to the road, I realized I had, perhaps, passed up a rare find. Would this particular strain remain dwarf under cultivation? Goldenrods are notorious for stretching their stems in favorable situations, and *S. missouriensis* and its close relatives are spreaders. We should surely be willing, nevertheless, to test a beautiful and novel variation. Typical *S. missouriensis*, as I know it, forms basal rosettes of glossy, linear-lanceolate leaves, entire or sometimes serrate, with reduced similar leaves along the stems. The golden panicle is somewhat narrow, its branches ascending, the general stance erect. Its early flowering gives it a special value.

The particular variety, or form, that I know as *Solidago glaberrima* is also called *S. missouriensis* v. *fasciculata*. It is the only goldenrod to inhabit successfully the heaviest of the gumbo clays near my home, and it is infrequent there. As do all goldenrods, it prefers sandy loams or sands. The inflorescence is distinctive, a broad-based pyramidal form with a nodding or side-tilted tip, on the pattern of some admired taller species. *S. glaberrima* begins flowering in July. A selection that I brought from a sandy locality to my garden flowers usually at eight to 12 inches; with abundant moisture it reaches 16 inches. It is a very moderate traveler, and its charming flower is full repayment. This and other segregates are common over the Plains region and eastward and westward as well.

Low, gray throughout, and with a compact and billowy inflorescence, *Solidago mollis* is closely confined to the Great Plains from central Canada to northern Oklahoma and Texas. Its dense, grayish leafiness is a splendid foil for the glowing, deep golden flower masses, borne at six to 12 inches in August and September. This low form is very beautiful. There are taller variants, some of which have been named. All spread by rather deep rhizomes, a trait to be considered when bringing them into the garden. At Prairie Gem Ranch, *S. mollis* has not been difficult.

Not only for the multitude of species are the solidagos troublesome to define. All too often attempts have been made at definition, separation, and recombination without adequate knowledge of the material in hand. As Dr. H. D. Harrington, author of *Manual of the Plants of Colorado*, has observed, "The nomenclature has become involved." **Solidago nemoralis** is a strong case in point. Here is a species with such wide variations that a description written to cover all variations fails to delineate any of them. Local floras of states or of wider areas tend to depend on material in their herbaria, which is not necessarily representative of what the species or the variations may look like elsewhere. There seems, however, to be general agreement that **S. nemoralis** has a branched caudex—does not travel by means of rhizomes; that it forms a more or less persistent basal mat of leaves, ashy gray with fine pubescence, mostly oblanceolate, mostly shallowly and remotely toothed. The many flowering stems and diminished stem foliage also are grayish; and for the Plains at least, the general height is 18 to 24 inches. It is chiefly in the inflorescence that conspicuous, wide variations occur. Commonly the panicle is composed of numerous slender, ascending branches, broadening somewhat airily to six inches or more, then tapering to a bent or nodding tip, with a total length of 10 to 12 inches. With several crowding stems in flower at one time, in a deep yellow, the effect is very fine. At Iron Mountain in the Black Hills occurs an extreme form with the slender branches rebranching and arching outward to form a 12- to 15-inch panicle, with rounded top and no conspicuous tip. The total height of the plant is 24 inches or more.

From impressions gained from state and provincial floras, I gather that the more common form is that which has been known as **Solidago pulcherrima**, now considered a variety of **S. nemoralis**. In its most strict form, its inflorescence is a simple rod, with branches so short as to be hardly noticeable, the tip nodding, the height 10 to 15 inches. It is most attractive where it grows in full sun and in a scanty soil among rocks or in very lean clay. In the garden this narrow form changes in appearance, for the stem readily reaches 20 inches, and the branches lengthen enough to break the compactness of the rod and lessen the neat dwarf effect. But grown side by side with the type, it still retains something of its distinct character. Both are lovely in September in their medium gold. The various forms of **S. nemoralis** are frequent from the central area of the Great Plains in Canada through Nebraska, becoming less common in the western portions of Nebraska, Kansas, and Oklahoma. They extend far eastward also.

In August and later the filmy, light gold plumes of **Solidago pallida** appear on slopes in the Black Hills like beautiful, small illuminants in the half-shade of the pines. One to five or more stems, diverging to give room for the plump, upright inflorescences, rise from a generous mat of light green, wide and entire, long-petioled, oblanceolate leaves usually 16 to 20 inches long. At close range one notes a delightful gentle and sweet fragrance.

In my garden *Solidago pallida* has not been exacting as to soils and from half-shade has seeded moderately into stronger light. It has excellent drought-endurance and is nonspreading. Notable in the Black Hills strain is the width of the leaf, as much as two inches, a measurement the plant keys reserve for the tall but otherwise similar *S. speciosa*, whose range is far to the east beyond the Plains. *S. speciosa* v. *rigidiuscula* occupies the intervening space. It has a narrower leaf, an inch or less wide, and it is intermediate in height between the two species. The particular species *S. pallida* apparently occupies the Black Hills, portions of eastern Wyoming, western Nebraska, and northern Colorado.

**Solidago petiolaris (S. angusta, S. wardii)** is an attractive southerner with an excellent garden presence. It flowers in September. From a widening crown, without rhizomes and without a basal leaf mat, several leafy stems branch upward into many erect, elongated racemes or rods of fragrant and rich golden flowers. Leaves are of medium size, irregularly toothed, and, although finely pubescent, are shining and light green. Stems reach 24 to 28 inches. The plant is native from southern Nebraska into Oklahoma.

On the northern Plains, **variety *humilis*** of the wide-reaching **Solidago rigida** often chooses difficult footings over its extensive range. These it fills boldly and gracefully with basal mats of prominent foliage and stems of a height adjusted to the regional, or seasonal, moisture supply. The plants carry wide and dense, somewhat flat-topped corymbs of rich and textured gold in August and September. It is the relatively low stature, 20 to 24 inches—capable of extending to 36 inches—that has gained it the designation v. *humilis*. Eastward from the Plains it grades into the much taller and coarser *S. rigida* v. *rigida*. In southern Colorado, southwestern Kansas, and farther south the species tends to become rare. Its many-stemmed floral display and non-traveling habit make it acceptable in the garden.

## *Sophora*

A low plant, usually eight inches or less, **Sophora sericea**, now known as **S. nuttalliana**, of the pea family is a deciduous perennial of the prairies from South Dakota and Wyoming to Texas and Arizona. From spring well into summer short racemes of light cream, with a touch of soft purple, are freely borne above light green or slightly glaucous, rather dainty pinnate leaves. For some reason infrequent in the wild, in the garden its creeping rootstocks have outdistanced all others.

## *Sphaeralcea (Malvastrum)*. Scarlet mallow, flame mallow     plate 106

The most arresting color on the Plains from early May to July belongs to *Sphaeralcea coccinea*, well known as *Malvastrum coccineum*. The five wide petals and prominent pistil column mark it as a relative of the hollyhock, though this flower is only an inch or so wide and the short, tapering spires grace a plant that rises to an average of eight inches. There is no closer description for the vibrant color than scarlet, though the tone varies even among plants in a community. Its brilliancy is set off by the gray-green, rough-hairy leaves which resemble proportionately small, deeply incised hollyhock leaves.

Scarlet mallow is so adapted to the Plains environment that perhaps no other species is more uniformly distributed from southern Canada to Texas; its total range is even wider. Strong ground-gaining roots, to be well considered when placing **S. coccinea** in the garden, enable it to establish showy colonies in disturbed soil, as along roads, or with disturbing readiness in the garden. Mature roots of six to eight inches transplant well. Prudence dictates putting this mallow in an enclosed space.

## *Spiraea*. Meadowsweet, rockmat

**Spiraea lucida** (**S. betulifolia** v. **lucida**) thrives along a cleared roadside in the Black Hills, where it still receives partial shade from the tall pines on either side of the road. It may thicken to a hedge, but altogether this meadowsweet is a rather gentle plant, even fragile against strong contenders for space. In habit it is permanently woody only near the base, from which rise a few slender, upright stems to maintain through the season a herbaceous effect, lightly furnished with shining, deeply incised, obovate or acutish leaves. The stems are crowned with wide corymbs of closely set, little creamy white flowers in a filigree of creamy stamens. In my garden the plant grew well when given much midday shade and the advantage of water from the cistern, but was eventually crowded out; it likes free space, where it may determine its own density of growth, and no rough competition. It flowered well at 10 inches or less and may double that height with good care. In the Plains region *S. lucida* is frequent in the Cypress Hills as well as in the Black Hills; otherwise it is native in the northern Rockies, reaching to Colorado.

In Spearfish and other canyons of the northern Black Hills *Spiraea caespitosa*, now called *Petrophytum caespitosum*, known by the common name of "rockmat," forms very low mats with creeping stems and rosettes of tiny, gray-hairy, spatulate, evergreen leaves. In summer it produces short, upright, densely flowered, white spikes. Its habitat is in much-shaded limestone crevices; its range, with this outpost as an exception, is in the lower zones of the western mountains.

## *Stachys*. Glistening mint, hedge nettle

In flower in June and July and later, *Stachys palustris* v. *pilosa* (*S. scopulorum*) bears with a gala air its numerous broad, tapering, and somewhat leafy spikes of bright rosy lilac, all in a sparkle of glistening hairs, at a height of 20 inches or more. The serrate, broadly lanceolate leaves carry a prominent pubescence and the stems an abundance of longer, crystallike hairs that have no sting.

This western variety extends throughout the Canadian area to Colorado, Nebraska, and Minnesota. In the competition of the wild, the plant chooses moist places; in the freedom of the garden, it readily spreads into a wide clump, if not restrained.

## *Stanleya*. Prince's plume, stanleya      plate 107

A tall and showy perennial of the mustard family—very unlike any other mustard—to be expected in badlands or other bare ground is *Stanleya pinnata*, the specific name covering several varieties. From a strong basal cluster of prominent thickish, glaucous, partly pinnatifid leaves arise several stout stems, with diminishing leaves, to produce spectacular, broad, tapering plumes of luminous medium to light yellow about midsummer. The raceme may be four or five inches wide at the base where flowering begins; the long-pediceled flowers are spidery with narrow blades and spurs. Several inches of the length-ening raceme are in flower at one time. The plant's native soil is often shaly or loose, unacceptable to many other species, so that stanleya has space of its own; this may be the secret of its persistence or disap-pearance in the garden. Perfect drainage and alkalinity may be requis-ites. Small plants are difficult to find, but seed is borne abundantly in very long, slender pods. *S. pinnata* ranges well into Montana, includes portions of the Dakotas and Nebraska, much of Kansas and Colorado.

## *Stenosiphon*

Conspicuously slender, straight and erect, simple or branched, tall (three to five feet), with airy flowers of dazzling white in long, tapering racemes, **Stenosiphon linifolius** attracts instant attention and admira-tion. It is found from central Nebraska through most of Kansas and in widening range to central Texas. Perhaps it is not destined for gardens, though I grew it for a time when I brought roots from Kansas; an unacceptable soil and dryness may have brought about its failure. In its second year it did not come up where planted; but several feet away a few new plants, apparently from lengthy rhizomes, grew and flowered. Of the evening primrose family and closely related to the gauras, the sparkling flowers are poised by slender, half-inch, floral tubes in a loose cluster and from July to September ascend the terminal foot or more of the stem. The flaxlike leaves, to two inches, and the stem are light green and slightly glaucous. In its native wilds *S. lini-folius* stands alone or in a loose group.

## *Talinum*. Sunbright, fame-flower, talinum      plate 108

The talinums I have known have succulent leaves and fleshy rootstocks, well fitted to conserve their moisture-content under extreme exposure. **Talinum calycinum** and **T. parviflorum** are the Plains species, and the latter especially, when forced out of the ground by frost, endures extreme cold and drying sun for weeks without impairment of its ability to grow when replanted. *T. spinescens* of the Northwest, from the garden of Carl S. English, Jr., in Seattle, Washington, has flowered here for 20 years, surviving recurrent years of subnormal moisture, but its seed has never matured. *T. rugospermum* from the east central states, when uprooted from an unwanted position and thrown on the ground in a shaded place, has opened flowers for three days at the irregular late hour. These delicate-appearing plants of refined character and scale, all delightful in their afternoon abundance of bloom, continue from early summer to fall.

Very short, spreading, fleshy stems branch from the rootstock of *Talinum calycinum*, each to carry an ample complement of the short, terete, succulent leaves. Above the leaves arise slender, stiff scapes which divide upward by short steps, ultimately to eight inches, to continue the daily show. The inch-wide, five-petaled, daintily cupped blossoms are of a lovely hue — purplish pink. Most frequent in central Kansas, *T. calycinum* ranges into Nebraska, Colorado, Oklahoma, Texas, and Arkansas and Missouri. In two trials in my garden, it did not persist. Is it short-lived? Self-sown seedlings followed, but I ultimately lost the line. There are more reliable talinums.

From a tiny tuft in hardpan and gravel or anchored by tenuous feeder roots in a shallow basin or fissure of disintegrating rock, *Talinum parviflorum*, safe from rough aggressors, brightens sunny or partly shaded places over the Plains states from southern North Dakota to Texas and contributes to the flora of bordering states from Minnesota to Arizona. Hardly ever does it achieve full development in the wild; in the garden, with a measure of freedom in a screelike footing, its crown of green may widen to four inches and the many threadlike, branching scapes, up to five inches long, support an open-hearted show for an unbelievably long season. The color is much like that of other talinums, perhaps a little deeper pink with a hint of purple; the flower is about half an inch wide. A few miles from my home, in gritty badland clay, *T. parviflorum* brings a ruddy glow to an acre or more of sparsely grassed pasture.

Having mentioned *Talinum rugospermum*, may I say a word for this little-known treasure? It came to me from a well-known botanical garden under the name *T. teretifolium*, a name also applied years back, to *T. calycinum* in a Great Plains checklist. In *Flora of the Prairies and Plains of Central North America*, Rydberg noted that *T. rugospermum* ranges from northwestern Indiana to Minnesota and that it has been confused with the eastern *T. teretifolium*, whose area is given by Wherry and by Cronquist as Delaware, Pennsylvania, and West Virginia to Georgia and Alabama. In addition to some minor differences in form, *T. teretifolium* is a flower of the early afternoon, *T. rugospermum* of the later afternoon. *T. rusgospermum* prefers a sandy scree, thrives in its own close company, survives in the difficult climate where I live, and provides lovely color over a very long season. Its flowers of five cupped petals are as much as three-fourths of an inch wide and are carried at eight or nine inches.

## *Thalictrum*. Meadow-rue

In *Thalictrum*, the Plains have little to offer the average garden. *Thalictrum dasycarpum* ranges across much of this continent, including the Great Plains, in woods and where extra moisture is available. There it makes way for itself with such freedom that only an out-of-the-way place affords room for it; and there its voluminous foliage, somewhat like that of columbine, and its filmy inflorescences of creamy white or purplish are admirable at a distance in spring to late summer.

*Thalictrum venulosum* inhabits quite dry places, and its colonizing is fairly restrained. Its mounds of somewhat glaucous foliage rise to eight inches and retain their fresh and neat appearance for the entire growing season. The slender, arching flowering stems reach 24 inches. The inflorescence is bronzy in effect, and the bronzy yellow, pendent anthers are vibrant with the least breath of air. With midday shade and ordinary moisture, the plant maintains itself well and travels moderately. It is native to the light woods of Canada and the northern Plains states, and to the lower mountains of Colorado.

## *Thermopsis*. Golden pea, golden banner    plate 109

Broad, packed racemes of glowing medium yellow in close or looser colonies—such is the impact of *Thermopsis rhombifolia* for several weeks, including the month of May. The florets are over half an inch wide, nicely plump, well nourished in effect. Most stems carry only one full raceme, at six to 12 inches. The leaves, rather stiff and harsh, slightly grayish, suggest those of lupines. They are in threes, broadly lanceolate, entire. Conspicuous sickle-shaped pods, brown when ripe, carry 10 or more tiny discus-shaped seeds. Smaller plants are readily transplanted, if one digs deep enough to secure feeder roots with a section of the wandering rootstock, which serves as both root and rhizome. Over the many years in my garden it has not traveled far; in my pastures, choosing either stiff gumbo or the looser mud-shale, it has formed large patches. By no means seen everywherer, *T. rhombifolia* appears now and again, in shale or loam or sand, from well up in Canada to Colorado, making a broad swath of color in the spring. The plant pictured in plate 109 was growing near Carpenter, Wyoming.

## *Townsendia.* Easter-daisy, townsendia     plates 110, 111

Wintering as a completely evergreen bun of narrow leaves close to the ground, and guarding its quota of autumn-set buds, *Townsendia exscapa* joyously responds to the gentle light and warmth of early spring with wide disks and short rays of soft gold and glowing light pink. Fittingly, it is called "Easter-daisy," a name which struck the fancy of gardeners and which has persisted. Yet how many know the plant, other than devoted specialists who study its needs and meet with a measure of luck? It seems a long time since Louise Beebe Wilder termed it "inscrutable." Why, indeed, has it taken on an exclusive, high-alpine pattern, then chosen the lower, drier Great Plains for its chief habitat? What structure lies beneath the scapeless flowers and the closely clustered, narrow leaves, only dissection will disclose. And by what characteristics and faculties has it maintained itself in a trying climate and against tidbit-seeking jack rabbits and other predators?

Conforming to a type structure shared by many of the finer jewels of the Plains, *Townsendia exscapa* is supported by a rather shallow, branching taproot and forms a branched crown near ground level. The very short stems are thickly set with two-inch or shorter linear-oblanceolate leaves. The flower buds remain green against any odds of winter weather and hurry toward bringing out every blossom within a few days. The neat, wide, up-facing flower heads rest upon the faintly gray cushion, nudging each other. At the time of heavy setting and maturing of seed, the plant is especially vulnerable; hard freezing, or drought, forestalling the immense effort, may save the plant from complete exhaustion. Lean, shaly clays, dune sand, or scree, affording excellent drainage and not the most rapid drying, are the plant's choice of footing. A narrow crevice in a flat expanse of rock harbored the largest specimen I have seen. There slight moisture drained to the site from light sprinkles, the fissure admitted no excess, and the rock surface kept the leaves and stem dry. The spread measured eight inches, the height little more than two.

One April, on a sparsely grassed, gumbo slope appeared an Easter-daisy, eye-catching as always; nearby another. Then, covering an acre or two, there must have been three or four hundred. Amid the pink ones was a lone albino. Never before had I known such numbers and never again would this spectacle be repeated. At the present time, only a few plants are found in any habitat; perhaps this registers a low point in a cycle. In the garden it is necessary to fence *T. exscapa* from rabbits when green feed is scarce.

*Townsendia hookeri* has been dogged by errors throughout its history of 140 years. It has long been known as *T. sericea*, a name synonymous with *T. exscapa* — if the tangles are all resolved.

Gardeners and botanists who know only *Townsendia hookeri* still mistake it for *T. exscapa*. A current key separates the two species on the basis of a tuft of hairs (microscopic, or course!) on the apex of the involucral bracts; the tuft is present in one species, absent in the other. For practical purposes: *T. hookeri* is the smaller in leaf and flower, grayer with appressed, ashy hairs; earlier in flower by two weeks, the rays somewhat brownish in the bud, usually white when open; the seeds smaller and readily distinguishable. The leaves are more narrowly oblanceolate-linear, averaging about an inch in length, and are more crowded, presenting a finer-textured tuft. Grown in much shade, the stems may lengthen to two inches. It has a definite preference for limy places. The range of *T. hookeri* is difficult to delimit, because of uncertainties in names and identifications. I have recognized it from near the Colorado line in the Nebraska Panhandle and in Wyoming, up through those states and the Dakotas to the Missouri River, and in western Montana and southeastern Alberta.

*Townsendia hookeri*, though lacking some of the glamor of *T. exscapa*, is a treasure for the rock garden. At Prairie Gem Ranch it is easier to retain, better able to perpetuate itself by seed, and longer-lived than *T. exscapa*, though, like the other, it may die from overexpansion. Its compact habit lends it distinction when out of flower. As for color, there are localities in the Black Hills and on stony prairies in northern Wyoming where the flower is a light but definite pink; and in southern Wyoming, a colony arrayed in deep pink has recently been found.

There are some 20 species in the genus *Townsendia*, roughly a third of them biennials; some with stems as much as a foot long. *T. parryi*, a biennial flowering from May to July, is a magnificent, two-inch or larger daisy of glowing lavender. It is amenable to my garden and propagates itself in scree. This townsendia is native to the Rockies from Alberta to Wyoming.

A biennial of the Plains is *Townsendia grandiflora*, which somehow has gathered, on paper, a reputation of finery; the reason for its specific name is far from self-evident. Its heads are of very ordinary breadth and the rays a translucent white with a pinkish brown backing, which shows through as a smudge. It seems to care only for the high, exposed rims of rough-country breaks. There it displays its only interesting feature—stems of a few inches arching from the crown to a horizontal position slightly above the ground, with the daisies facing upright at the tips. No more than a novelty in the garden, it left no progeny in my few trials. Persistent, puzzling reports of color in *T. grandiflora* may be based on mistaken identification. Several of the lengthy-stemmed biennials extend southward in the Colorado mountains and foothills and into New Mexico, and some of them have color.

The last member of the Plains townsendias came to my attention in a small herbarium at Canadian, Texas. The *Townsendia texensis* specimen observed there had been collected on the rim of Palo Duro Canyon, a fork of the Red River drainage. It had a sparingly leafy, upright stem; the flower, somewhat shriveled, could have been as large as that of *T. parryi* and of much the same vibrant lavender; dried, it appeared as dark violet-blue. The species is worthy of investigation. herbarium specimens, elsewhere, indicate a life-span as a biennial; a height of about eight inches; and a range through most of the Texas Panhandle and east on the Canadian River drainage to Roger Mills County in Oklahoma.

## *Tradescantia*. Spiderwort    plate 112

Although the fragile, three-petaled flowers of the spiderworts fold by noon or earlier, morning brings a fresh display of their elaborately patterned beauty, and their flowering season is long.

Wide and long bracts subtend the flower clusters of *Tradescantia bracteata* and provide a distinguishing characteristic, together with a height of six to an occasional 12 inches, and a strong rhizomatous, colony-extending faculty. This roving propensity bars the species from select places in the garden but seems not to deter many spiderwort fans. The species favors light loams with good drainage. Flowering terminates as moisture is exhausted, though it may continue from spring into August. Often in a small area in the wild, the color of *T. bracteata* will range from sky-blue to mauve-blue to very dark, from light lavender through orchid and heliotrope to deep purple, and from pale pink, near apple-blossom, to deeper tones bordering on purplish red. Occasional albinos are found. The species ranges over the Dakotas, including the lower Black Hills, much of Nebraska, the eastern two-thirds of Kansas, and indefinitely into bordering states of the East.

Preferring dunes and especially sandy soils, ***Tradescantia occidentalis*** occupies the greater portion of the Plains states and has been reported for Utah, and Minnesota and Wisconsin. With stems quite erect, reaching about 14 inches, with flowers at the apex, it does not depart from the close clump habit. It is long-lived. Northern strains are always a work-a-day blue, with stem and leaf bluish green; southern plants are rosy mauve. Minor variants have been called ***T. laramiensis*** and ***T. universitatis***.

A very hairy little spiderwort, flowering freely for several weeks in early spring, is ***Tradescantia tharpii*** from central Kansas and Oklahoma. I received this spiderwort from Darwin Andrews many years ago. It has kept its allotted space among other gentle-mannered plants in the half-shade of my lath house, and appeared again each spring to draw its sustenance mainly from the native heavy clay. Of rock garden proportions, it puts up a number of stems about seven inches long in a close group and flowers in a pleasant, medium purple-rose. It is said to have a purplish blue form. Doubtless the plant may be divided; it has never produced seedlings. In some references, the species is called ***T. brevicaulis***.

## *Verbena.* Verbena

Recognized at once by its resemblance to the familiar garden annual, though with smaller florets, ***Verbena bipinnatifida***, a perennial but probably everywhere short-lived, makes up for any deficiencies by its indefatigable yields of lengthening racemes in violet-blue, moderate in hue and very pleasing. The specific name well described the form of the leaves, which are of medium size and plentiful. The stems spread widely upon the ground and continually branch to maintain a constant sheet of bloom. Whether the plant develops from an original taproot or from adventive new crowns along the self-layering stems, flowering begins very early and declines only with severe fall frosts. From seed, *V. bipinnatifida* may flower by early June. It is native from South Dakota to Texas. To endure the winter, the species must be grown under conditions of relative but not extreme dryness. The widening mat may reach 30 inches, the height five or more.

The leaf of ***Verbena canadensis*** is ovate in outline, sometimes doubly toothed. Although the plant may cover the ground well, the stems often rise to eight inches or more. The florets are larger than in *V. bipinnatifida* and the clusters often two inches wide. Their color varies from pinkish lavender to vivid purplish pink. The flower is richly fragrant. Doubtless named for its occurrence along the Canadian River of the southern Plains, the species ranges from Kansas and southern Colorado to Mexico, also to Illinois and far to the southeast. The High Plains strains are hardy at Prairie Gem Ranch.

*Verbena hastata*, the swamp verbena, a tall species occurring throughout the North American continent, finds habitat sparingly in the Plains states and provinces. It branches widely, upward, to hold its narrow racemes strictly upright. The color, violet-blue, may be so pale as to be uninteresting. The plant often forms close colonies.

From June to August, roadsides and pastures of lean to rich loams show great patches of *Verbena stricta* whose thrilling color, an intense purple, is rare in its season. The plant grows very erect, its many narrow spikes several inches long when in full flower; its height is usually 18 to 20 inches. The oblong-oval leaves, rather coarse and sharply dentate, are roughly hairy, as are the stems. In the garden *V. stricta* spreads freely by seed but is easily controlled. It is native over the Plains states from southeastern North Dakota to western South Dakota, south to New Mexico, to states along the eastern border of the Plains, and has been introduced in a much wider area.

## *Vicia*. Vetch, wild pea

On the Plains and eastward to Minnesota, also far to the west, an excellent forage plant, *Vicia sparsifolia*, half reclining in somewhat of a tangle, is plentiful on all the gumbo clay far and near, until it becomes dormant early in the summer. It is much too infiltrating in my garden. The leaf is pinnnate, with narrow leaflets and a short tendril at the tip. Many short racemes bear crowded, small pea flowers in two shades of bluish purple. The flowers are in themselves nicely rounded and pretty, but I have lost interest after years of pulling this weed from reserved spots. The roots and slender rhizomes are deep-seated, ineradicable, and insufferable. Variants in two-toned pink and in an intriguing dark purple-blue have been noted. *V. sparsifolia* ranges over most of the Plains and far to the West. Beware!

*Vicia americana* resembles *V. sparsifolia* in general features, but is a vine growing to 40 inches, is less of a pest, and is less seductive with its restrained flowering. It is occasional in the Black Hills and crosses the North American continent. In modern taxonomic treatments, **V. sparsifolia** is used as a synonym for **V. americana v. minor**.

## *Viola*. Violet     plate 113

The early yellow **Viola nuttallii** is so thoroughly adjusted to the environment of the Great Plains and occupies so large a proportion of the region that it may have originated here, though it is not now an endemic. It challenges the region's extreme measures of sun and dryness in the growing season and sidesteps the dry heat of summer and fall with complete dormancy. **Viola pratincola**, the lone blue species that has adapted itself to conditions of sun and low rainfall, attempts to maintain its verdancy throughout the season, but under intense stress it too resorts to dormancy. Other violets of the region, whatever their acquired facilities, are to be sought in tempered situations and are met with less frequently. **Viola montanensis**, **V. nephrophylla**, **V. pedatifida**, **V. rugulosa**, and **V. vallicola** are the more valuable kinds.

Given a modicum of humus in its root-run and the half-shade, the retarded drying, and the better humidity of the lath house, **Viola adunca**, the quizzical little old man in deep blue, accepts the environment of Prairie Gem Ranch with charming grace. High or low in the Black Hills, it seeks similar conditions and probably nowhere ranges farther south, except in the higher mountains of Wyoming and Colorado. Northward, making use of shady places or taking to the parts of prairie that are not too dry, it goes to Alaska, westward it reaches to California, and eastward to New Brunswick. This violet may present a wide crown of small, heart-shaped, finely round-toothed leaves in a well-developed plant, but it often sends out a number of slender, divergent, and procumbent stems, thus scattering its flowers. It has a long blooming period and, with good moisture in the fall after the drought, will again produce a few flowers.

A somewhat similar plant is **Viola conspersa**. It was out of flower when I first found it on a shady roadside east of Saskatoon, Saskatchewan, in late June. A faint purplish tinge in leaf and stem drew my attention. Canadian authorities say the flower is a pale violet or almost white. Its range is generally more eastern and southeastern than Saskatoon.

A third small violet and a marvel for blooming is **Viola montanensis**. The strain I have from rich, shaded locations in the Black Hills has leaves an inch and a quarter from cordate base to tip, more broadly ovate than the average in **V. adunca**, and regularly grayish with fine hairs. Its short stems typically remain within the leaf mass, and the whole is generously covered at the height of the season with lovely little blossoms in light blue. This lasts well into June. In low, moist pasture in the Hills it may be for a time dominant; in a watered lawn, so low is this violet that it sparkles undaunted between mowings. With several hours of midday shade, it is surprisingly drought-resistant. Beyond the Black Hills, **V. montanensis** may be found only in the Rockies.

Even in the most promising sites my garden affords, **Viola nephrophylla** has always succumbed to prolonged drought. It is indeed a wet-soil kind—found along brooks and springs. Its range almost spans the North American continent, but is mainly northern. In Canada it is to be seen in woodlands, along stream margins, and on prairies. Farther south it occurs in locations providing dependable moisture, as in the Black Hills and in the foothills, above 5,000 feet, in Wyoming, Colorado, and New Mexico. **V. nephrophylla** is stemless and non-rhizomatous. The moderately wide leaves and the fine deep violet flowers, which are held well above them, have a marked clearness and freshness.

"One of the outstanding spring flowers of the western prairies," someone has said of **Viola nuttallii**. Although it is a flower of moderate size, its impact is magnified by the scintillating reflections of its textured gold petals, by its prolonged season of bloom, and by its wide range. In close patches or scattered, it is a prominent color-bearer across the sun-drenched expanses from northern Kansas into the southern Canadian Plains. Eastward from the Plains **V. nuttallii** extends sparingly to Missouri and Minnesota, and westward into the foothills regions and down to New Mexico. For earliness of bloom it vies with the pasque flower, the first phloxes, and **Townsendia hookeri**, then carries on its festive display for many weeks. Its first flowers open almost upon the ground, then higher as the days grow warmer. **V. nuttallii** produces stems, but for most of the season the nodes remain very short, clustering the leafage quite low. Just above the excellent foil of oblong-lanceolate, firm, and low-gloss leaves appear the vibrant "Johnny-jump-ups." After liberal seed ripening, the plant retreats to its underground crown to await another spring.

**Viola pallens** occurs in moist canyons of the Black Hills at about 6,000 feet. White-flowered and very faintly fragrant, this violet has broadly cordate-ovate, blunt-tipped leaves of rich-textured, deep green which are deeply corrugated in a strikingly beautiful pattern. It has a wide range outside the Plains.

"And violets are blue," as every sentimentalist knows. The common meadow violet, or woods violet, or dooryard violet, needed little in the way of description; it was lowly, pleasing in color, and its flowers and intriguing heart-shaped leaves came directly from the ground. Close observers who wished to distinguish it from other violets followed the teachings of Brainerd and called it *Viola papilionacea*. The range of the species was delimited as the area from Massachusetts to Georgia, and westward to Minnesota and Oklahoma. Gates, of Kansas, credited *V. papilionacea* to most of that state, including with it *V. retusa*, found in moist places, and *V. pratincola*, of drier ground. William Chase Stevens, after his many years of detailed studies, wrote of it in *Kansas Wild Flowers*, "Although lacking the fragrance of the English violet, our common blue violet is so constant, so sweet and amiable, and so welcome an associate in the life of the people, that it shares with the rose alone the distinction of being chosen as state flower of four of our States."

In her bulletin, *The Violets of Colorado*, Alice M. Spotts records the difficult-to-distinguish *Viola retusa* as occurring in shady places and along streams from central Kansas to the mountain front and the foothill districts in Colorado. *Viola pratincola*, somewhat smaller in plant and flower, occupies open areas on prairies and hills and extends in range to North Dakota and Minnesota. It is doubtless the one frequently seen in astonishingly dry places through the northern Plains south of Canada. The flower is smaller than in many similar species, and less attractive in its lighter, opaque effect. It blooms briefly in May.

A fine, large blue violet, either light or medium dark, with a small, bright orange center, *Viola pedatifida* blooms over a long season. It differs from other violets of the region in its many-toed "bird's-foot" leaves. It is present from well north in Canada to New Mexico; it reaches also to Arizona and into the midland states as far as northwestern Ohio. In the Plains strains its drought-endurance is remarkable. It is one of the most satisfactory violets that can be grown; stemless, free-flowering, nonrhizomatous, but forming wide crowns which may be divided. There is a beautiful white form.

The downy yellow violet, *Viola pubescens*, an easterner, was a member of a small company—including the bloodroot, *Sanguinaria canadensis*—that in remote migrations extended their ranges westward and attained fastnesses in the Black Hills, but which have disappeared elsewhere from the High Plains. In the Black Hills, *V. pubescens* lends charm in heavily shaded areas where huge rock masses shed water and cater to its colonizing. There it looks out, perchance, to where *V. pedatifida*, *V. pratincola*, and *V. vallicola* bask in stronger light. In my garden by a north wall, *V. pubescens* survived and flowered for three years, seeming not to reject the high pH, but obviously it lacked moisture.

*Viola pubescens*, along with *V. eriocarpa*, "the glabrous *pubescens*," is to be found in moist woods at lower levels from Manitoba to Oklahoma. In Kansas and Nebraska, *V. eriocarpa* is reported westerly to about the 1,000-foot contour. These broad-leaved, stemmed species grow 10 inches high, and their soft yellow tones are pleasing.

*Viola rugulosa* and *V. canadensis* are beautiful white violets of shady haunts, with stems up to a foot or more and broad, heart-shaped leaves. The former ranges from Nebraska to Alaska, being most plentiful through Canada. It extends into areas bordering the Plains on the east and reaches westward to Washington. *V. canadensis* ranges across the North American continent but occurs scarcely or not at all on the Plains. Both are recorded for the Rocky Mountains. For garden purposes, the two species are very different entities. Anywhere within its range, dense and wide or more scattered colonies are built by the strong, rhizomatous roots of *V. rugulosa*. As a rule, the other spreads exclusively by seeds. I have known only those *V. canadensis* plants sent to me from the East; they were unsuited here and did not endure. As do most Plains dwellers, *V. rugulosa* thrives while moisture is plentiful, then undergoes long periods of drought safely. Its handsome foliage and flowers bear an air of crisp neatness; the petals are well rounded, a small golden jewel at their center. A petal-backing of purplish pink sometimes shows through. There may be pinkish or violet lines on the face; in some strains, the flower is pale pink throughout.

The exquisite golden *Viola vallicola*, which is often confused with *V. nuttallii*, inhabits the richer, moisture-retentive soils of valleys; it adapts to gardens where greater rainfall makes the other impracticable to grow. The two species have a casual resemblance. *V. vallicola* is distinguished by its root, which branches from the crown, as against the branching taproot of *V. nuttallii*; by darker, less glossy, elliptical, round-tipped leaves, in contrast to the lanceolate leaves of the other; and by its definite basal leaf mat and shorter stemming. The petals average wider in *V. vallicola*, and although the same tone of gold is present in both species, I sense a richer glow in *V. vallicola*. The capsules and seeds of the two species are markedly different. In my garden *V. vallicola* thrives in half-shade; in such shade *V. nuttallii* is often attacked by a rust. It needs sun. In 30 years here, no intermediates have appeared.

*Viola vallicola* ranges from the Black Hills—and a few miles out on the prairie toward Prairie Gem Ranch—to its maximum concentration in the central portion of the Canadian Plains, including the Cypress Hills. It is recognized in the Colorado mountains and in Utah, Idaho, Washington, and British Columbia.

In the 1930s, in Phillips County, Montana, near the Canadian line, Mrs. L. B. Nelson found a double yellow violet in partial shade at the foot of a slope. From one of three divisions of the original plant, given to me by Mrs. Nelson, the stock has been maintained by occasional division at Prairie Gem Ranch. No seed is produced. This I have named 'Gold Nugget.' Flowers of about 20 petals are borne with great freedom, and production continues beyond the blooming season of the normal single strain.

## *Yucca*. Yucca, soapweed, spanish bayonet
## plates 114, 115

Yuccas are evergreen shrubs and trees of the lily family, principally of the southern United States and Mexico. One species alone, *Yucca glauca*, ranges far northward, traversing the Plains states and a marginal extension eastward, and has advanced into Canada in a small locality in Alberta. Most yuccas form an elaborate rosette of narrow, stiff, sharp-tipped, densely crowded, basally overlapping leaves directly from the rootstock at ground level or, in older plants, sometimes from short stems or trunks. Strong rhizomatous roots at varying depths add new crowns to enlarge close groups or to widen colonies. The flowers are borne in May, June, or July on strong, upright stalks, simple or branching, in racemes or panicles of usually drooping, more or less closed bells of greenish, creamy, or variously tinted white. In favorable sites and soils yuccas create striking floral spectacles. In the winter landscape, the plants hold their normal lively deep green.

Even though the range of **Yucca baccata** is southern Colorado to western Texas, Arizona, and Nevada, it dwells at high altitudes there and thus is hardy enough to thrive and flower at Prairie Gem Ranch. Its leaves are bold, deeply channeled, up to a yard long, and at most an inch and a half wide. It has grown into a dense mass of rosettes several feet wide. The flower stalks hardly rise to the height of the leaves. The closely set corollas on long, tapering segments, shaggy in effect, are light cream to white, flushed with pearly pink. **Y. baccata** blooms ahead of the local **Y. glauca**; but since the pronuba moth, which fertilizes yuccas, does not make its appearance until the flowering season of **Y. glauca**, only once in the many years I have grown **Y. baccata** has fruit been borne. This edible fruit is mellow when ripe and has a texture and flavor somewhat like that of papaw.

The leaves of **Yucca glauca** are very narrow, a quarter of an inch across, and have conspicuous white-line margins from which narrow, spiraling fibers curl away at intervals. The leaf length is commonly 18 inches; the leaf tips are needle-sharp to protect the plant from browsing; the leaf arrangement is splendidly symmetrical. The flower stalks are stout enough to carry upright the heavy-textured blooms or the much heavier burden of the seed capsules. The large columns of dark green fruits maintain an architectural effect for a long season, as later the capsules, ripened to light brown shades and partly opened, release to the winds the abundant seeds remaining unconsumed by the moth's larvae. No soil seems too poor or exposure too dry for this plant, but it flowers only in response to good moisture. The glossy, black, waferlike seeds germinate readily. Young plants of six to eight inches, either seedlings or offsets, with a like length of the coarse rootstock, either whole or severed, are readily transplanted; with the precaution that a moist root-run be maintained until new feeder roots have developed for a year. Root cuttings, covered by four inches of soil, are effective for propagation.

Little has been done toward color selection in **Yucca glauca** as far as I know. From a clump of a few crowns, later to be destroyed by road building, I brought to the garden a plant whose sepal segments were strongly tinted with red. A report of a similar specimen came from Colorado, and of a **Y. glauca** nearly black in hue from Nebraska. One late June a friend asked if I would be interested in a red-flowered yucca. How red, I cautiously sought to know. "A really all-over red," as he described it. Some days earlier, when he had been helping a neighbor with fencing in a high summer pasture in the Black Hills, he had seen the rare flower. The plants about the canyon home were still in full bloom when we arrived. We rode a small tractor part way until the climbing became too steep, then walked perhaps two miles. But on that hot southern slope every plant was out of flower. I dug some offsets from a cleft in the fractured sandstone outcrop in which the entire colony was imbedded. Two years later I made the long trip alone and on foot for more stock. The cattle, which have a special fondness for yucca buds and flowers, had left two buds in the colony to open fully. Their vivid light crimson bells beckoned from a hundred yards away. At close range I discovered that the plant bearing the thrilling color grew from a narrow fissure on the opposite side of the slope from where I had dug previously. Spade and heavy miner's pick were ineffective in getting at its root. I needed dynamite. A few new starts were secured from the old wide crevice to carry back to my ranch. From the earliest accessions to the garden, the lone survivor in its eighth year produced its first stalk of blooms — in almost the ordinary *Y. glauca* light greenish cream, the outer segments weakly flushed with red. The explanation must be that the colony in the sandstone comprised more than one strain. Perhaps the end of the red yucca trail has not yet been reached; there remain in the garden young, unflowered plants.

Again in a propitious year I made the pilgrimage to the high pastures. Along the farther margin of the table-topped last ridge ran a fence; on the near side, cattle had already stripped the numerous patches of bud and blossom. Beyond the fence a long, descending, and undulating terrain staged a veritable yucca paradise. Recurrent groups and colonies, among rocks or in grassy expanses, stretched into the distance. Flowering was at its seasonal height. In the offing were spots of color which drew like magnets. Into this pasture the cattle had not yet been turned.

A first engrossing discovery bore short columns of bells, much dwarfed, like inch-wide pearls. The stone blocks of their footing were readily pried apart, and good roots were secured. Every columned prospect bearing a strong red signal, at whatever distance, had to be investigated. But close inspection disclosed only flecks of crimson mingled with flecks of pure green upon a cream base — an effect short of ideal. A contrasting stew of fine specks of green and mauve and cream and red resulted in a shocking repulsive drab. From these it was a relief to turn to charming, smooth flushings of pink or red upon cream-white, and to discover an impressive all-over mauve-pink; then a lone colony of tall spires arrayed in deep maroon outer parts with greenish cream inner, a striking variation.

Now and again I noted especially showy spires with perianths spread wide, saucerlike, crowded and facing outward for space. Some were of plain cream, others blushed with clear, soft pink. Elsewhere I saw occasional branched stems, though the typical inflorescence of **Y. glauca** is a simple raceme or spire. Crossing some minor ravine, I reached the brink of a sharp canyon. Yuccas tumbled over the broken rim, and there stood two marvels with wide-angle branches arching upward like handsome candelabra. Along the rim a group of proud cream-white spires attained a full six feet; these were simple columns of fresh and crisp bells, with a few unopened buds above, a few withered flowers below.

Contemplating these tall marvels, I suddenly realized, with a sense of exhaustion, that the scene had dimmed and that the sun had long been down. The afternoon had been spent in seeking out attractions for intimate evaluation. But the colony of the crimson glory I had come so far to revisit still lay a vague distance beyond.

I turned back and took the trail across the plateau portion of the high ridge. In dim light, I could see that the park stretched diagonally down the slope at a moderate grade for a half-mile to a saddle, where it would switch back and pass directly below my position. The load of plants, pick, and spade was burdensome. Hesitating only a moment, I chose the pathless shortcut through the precipitous north-slope woods. There could be no question of direction, the right way would always be in descent. Under the trees the enveloping darkness soon became total. Using my spade as a prospecting rod, I tested the firmness of the land before taking each step. Where no tree trunk might aid my sense of balance, the undergrowth, familiar enough to the touch, was untrustworthy. The friendly feel and known strength of the needles and twigs of occasional young pines were comforting. Only in one place did my spade fail to touch bottom. A few steps sideways led to another descent. At last came a vague dimness ahead, perhaps a treeless space or an outlook above the woods; then the trail.

The way was still steep and rocky. I had to exercise caution in taking every step, with my spade serving as a cane. The trail turned again, and in the last mile the light became more definite. The moon had risen; its pale light was being thrown back from the main canyon wall beyond the highway.

Possibly the most valuable find of that day was the type with open widespread corollas, appearing in various scattered colonies. Here were disclosed to intimate view the inner parts commonly hidden in the familiar drooping yucca bloom. One needs the fully open flower at hand to appreciate the effect of greater volume of the wide, crowned raceme.

A few plants each of several of the most select color and type variants are now in my garden and, aided by cultivation, are advancing in the deliberate manner of yuccas toward maturity and flowering.

A sequel to the events of that day of exploration: In September there should have been a seed harvest but to all appearances, the cattle had entered the paradise to feast and fatten on flowers or tasty young pods. My search of this vast area revealed only one capsule that had escaped to ripen; it was on a plant I had not marked.

The third member of the trio of species distinctive of the Great Plains region, **Yucca harrimaniae**, I secured many years ago from the D. M. Andrews Nursery. Its rosetted leaves are relatively short, about a foot, and wide, a half-inch or more; the flower stalks are more slender than those of *Y. glauca*; the drooping bells are similar. In the garden, offsets appear at a little distance from the mother plant, but the colony widens very slowly. The species tends to produce new crowns at the foot of a spent flower stalk, thus building a taller trunk, sheathed by the drooping, brown leaves of old rosettes. The names **Y. coloma** and **Y. neomexicana** are synonyms.

On the precipitous, hot southwestern slope of the volcanic Carrizo Mesa in southeastern Colorado, I found a sizable stand of **Yucca harrimaniae**. It was my first recognition of the species in the wild. Closely neighbored by **Y. glauca**, it was readily distinguished. In an earlier year, in New Mexico, I discovered a few rosettes of an apparent dwarf amid a large number of **Y. glauca**, the plants only about six inches high. Now, after several years of special care and of anticipating bloom, the leaves still measure no more than 10 inches. They have the proportionate width of those of **Y. harrimaniae**. Will the flower stalk be dwarf? It is an absorbing speculation.

## *Zigadenus*. False camas, poison camas, death camas, zigadenus, zigad     plate 116

Two of the more attractive species of this genus are habitants of the Great Plains. They are June- and July-flowering bulbs, in habit closely resembling the blue-flowered, true camassias. The generic name *Zigadenus* — or *Zigad* — is desirable for familiar usage, since other common names are somewhat inadequate. The one most often heard, "death camas," is pure melodrama. *Zigadenus* is not all that bad. Synonyms appearing in older manuals are *Anticlea* and *Toxicoscordion*.

*Zigadenus elegans* bears 18-inch panicles of six-pointed stars, three-fourths of an inch wide, above mostly basal, grasslike leaves. The petals are pale, tinted greenish yellow, with delicate green and purple accents. The slender, elongated bulbs slowly proliferate into a culster, and the resultant close group of airy and graceful panicles is a pleasant reward for the care given them. Good soil and half-shade are appreciated. This species is frequent in the higher Black Hills and at lower levels northward, especially in suitable habitats throughout the Canadian area; in the rockies it is found at higher elevations, as far south as New Mexico.

*Zigadenus gramineus* carries its smaller stars in a crowded raceme, at 10 to 16 inches, from a whorl of long, basal leaves. Their light straw-yellow is brightened by an aura of golden anthers. In the wild it is often plentiful enough to spread a light veil over the fresh green pastures in June, on heavy gumbo and on the wild badland loams where it is at its best. Its range covers portions of western Nebraska and the Dakotas, Wyoming, Montana, and south central and southwestern prairie Canada.

In some systematic treatments, *Zigadenus gramineus* is considered a variety of the coarser-appearing *Z. venenosus* from farther west. Both contain alkaloids in amounts to justify the name "poison camas," and are dangerous to humans and cattle *if consumed in quantity*. Cattle regularly avoid the flowering plant, if grass is abundant. When eager for the new grass of May, doubtless they take some of the new leaf growth of the camas. Veterinarian authorities, however, in the typical grazing areas, have been unable to trace any seasonal disorders, such as "grass-tetany," to *Z. gramineus*. Cases of human poisoning, from ingesting the bulbs in the mistaken belief that they are those of the true camassias or other edible kinds, have been reported. *Z. elegans* is rated practically free from the dangerous elements.

## *Zinnia*. Zinnia    plate 117

A golden gem of the southern Plains—southwestern Kansas, southern Colorado, to northern Texas, and to Arizona—the very dwarf, hardy perennial *Zinnia grandiflora* is so different from the familiar garden annual that one questions the generic name. Then one ponders the specific name, for the flower is only about an inch wide. The four or sometimes five shallowly cupped and spreading rays are so wide they complete a rounded circle about the very narrow cluster of disk flowers. The color of the disk may be a trifle deeper than that of the rays, but often it is an enchanting flash of luminous brick-red. The leaves are narrow, up to an inch long. So many fine stems are sent up from the crown to six inches or so, each carrying a flower head, that the massed bloom completely hides the foliage. The gentle glow of the flower is highly satisfying. In a sizable colony, which is built by seeding and by rather slow root extension, this maximum blossom effect may impress one as a "grandiflora" achievement. Furthermore, the show runs from June through August.

In sunny pastures or in bare ground taken over at the roadside, the variations in flower size and in disk coloration suggest that much seeding has aided in extending and maintaining the stands. Nowhere does the species appear weedy in its native lean and rather heavy, well-drained, and often dry soils. The finest displays I have seen in the wild had not lacked moisture—rainfall had been fair—yet even there no rapid colonizing appeared. In my garden *Z. grandiflora* has been resistant to drought and to cold; and, when moisture is present, its exuberant flowering is a rare delight. Freer increase would be welcome.

# The
# Great Plains Plants
# in the Wild and
# in the Garden

The high, open prairies of the Great Plains constitute a harsh environment for plants. There are long summer days of intense light with no intervening mountains or hills or trees to shade the plants. Afternoon temperatures on many days in July and August hover in the nineties and frequently rise above 100°F. Summers are marked by infrequent rainfall; the annual average for most localities varies from 20 down to 12 inches, with records much higher or lower as exceptions. Drying westerly winds come quickly, and surface soil as well as foliage becomes dry within a short time following a typical shower. The relatively high elevation and low humidity are responsible for the general absence of dewfall during the warm seasons. But the same factors bring mostly cool nights, welcome intervals when the plants may regain their moisture balance.

Weather cycles, which can determine environment on the Great Plains, are difficult to define. Variability in the weather is so common and so disruptive of weather patterns in the region that only by taking an average for a period of years can a general rule be formulated; and rules are still subject to revision after a hundred years of weather watching.

Certain environmental factors, which I have already touched on, are clearly in evidence and, having a geographical basis, are fairly constant characteristics of the Great Plains. Because the Plains are located in the interior of the continent, because they are at a relatively high altitude and on an eastward slope, and because moisture-controlling mountainous regions border the Plains on the west, rainfall and humidity are low and evaporation is hastened by sunshine and wind. In consequence, a light cover of vegetation, neither dense nor tall, distinguishes the region. Dominant are the short grasses or mid-grasses, depending on topography and soil types, but space is shared by the great numbers of flowering plants, with a light contribution of shrubs and a few sometimes conspicuous but mostly weedy annuals. Such are the flora that cover the vast prairies. They are the successful competitors for moisture, adaptable to the long droughts and tolerant of the wetter periods. Trees are thus restricted to the higher and more rugged areas and to streamsides.

Where vegetational cover is scant, more or less bare ground is exposed to wind and water erosion, with the unfortunate result being the removal of humus and retarded soil buildup. A leaner stratum of soil or subsoil remains, which is more impervious to moisture penetration and less moisture-retentive. This explains in part why areas with such clay "gumbo" around Pierre, South Dakota, are pastured rather than farmed.

The distinguishing features of the wild flowers of the Great Plains represent the sum of the evolving characters the plants have found effective in their long and successful adjustment to this stressful environment. For example, the seeds are coated to restrain germination until there is ample moisture present to dissolve this covering and sustain the plantlet while its plunging root finds safety at a good depth. And the green parts hurriedly develop a protective armament to meet the exigencies of coming heat and drought.

The fact that there are so many special types of flowering plants widely distributed over the region indicates a general adaptation to this distinctive environment. Very noticeable are the low and compact, or "bun," types growing from a taproot, sometimes spreading into a mat, with their mass of foliage directly upon the ground, and with very low scapes or flowering stems; this pattern is repeated in *Arenaria*, *Astragalus*, *Erigeron*, and *Eriogonum*, in *Haplopappus*, *Lesquerella*, and *Oxytropis multiceps*, and in *Townsendia* and others. By means of short stoloniferous roots, or stems that put down new roots as they advance, or merely extending trailing stems, others attain the mat or even the bun effect. Examples include *Antennaria*, *Hymenoxys*, *Phlox*, and *Potentilla*. Hardly meeting these patterns, *Leucocrinum montanum* and *Lewisia rediviva* have no stems at all—both their foliage and abundant blossoms arise from an underground crown; but their outlines are also rounded and very low. All these forms result from the plants' adaptive effort to provide their own microenvironment, to shade their parcels of ground fully or to a high degree, and to guard their covered areas from drying winds.

Another special plant type of notable occurrence arises from a branching taproot, and puts out from a short, stocky stem numerous fine branches to form a dense low bushlet. These plants cast a less effective patch of shade than the bun types, and may permit some air to pass beneath them. Included in this group are *Gutierrezia sarothrae*, *Hedeoma drummondii*, *Melampodium cinereum*, *Oenothera lavandulaefolia*, *Oenothera serrulata*, and *Scutellaria resinosa*, all of which have a tendency to shrubbiness.

During periods of drought some specialized evergreen subjects, from *Townsendia* to cactus, meet emergency demands with closable pores to reduce loss of moisture. Other adapted types are provided with fleshy, moisture-storing roots which tide them over lengthy periods of drought. They may remain green for the full summer season and maintain long seasons of bloom.

Such tiny tubers as *Anemone caroliniana* and *Lithophragma parviflora* hasten to flower and ripen a crop of seed, then without apology resort to the safety of underground dormancy. Great Plains bulbs and corms follow a similar schedule. The species of *Dodecatheon*, *Leococrinum*, *Mertensia*, and *Microseris*, and *Clematis fremontii*, *C. scottii*, and *Lewisia rediviva* and some violets employ moisture-storing roots to support a lavish season of bloom; then they too dodge the hot and dry months by going underground.

The adaptations in leaf form and texture by which many of our plants withstand the ardent forces of nature are to the casual observer a never-ending wonder. To the newcomer from a milder climate, the variations in stem and leaf coloration from plain green are at once apparent. Notable are the glossy and light-reflecting, waxy, blue-gray-greens, and the shades from faint gray to sparkling silver to white that characterize the protective hairs; whose texture ranges from the finest velvet to coarse and kinky. The glossary of a local checklist attempts to define a dozen distinct forms of hairiness—and there are others. In such coverings the plant admirer may perceive decorative effects; the plants themselves find the attire a useful way of shielding their sensitive inner parts from intense light and evaporation. The effectiveness of this means of protection is indicated by its wide application by many species, as balanced by the fewer species favoring waxy or high-gloss surfaces. Yet even on the Plains, in odd spells of weather individuals or colonies meet their limit of endurance and succumb. You may go back to check a certain plant, and find it missing, especially on the heavy soils. The gravelly knolls or ridges are the safer habitat.

In the long hours under the open sky many plants have found their normal functions well served by reduced leaf surface. A prime example is the completely skeletonized leaf pattern of *Astragalus ceramicus*, the bird-egg pea. Even the stems of the ten-inch plant approach in slenderness the pinnately arranged, stripped leaf veins, and in certain light the plant's shadow on the buff-colored sand makes a clearer image than the plant itself. In this species with flowers small and pale, we await with interest the development of the astonishing fruits, or pods, highly inflated to the size of a bird's egg. Exceeding an inch in length, fragile looking, and pale green, they are strikingly speckled and streaked with brownish pink and purple—chiefly with reference to the atttachment to the pedicel, rather than to the large end of the "egg." In numerous other species reduced leaf surfaces are to be observed in linear and channeled forms and variously divided blades.

To sum up: many of the wild flowers have developed special features to adapt to the difficult enviroment of the Great Plains, features ranging from a low and compact shape, to closable pores and moisture-storing roots, to early dormancy, to variations in leaf form, size, color, and texture.

When we began to grow a nursery stock of the native ornamentals at Prairie Gem Ranch, the natural choice of terrain was the acre conveniently adjoining the lawn on the south which had been planted in vegetables and small fruits. Two rows of ponderosa pine and a hedge of common lilac on the west afforded some wind protection, and on the north a hedge of 'Harrison's Yellow' rose. The plot was convenient for other hardy roses, a chosen trio of French lilacs, and annuals such as larkspurs, verbenas, poppies, even nasturtiums. These exotics thrived, as did the vegetables, in the better years, with clean cultivation and some fertilizing from poultry and barnyard sources.

For soil, there was no alternative, at first, to the native stiff gumbo clay, which was difficult to manage though rich in minerals and productive when rainfall was adequate. It was an early and pleasant discovery that the indigenous flowers of the neighboring prairies responded remarkably well to garden care, whether they were transplanted from badland soil, sandy loam, or dune sand, and would thrive in the gumbo when freed from competition. Planted in ground-level beds, 36 inches wide—between 18-inch paths of bare soil—the plants were spaced for growth without crowding. Away from the competition of grass, and carefully weeded, they could use the conserved moisture supply. But too often even these natives suffered in the gumbo from drought.

How to improve moisture penetration and retention? In a dashing rain the gumbo is soon "puddled" and water runs off in a sheet. The close-textured soil absorbs moisture slowly by capillary action, and any surplus is conducted steadily downward to depths even beyond the reach of roots. With the surface soon dry, capillary movement is reversed, and the moisture that is again brought to the surface evaporates. Always low in humus content, the gumbo dries out to extremes. In my first effort at improving the soil, I combined equal measures of coarse sand, barnyard fertilizer, and gumbo; and put the mixture in two small beds under the eaves—but like everything else, plants there were subject to drought.

Remember, we have gardened successfully, by local standards, with less than 15 inches of rainfall annually, at the altitude of about 3,300 feet. Our available water supply was stored in cisterns and dams, with extra water brought to the garden by *bucket and cup.* I will touch on only the highlights of success.

We conducted soil studies for years. Soils for small or larger tests, a grain-bagful in the car trunk, or a ton trailer-load, were available from various sources for the loading and hauling. This was especially true in the pasturing areas where soil, or earth, is not highly regarded, or indeed is rated as so much dirt under the feet. Along a pasture trail, convenient for hauling, and near a pit where gravel for road surfacing had been taken, were sand, gravel, and a mellow clay loam, remnants from an ancient stream course. This nonsticky loam continues to serve well in my scree mixes—corresponding to the "one part of ordinary garden soil" of the usual formula.

In Wyoming, 150 miles from home, I asked for permission to dig plants of **Lewisia rediviva**, bitter-root, growing in its native firm loam where sheep were pasturing; and to load my trailer with the soil. The reply was, "Anywhere out there, so long as you don't leaves any holes; help yourself." But that soil, as a replacement for my gumbo to a depth of a few inches, grew the bitter-root no better than my prepared mixtures. It takes moisture well but dries out quickly, and is obviously low in humus.

Perhaps the nicest High Plains soil I have found was in the extreme western range of **Anemone caroliniana** in the Pine Ridge country a hundred miles to the east. The dainty plants grew in wide, white-flowered sweeps with occasional patches of the striking blue form, in a light turf of buffalo grass, small sedges, and other low vegetation. Here, apparently, the turf had effectively held the basic loam with decaying vegetable matter and an increment of windborne dust, until a rich humusy loam had been built up. My ton from that fortunate spot is used sparingly in mixes for this special jewel.

At last, after some years of battling the clinging wet gumbo on over-shoes and digging tools at those busy times when plants were dug up and shipped to customers—I had to scrape my hand tool with a putty knife after every thrust—the need for a workable medium for my stock plants became pressing. A first bed, completely replacing the sticky clay, would accommodate the essential portion of the roots of most of the native perennials. I excavated a sizable bed to a depth of 8 inches, and carted the waste gumbo away. I compacted the refill mixture of sand, limestone chip, and screened, milled peat moss by trampling as it was brought up to ground level. This first scree bed found ready use as a rooting ground for prickly pear cuttings. It proved well suited to cactus, including a carmine-flowered **Opuntia poly-acantha**, a choice stock purchased in Colorado which had not thrived in the heavy soil. When the cuttings were watered lightly every second day for three weeks, roots were well started. The planting was then left to nature's care and results for the balance of the season were highly pleasing. Cactus bloom from cuttings is not guaranteed in the second year, but in this footing some plants bloomed then, including the red-flowered one. Various windborne seeds from nearby sources also found the bed an inviting starting ground.

A year or two later, as I was returning from an exploring trip through western Oklahoma, the Texas Panhandle, and eastern Colorado with some 600 plants, about half of them cacti, the balance various perennials, I recalled the many soils in which the plants had grown and came to the conclusion that the formula for my scree bed could well have included a portion of nonsticky clay loam for added moisture capacity. Beds for the entire 600 plants were thus prepared. The mix has proved so effective that I now rate it standard for my environment, excellent for full sun or half-shade. It is not perfect for every plant I wish to grow, but the missing element may be a more uniform moisture supply.

The scree mixture is as follows: two parts sand, with one part each of limestone chip, peat moss, and good clay loam. This assumes the roots have access to additional mineral nutrients in the deeper soil or subsoil. Let us now consider the role of each soil component in plant growth. Sand: even clean coarse sand is agreeable to starting plants; it takes moisture like a blotter and does not retain an excess. Limestone chip: with or without a portion of crusher dust, it aids in moisture absorption, retains a large amount of moisture and supplies lime for cacti, evening primroses, creeping phloxes, and other lime lovers, and poses no obstacle to the great number of tolerant prairie natives. Peat moss: the prime moisture retainer, the most independent of capillary pull, always sought by fine feeding roots. Good clay loam: a soil of tillable texture lacking stickiness or clinging wetness—a "good garden soil."

The foregoing describes the effort at Prairie Gem Ranch to provide an efficient growing medium and to conserve all possible moisture in the root-run. Together with the natural slope of every portion of the garden, the formula provides adequate drainage for the local rainfall. Here there is no subsoil problem other than slow absorption; there is no water table, but always an unfillable reservoir of relatively dry subsoil.

In preparing to grow the dry country plants, drainage is the first consideration. In most areas of their native region, drainage is well taken care of by the slope of the land. The water-shy plants may grow well on a downslope, but they leave off abruptly as they meet the line where water may now and again flood the ground. In a garden where drainage is a problem, raised beds, or a substratum of gravel, or a tile system leading to an outlet may relieve the situation.

Since the Plains plants are so constituted—adapted and equipped—to endure a shortage of moisture and to thrive under an occasional abundance, my root-run formula may be varied in climates with abundant rainfall if thorough drainage is maintained. More sand or leaner loam or less humus are effective in lowering unwanted moisture. Starting plants in clean sand, or growing them permanently in it, is recommended. To keep leaves and stems at their driest, use a covering of stone chips, as much as half an inch deep, which will hold the sensitive parts of the plant away from the wet ground. Thin slabs of stone buried at an angle also meet the need for dryness. A rock gardener in Pennsylvania grows all the Great Plains plants in sand beds six inches deep, placed on top of regular garden soil. Lower temperature through the heat of the day is important to many plants—not just newly set plants—and is effective against smothering humidity. It may be attained by positioning plants on a slope away from the sun, or by the shade of distant objects, or by temporary low shade.

The recommendation, given in Prairie Gem Ranch catalogs, that newly set plants must have complete airtight shading for protection against strong winds and low humidity, when the air temperature is above 70°F, has often been called into question. The argument against it is simple: "The plants would smother." The affirmative stand is time-tested and definite: there is no other way, with limited water, to protect a plant that must not wilt. With adequate moisture surrounding the roots, a tin can or other airtight cover, large enough to leave the foliage free of contact, is pressed slightly into the soil in early morning while the plant is fresh, and removed in the evening when the temperature has dropped. Proper humidity is maintained in the airtight compartment, and the plant remains fresh. Water is applied every second night as the plants are uncovered. A small pit dug beside the plant is troweled so as not to interfere with the roots, filled with water to less than overflowing, and refilled as the water soaks away—four times—and then the pit is refilled with dry soil. Such watering is continued until a good rain comes or until it is certain that the plant is well rooted. This care might be called "desert gardening," but it is effective. It is important to keep the ground about the plant dry, so that it serves as a mulch to retain moisture at a deeper level. Second-night watering is also used for cactus cuttings in July, the favored rooting season. The calloused part is set deeply enough in clean or relatively clean sand to hold the cutting upright. Water is applied with a sprinkling can to wet the rooting medium to a depth of three or four inches. The texture of the sandy medium guards against excessive drying. Airtight cover is not required for cactus, though lath shade, 20 inches off the ground, is beneficial in avoiding sunburn.

I hope this section has been helpful to gardeners who grow the distinctly endowed flowering plants of the Great Plains.

# The Botanical Contributions of Claude A. Barr

## Ronald R. Weedon

Claude A. Barr made an impressive number of contributions to systematic botany and to horticulture. A specialist on the Great Plains natives, he discovered species of flowering plants as well as a number of genetic variants including previously unknown color forms. He introduced a great many native plant species to global horticulture. Barr also added to our knowledge of rare and endangered species, a subject of interest to him long before it was a subject of general interest in our part of the country.

*Astragalus barrii* Barneby appears to be Barr's most outstanding discovery of a species. He brought this *Astragalus* to the attention of R. C. Barneby, who named it after him. The species is not known to be common but is locally plentiful in several locations in the High Plains of southeastern Montana, eastern Wyoming, and southwestern South Dakota (Barneby, 1956, 1964). Endemism is rare in the Great Plains; thus the discovery of this species is most interesting. Barr's milkvetch is of interest to horticulturists because of its cushion habit and relatively large flowers. As a result of Barr's work with *Phlox*, several notable taxa were discovered, particularly *Phlox andicola* Nutt. v. *parvula* Wherry, whose morphology is intermediate between that of *P. andicola* and *P. hoodii* (Rich. Wherry, 1955). Barr also found a beautiful diminutive pink phlox strongly reminiscent of *P. alyssifolia* Greene but yet different, a genetic variant (Smith, 1970) which he labeled 'Flag Mountain' for the place where he first saw it. In addition, Barr contributed specimens and information regarding possible *Phlox* hybrids or populations of various ploidy levels in the central Great Plains. Barr's work has added to our understanding of genetic variation in *Potentilla concinna* Richards, a cinquefoil which is beautiful in rock garden settings.

A recognized authority on cacti of the Great Plains, Barr gave horticulture several hybrids and a number of beautiful color forms, including *Opuntia* 'Apache', with showy carmine flowers and impressive spines, and *Opuntia* 'Desert Splendor', with magnificent large carmine flowers. For *Opuntia polyacantha* Haw., plains prickly pear, Barr recorded many color forms, among which are 'Giant', with large yellow flowers, and 'Red Head', with very red spines and bright red-centered yellow flowers. Among the hybrids, highly noteworthy are *Opuntia* 'Super-rutila' (*aurea* X *rutila*) with bright carmine flowers, *Opuntia* 'C. Arno' (a hybrid involving *O. fragilis*) with pink, nearly red flowers, and *Opuntia* 'Smithwick' (*compressa* X *fragilis*), a variant twice the size of *O. fragilis* (Nutt.) Haw. with bright yellow flowers.

A spectacular color form discovered by Barr was named *Aster kumleini* Fries, f. *roseoligulatus* by Benke (1939). This aster with rose-pink ray flowers is now recognized as a variant of *A. oblongifolius* Nutt. Barr named it 'Dream of Beauty'. He also found a deep blue color form which he named 'Prairie Gem Blue', as well as a variant with lacy-rayed silver blue ray flowers which he left unnamed. Other aster variants of note are *A. laevis* L. (*A. geyeri*) 'Black Hills', a superb large-flowered strain of an unsurpassed soft blue, and a genetic variant of *A. ericoides* L. which Barr considered as a variant of *A. batesii*. Within a relatively closely related genus, Barr selected *Erigeron flagellaris* Gray 'Prairie Gem', a variant that is smaller, greener, and of a less invasive nature than the typical *E. flagellaris*. He also had excellent success with several other impressive daisy fleabanes.

Other horticulturally desirable clones selected by Barr include a dark rose form of *Antennaria rosea* Greene, a pink-flowered variant of *Clematis hirsutissima* Pursh (*C. scottii*), and two outstanding color forms of *Dodecatheon pulchellum* (Raf.) Merr., the one 'Prairie Ruby', an intense velvety ruby red, the other 'White Comet', a pure white with a thread of gold at the petal base. *Leucocrinum montanum* Nutt., sand lily, is one of the best examples of Barr's ability to select variants of great horticultural value from natural populations. Of great interest is his work with *Nemastylis geminiflora* Nutt. (*N. acuta*), an introduction from southeastern Kansas, known as prairie iris or blue tigridia.

Barr discovered *Rosa arkansana* Porter 'J. W. Fargo', a beautiful many-petaled tetraploid named by N. E. Hansen (Moon, 1958). He also made note of the several color forms of *Tradescantia bracteata* Small. The very impressive 'Gold Nugget' form of *Viola nuttalli* Pursh, which Barr considered a variant of *V. vallicola* A. Nels., now a synonym, was one of the most outstanding plants in his garden. One of his most notable discoveries in the field was his observation of red and black color forms in populations of the usually cream-white *Yucca glauca* Nutt., one of which received the name 'Pink Brilliant'. Barr made a number of very interesting plant introductions in the genera *Anemone, Astragalus, Oxytropis, Campanula, Dalea, Mertensia, Oenothera, Penstemon, Polygala, Senecio, Solidago,* and *Townsendia,* among others.

Barr made significant observations about the ecology of *Penstemon haydenii* S. Wats., blowout bluebells as it is known locally, Nebraska's candidate for designation as an endangered species. This plant is so rare that there are only twelve populations in five counties and a total of about three thousand individual plants known currently, confined to blowouts and their margins in the unique Nebraska Sandhills. Barr's important collection of plant specimens, notes, and observations are currently being studied by the South Dakota Natural Heritage Program, a cooperative effort involving the Nature Conservancy and the South Dakota Department of Game, Fish, and Parks, devoted to the inventory of rare and endangered species of plants in that state.

### Literature Cited

Barneby, R. C. 1956. Pugillus Astragalorum XIX: Notes on *A. sericoleucus* Gray and Its Immediate Relatives. *The American Midland Naturalist* 55(2): 504-7.

————. 1964. Atlas of North American *Astragalus. Memoires of the New York Botanical Garden* 13:1-1188. Parts I and II.

Benke, Hermann C. 1939. New Color Form in South Dakota Aster. *The American Midland Naturalist* 22(1):212-13.

Moon, Mary H. 1958. Plantsmen in Profile, VI: Claude A. Barr. *Baileye* 6:106-10.

Smith, Dale M. 1980. Personal communication.

Wherry, Edgar T. 1955. The Genus *Phlox. Morris Arboretum Monographs* 3:1-174.

# Glossary
# Bibliography
# Index

# Glossary

**Adventive**. Introduced into an area.

**Aerole**. In cacti, a specialized spine-bearing growth center on the stems.

**Anther**. The pollen-bearing part of a stamen.

**Anthesis**. The period when a flower opens.

**Apomixis**. A process of seed production involving the specialized generative tissues but not involving fertilization.

**Aril**. An appendage that wholly or partly encloses certain seeds. (The red covering of the bittersweet seed is a good example.)

**Atragene**. A trailing or climbing group in *Clematis* whose spreading sepals are petallike, commonly blue or purple, showy.

**Attenuate**. Slenderly tapering.

**Aurator**. A good name in *Penstemon*, including several Plains species that are often difficult to grow in new environments.

**Axil**. An angular space formed where two plant parts are joined.

**Badland**. A greatly eroded area of sterile soils subject to long periods of drought. Often scenic, spectacular.

**Banner**. The prominent upper petal in the flower of the pea family.

**Bilabiate**. With upper and lower lips, usually referring to the corolla; sometimes also to the calyx.

**Bipinnate**. Doubly pinnate, the primary pinnae themselves pinnate.

**Bract**. A leaflike part from whose axil a flower or an inflorescence arises.

**Bracteate**. Bearing bracts.

**Calyx**. The sepals collectively, usually green, or in some flowers showy-colored; in the bud, encloses the inner parts of the flower.

**Caudex.** The persistent portion of an herbaceous perennial from which root and stem originate.

**Cholla.** (Pronounced Choy-a.) Any of the slender, jointed, treelike opuntias.

**Cleistogamy.** Self-fertilization in nonopening flowers, as in some violets.

**Compound.** Composed of two or more like parts, as a leaf with two or more leaflets.

**Cone.** In the composite family, a mounded or elongated disk.

**Cordate.** Heart-shaped with the point outward.

**Corm.** A bulbous but solid underground base of a stem.

**Corolla.** The petals collectively, usually colored other than green.

**Corymb.** A flat-topped or convex cluster of flowers with the outer flowers opening first.

**Corymbose.** Corymblike, or in corymbs.

**Crown.** The juncture of stem and roots.

**Cultivar.** A plant of garden origin, often much modified from its ancestors.

**Cyme.** A flat or convex flower cluster with the central flowers opening first.

**Cymose.** Bearing a cyme or cymes, or having the nature of a cyme.

**Digitate.** Having radiating divisions or leaflets suggesting fingers.

**Disk.** In the composite family, the central cluster of tubular flowers of the head as distinct from the rays.

**Endemic.** Native or indigenous to a particular region.

**Epidermis.** A thin layer of cells forming the outer skin, shell, rind, or the like of a seed plant or fern.

**Falls.** The outer, often drooping, perianth parts in some members of the iris family, especially in *Iris*.

**Filament.** The stalk of a stamen.

**Floret.** A small flower, usually one of a dense cluster.

**Fusiform.** Spindle-shaped, swollen in the middle and narrowing toward each end.

**Generic.** Pertaining to a genus.

**Genus.** A category of classification used for a group of closely related species or for a lone species with no close relatives.

**Glabrescent.** Nearly glabrous.

**Glabrous.** Lacking hairs; smooth.

**Glaucous.** Gray, grayish green, or bluish green due to a thin coat of waxy particles.

**Glochid**. A minute barbed spine found on the aeroles of prickly pears and chollas.

**Gumbo**. See Mudshale.

**Habit**. The characteristic form or appearance of a plant including the posture and texture of its parts.

**Habitat**. The kind of place where a plant naturally grows.

**Head**. A dense cluster of stalkless or nearly stalkless flowers, as in the composite family.

**Herb**. A nonwoody plant, often a perennial, with stems dying back to the ground each year.

**Herbaceous**. Herblike.

**Humus**. The dark organic material in soils that is produced by decomposition of vegetable or animal matter. It is essential to fertility and retains moisture.

**Hypanthium**. A saucer-shaped, cup-shaped, or tubular expansion of the receptacle bearing the sepals, petals, and stamens on its rim.

**Incised**. Cut sharply and irregularly.

**Inflorescence**. The arrangement of flowers on a plant; the flowering part of a plant, including branches and bracts.

**Involucre**. A circle of bracts surrounding a flower or flower cluster.

**Keel**. A boat-shaped ridge formed by the two lower petals in the pea family flower.

**Lanceolate**. Much longer than broad, tapering toward the tip from below the middle.

**Leaflet**. One of the leaflike subdivisions of the blade of a compound leaf.

**Legume**. A pod formed from a simple pistil, usually opening down both sides, as in the pea family.

**Limb**. The widened or spreading outer part of a petal, sepal, or of a corolla composed of united petals.

**Linear**. Long and narrow, with essentially parallel margins.

**Linear-filiform**. Very narrow, almost threadlike.

**Linear-lanceolate**. A shape intermediate between linear and lanceolate.

**Loess**. A loamy soil, dried, sifted, transported, and deposted by wind.

**Microenvironment**. The restricted portion of the environment that affects plants directly; more often the portion of the general environment closest to the earth's surface; a very specialized localized environment thought to be particularly suitable for a given kind of plant or animal.

**Mudshale.** A clayey rock of nearly uniform texture throughout, laid down over the great Plains region by the Cretaceous muddy seas, and containing numerous fossils and limy concretions. The breakdown product of this shale, technically known as the Pierre, is the difficult, sticky, and unlovable soil called gumbo.

**Node.** The place on a stem or an underground part, especially a rhizome, from which a leaf, a branch, or new growth originates.

**Oblanceolate.** Lanceolate with the broader end toward the tip.

**Ochroleucous.** Yellowish white.

**Orbicular.** Essentially circular.

**Orophaca.** A group designation of ground-hugging and mat-forming trifoliate plants in *Astragalus.*

**Ovary.** The enlarged, lower part of the pistil that encloses the ovules.

**Ovule.** The reproductive structure within the ovary that may ultimately become a seed.

**Panicle.** A branched inflorescence.

**Pappus.** A series of hairs, bristles, or scales attached near the top of the mature ovary in many composites, often serving as a parachute in seed dispersal.

**Parthenogenesis.** The production of seeds without fertilization.

**Pedicel.** The stalk of a single flower of a cluster.

**Peduncle.** A primary flower stalk arising from a stem, bearing a lone flower or a cluster of flowers.

**Peneplain.** A formerly elevated area that has been reduced almost to a plain by erosion.

**Perianth.** The calyx and corolla together, or either of them if the other is lacking.

**Petal.** One member of the inner whirl of floral leaves composing the corolla.

**Pinnate.** With leaflets or other structures arranged on either side of a common stalk or rachis.

**Pinnatifid.** Pinnately cleft about halfway or more to the midrib.

**Pistil.** The seed-bearing part of the flower.

**Pistillate.** Pistil-bearing; usually applied to flowers that lack stamens.

**Playa.** (Spanish.) A depression in very flat terrain, often dry, occasionally a lake.

**Puberulent.** With a covering of minute, short, soft, often sparse hairs.

**Pubescent.** Covered with hairs.

**Pyramidal**. A uniformly tapering growth from base to tip (usually conical).

**Raceme**. An elongated unbranched inflorescence, with each flower borne on a separate stalk (pedicel) attached to the central axis.

**Rachis**. The axis of an inflorescence, or of a compound leaf.

**Ray**. In some composites, a marginal flower with an extended strap-shaped corolla.

**Receptacle**. The part of a flower stalk bearing the floral organs; or in the composite family, the part of the flower cluster bearing the florets.

**Relict**. A plant or animal species living in an environment that has changed from that which is typical for it.

**Rhizomatous**. Having rhizomes.

**Rhizome**. An underground stem, usually horizontal, usually putting out roots from the underside and leafy stems above.

**Sagittate**. Arrowhead-shaped.

**Scape**. A leafless or bract-bearing peduncle arising from a crown or from a very short stem.

**Scorpioid**. An inflorescence that is coiled at the tip before flowers bloom and which uncoils as they develop.

**Scree**. A sloping mass of detritus below an eroding cliff; any mixture of rock material, soil, and vegetable matter.

**Secund**. Arranged on only one side of an axis.

**Sepal**. One member of the outer row of floral leaves composing the calyx.

**Shrub**. A woody perennial smaller than a tree and usually with several stems.

**Spatulate**. Paddle- or spoon-shaped.

**Species**. A kind of plant the individuals of which are interfertile and which shows distinct differences from other similar kinds.

**Sport**. A notable deviation from the normal or parental type.

**Stamen**. The pollen-bearing organ of the flower, consisting of anther and filament (when present).

**Staminate**. Bearing stamens. Usually applied to flowers lacking pistils.

**Staminode**. A sterile structure occupying the position of a stamen.

**Stellate**. Star-shaped. Usually applied to branched hairs.

**Stigma**. The part of the pistil (usually the tip) that is receptive to pollen.

**Stipe**. A short stalk, especially that of a pistil.

**Stolon**. Any horizontal basal branch such as a runner that tends to produce roots and new plants at the nodes or apex.

**Style**. That part of the pistil that separates the stigma from the ovary (not always present).

**Subshrub**. Of shrubby habit including overwintering live stems above ground, but not truly woody.

**Subspecies**. A subdivision of a species exhibiting definite variation from the species type and often occupying its own geographical area.

**Succulent**. Juicy, fleshy, and thickened; also a group designation of plants having these characteristics.

**Taproot**. A primary root, stout and vertical.

**Tendril**. A slender, leafless, twining or clasping climbing organ.

**Terete**. Circular in cross-section.

**Tomentum**. A covering of longish, soft, entangled hairs pressed close to the surface.

**Trifoliate**. With three leaflets.

**Tuber**. A short, thickened underground stem serving for food storage and often for the production of new plants.

**Tuberculate**. With rounded, protruding bodies, as the nodules caused by nitrogen-fixing bacteria on the roots of certain plants.

**Umbel**. A flower cluster in which all the peduncles and/or pedicels arise from a common point.

**Variety**. A subdivision of a wild species of lesser rank than a subspecies; colloquially a kind of plant or species. See also Cultivar.

**Verticillate**. Arranged in whorls of three or more.

**Viorna**. The *Clematis* group with urn-shaped flowers.

# Bibliography

Albertson, F. W. 1937. Ecology of Mixed Prairie in West Central Kansas. *Ecological Monographs* 7:481-547.

Andrews, D. M. 1933. A Garden of Pentstemons. *The National Horticultural Magazine* 12(4):284-91.

Bailey, L. H. 1935. *The Standard Cyclopedia of Horticulture.* 3 vols. New York: Macmillan.

Bailey, L. H., and Ethel Zoe Bailey. 1941. *Hortus Second.* New York: Macmillan.

Barkley, T. M. 1968. *A Manual of the Flowering Plants of Kansas.* Manhattan, Kans.: Kansas State University Endowment Association.

Barneby, R. C. 1952. A Revision of the North American Species of *Oxytropis* DC. *Proceedings of the California Academy of Science* 27(7):177-312.

————. 1956. Pugillus Astragalorum XIX: Notes on *A. sericoleucus* Gray and Its Immediate Relatives. *The American Midland Naturalist* 55(2):504-7.

————. 1964. Atlas of North American *Astragalus. Memoirs of the New York Botanical Garden* 13:1-1188. Parts I and II.

Barr, Claude A. 1929. Installment Pruning. *South Dakota Horticulturist* 1(5): 13-15.

————. 1930a. Domesticating the Pasque Flower. *House and Garden* 58(4): 122. And 1931. *North and South Dakota Horticulture* 3(5):68.

————. 1930b. What Good Is the Buffalo-Berry. *North and South Dakota Horticulture* 2(9):10.

————. 1930c. Why Peonies Refused to Blossom. *South Dakota Horticulturist* 2(5):11-12.

————. 1931. The Mariposa Tulips. *North and South Dakota Horticulture* 3(6):87-88.

————. 1932a. Denizens of Slim Butte. *North and South Dakota Horticulture* 4(4/5):44-45, 58.

————. 1932b. Oriental Poppy. *North and South Dakota Horticulture* 4(6):72.

————. 1933a. Garden Adventure on the High Prairies. *Gardeners' Chronicle of America* 37(9):245-47.

*215*

————. 1933b. Weatherproof Plants for Dakota Rock Gardens. *North and South Dakota Horticulture* 5(3):30-31, 35-36.

————. 1934a. Beyond Garden Walls on the Great Plains. *Gardeners' Chronicle of America* 38(4):100-102, 104, 113.

————. 1934b. Jewels of the Plains. *North and South Dakota Horticulture* 6(3/4/5):35-36, 47-48, 60.

————. 1935a. Natural Gardens of the Black Hills. *Gardeners' Chronicle of America* 39(7):197-99.

————. 1935b. Thimble Flower in the West. *Horticulture* 13(3):59.

————. 1936a. Gardens of the Pahasapa. *Gardeners' Chronicle of America* 40(11/12):313-14, 316, 357-58.

————. 1936b. The Oxeye Daisy Comes to the Black Hills. *North and South Dakota Horticulture* 9(6):70.

————. 1936c. The Prickly Poppy. *North and South Dakota Horticulture* 9(2):23-24.

————. 1936d. Slants on Rocks. *North and South Dakota Horticulture* 9(8):90-91, 93-94. And 1939. *The Dakota Farmer* 59(8):173, 181-82.

————. 1938a. Carpets of Silver and Green Gray. *Gardeners' Chronicle of America* 42(5):145-46.

————. 1938b. *Erigeron salsuginosus. Gardeners' Chronicle of America* 42(6):174.

————. 1938c. *Oenothera serrulata,* a Group Species. *Gardeners' Chronicle of America* 42(6):173.

————. 1939a. *Brodiaea douglasi. Gardeners' Chronicle of America* 43(12):389.

————. 1939b. *Hedeoma campora. Gardeners' Chronicle of America* 43(1):28.

————. 1939c. Native Plant Finds. *Gardeners' Chronicle of America* 43(8):237-39.

————. 1940a. Another Reply to Mr. Hay. *Flower Grower* 26:300.

————. 1940b. *Calochortus,* Sensational American Tulips. Unpublished manuscript.

————. 1940c. *Clematis scotti. Gardeners' Chronicle of America* 44(2):59-60.

————. 1940d. Grapes in a Prairie Garden. *North and South Dakota Horticulture* 13(4/5):47-48, 60.

————. 1940e. *Ipomoea leptophylla. The National Horticultural Magazine* 19:56-58.

————. 1942a. Bitter-Root Steals a March. *Gardeners' Chronicle of America* 46(7):210, 213.

————. 1942b. Cimarron Evening Primrose. *Gardeners' Chronicle of America* 46(6):194-95.

————. 1942c. Growing the Pasque. *North and South Dakota Horticulture* 15(6):69.

————. 1942d. Mountain Gold. *Gardeners' Chronicle of America* 46(8):242.

————. 1943a. *Astragalus tridactylicus. Bulletin of the American Rock Garden Society* 1(4):75-78.

————. 1943b. Horticultural Notes. *North and South Dakota Horticulture* 16(4/5):47.

————. 1943c. Jewels of the Great Plains. *Bulletin of the American Rock Garden Society* 1(1):13-16.

————. 1943d. *Townsendia parryi. Bulletin of the American Rock Garden Society* 1(6):107-10.

————. 1944a. *Anemone caroliniana. Bulletin of the American Rock Garden Society* 2(5):90-91.

————. 1944b. *Hypoxis hirsuta. The National Horticultural Magazine* 23(4): 235.

————. 1944c. Three Alliums for the Great Plains. *Herbertia* 2:327-28.

————. 1944d. Through the Nebraska Sandhills. *Bulletin of the American Rock Garden Society* 2(6):105-8.

————. 1944e. Whip-Lash Daisies. *Bulletin of the American Rock Garden Society* 2(3):35-37.

————. 1946a. The Best Soil for Penstemons—Experiments with Different Soils. *Bulletin of the American Penstemon Society* 2:52-55.

————. 1946b. Handling of Plants from Nurseries or the Wild. *Bulletin of the American Penstemon Society* 2:55-57.

————. 1946c. How to Succeed with Plains Penstemons. *Bulletin of the American Penstemon Society* 2:39-40.

————. 1946d. The Life Span of Penstemons. *Bulletin of the American Rock Garden Society* 4(4):59-61.

————. 1946e. *Penstemon angustifolius. Quoted in* Juanita E. Jorgensen, Blizzard Belt Garden Notes. *North and South Dakota Horticulture* 19(3):44.

————. 1946f. Summary of Reports on Plant Behavior. *Bulletin of the American Penstemon Society* 1:16-39.

————. 1946g. *Viola montanensis*, a Gem. *Bulletin of the American Rock Garden Society* 4(6):107-8.

————. 1946h. *Viola nuttallii* and *vallicola. Bulletin of the American Rock Garden Society* 4(6):108-9.

————. 1947a. *Aquilejia jucunda. The National Horticultural Magazine* 26(2):134-36.

————. 1947b. Dwarf Western Asters. *Bulletin of the American Rock Garden Society* 5(4):65-68.

————. 1948a. *Penstemon albidus. Bulletin of the American Rock Garden Society* 6(4):62.

————. 1948b. *Penstemon eriantherus. Bulletin of the American Rock Garden Society* 6(4):61-62.

————. 1949. *Penstemon gracilis. Bulletin of the American Rock Garden Society* 7(4):60-61.

————. 1950a. The Engaging *Penstemon humilis. Bulletin of the American Rock Garden Society* 8(2):30-31.

————. 1950b. *Penstemon aridus. Bulletin of the American Rock Garden Society* 8(2):31.

————. 1951a. Cushion Astragali. *Bulletin of the American Rock Garden Society* 9(1):2-5.

————. 1951b. An Open Heart for Penstemons. *The National Horticultural Magazine* 30(1):29-31.

————. 1952. My Black Hills. *North and South Dakota Horticulture* 25(9/10): 74-75.

————. 1957a. Packing Plants for Shipment. *Bulletin of the American Penstemon Society* 16:57.

————. 1957b. Reports of Members. *Bulletin of the American Penstemon Society* 16:57.

————. 1958. The Germination of Great Plains Species. *Bulletin of the American Rock Garden Society* 16(1):9-11.

————. 1959. Reports on Behavior of Penstemons in Gardens and Evaluation by Members, List of Species Being Grown by Each Member. *Bulletin of the American Penstemon Society* 18:101.

————. 1960. The Purple Loco and Others. *Bulletin of the American Rock Garden Society* 18(3):65-67.

————. 1961a. The Hardy Cacti. *Bulletin of the American Rock Garden Society* 19(2):33-42.

————. 1961b. Reports on Behavior of Penstemons in Gardens—The United States. *Bulletin of the American Penstemon Society* 20:76-78.

————. 1962a. Annual Reports by Members. *Bulletin of the American Penstemon Society* 21:101-2.

————. 1962b. In the Kildeer Mountains. *Bulletin of the American Rock Garden Society* 20(3):80-81.

————. 1962c. *Phlox alyssifolia. The American Horticultural Magazine* 41(3): 170-71.

————. 1962d. Wildflowers of South Dakota and Its Environs. *Brooklyn Botanic Garden Handbook, Gardening with Native Plants (Plants & Gardens* 18(1):83-86).

————. 1963a. Hardy Cacti. *Brooklyn Botanic Garden Handbook on Succulent Plants (Plants & Gardens* 19(3):25-29).

————. 1963b. Western Prairies. Annual Reports by Members. *Bulletin of the American Penstemon Society* 22:160-62.

————. 1964a. Prairies. *In* Annual Reports on the Behavior of Penstemon in Gardens. *Bulletin of the American Penstemon Society* 23:83.

————. 1964b. Three Visits to Flag Mountain. *Bulletin of the American Rock Garden Society* 22(2):33-36.

————. 1964c. A Trip to Wyoming and Other States. *Bulletin of the American Penstemon Society* 23:48-49.

————. 1965a. Adventures of '65. *In* Annual Reports on the Behavior of Penstemon in Gardens, The Great Plains. *Bulletin of the American Penstemon Society* 24:149-53.

————. 1956b. How Shall We Say "Dodecatheon"? *Bulletin of the American Rock Garden Society* 23(1):33-34.

————. 1966. Short Trip Stories. *Bulletin of the American Penstemon Society* 25:25-26.

————. 1967a. A New and Exciting Strain of *P. grandiflorus. Bulletin of the American Penstemon Society* 26:90.

————. 1967b. The Prairie States. *In* Parade of Penstemons, Annual Reports. *Bulletin of the American Penstemon Society* 26:146.

————. 1968a. Alexander Butte. *American Rock Garden Society Bulletin* 26(4):114-16.

————. 1968b. The Low Altitude *Eritrichium*. *American Rock Garden Society Bulletin* 26(2):48-49.

————. 1969. Trip Stories. *Bulletin of the American Penstemon Society* 28:42-43.

————. 1970a. The Great Plains. *In* Reports by Members on the Behavior of Penstemons in Gardens. *Bulletin of the American Penstemon Society* 29: 81-82.

————. 1970b. Trips Near home; A Trip to Mount Rainier. *In* Stories of Trips to See Penstemons and Other Flowers. *Bulletin of the American Penstemon Society* 29:24-25, 27-28.

————. 1971a. Comments on *Oenothera Missouriensis incana*. *American Rock Garden Society Bulletin* 29(3):95-96.

————. 1971b. The Prairic States. *In* Annual Report by Members on the Behavior of Penstemons in Gardens. *Bulletin of the American Penstemon Society* 30:61-62.

————. 1972. Annual Reports by Members on the Behavior of Penstemons in Their Gardens. *Bulletin of the American Penstemon Society* 31:88-89.

————. 1973a. Annual Reports by Members on the Behavior of Penstemons in Their Gardens. *Bulletin of the American Penstemon Society* 32:98.

————. 1973b. The Life Span of Penstemons. *Bulletin of the American Penstemon Society* 32:124.

————. 1974a. Annual Reports by Members on the Behavior of Penstemons in Their Gardens. *Bulletin of the American Penstemon Society* 33:71-72.

————. 1974b. Evaluations of Penstemons Being Grown in 1946. *Bulletin of the American Penstemon Society* 33:95-113.

————. 1974c. How to Succeed with Plains Penstemons. *Bulletin of the American Penstemon Society* 33:113.

————. 1975a. How to Succeed with Plains Penstemons. *Bulletin of the American Penstemon Society* 34:28-B.

————. 1975b. Peat Moss Does Not Conserve Moisture in a Dry Soil. *Bulletin of the American Penstemon Society* 34:7.

————. 1975c. Reports by Members on the Behavior of Penstemons in the Garden. *Bulletin of the American Penstemon Society* 34:57.

————. 1975d. Sand Beds. *Bulletin of the American Penstemon Society* 34:7.

————. 1976. Reports by Members on the Behavior of Penstemons in Their Gardens. *Bulletin of the American Penstemon Society* 35:59-61.

————. 1977. Reports on the Behavior of Penstemons in Gardens. *Bulletin of the American Penstemon Society* 36:43.

————. 1981. *Dodecatheon*—The Shooting Stars. *In* Sharon F. Sutton, ed. *Alpines of the Americas, The Report of the First Interim International Rock Garden Plant Conference, July 18-25, 1976*. Organized Jointly by the American Rock Garden Society, Northwestern Chapter, and the Alpine Garden

Club of British Columbia, Seattle.

Beal, J. M. 1939. Cytological Studies in Relation to the Classification of the Genus *Calochortus*. *The Botanical Gazette* 100(3):528-47.

Beaman, J. H. 1957. The Systematics and Evolution of *Townsendia*. *The Contributions of the Gray Herbarium* 183:1-151.

Bennett, Ralph W., compiler. 1946. *A Tentative Manual on Penstemons*. Arlington, Va: American Penstemon Society.

Benson, Lyman. 1950. *The Cacti of Arizona*. 2nd ed. Tucson: University of Arizona Press.

Booth, W. E. 1950. *Flora of Montana, Part I, Conifers and Monocots*. Bozeman, Mont.: Research Foundation at Montana State College.

Booth, W. E., and J. C. Wright. 1966. *Flora of Montana, Part II, Dicotyledons*. Bozeman, Mont.: Department of Botany and Microbiology, Montana State University.

Brainerd, Ezra. 1921. Violets of North America. *Vermont Agricultural Experiment Station Bulletin* 224.

Breitung, August J. 1954. A Botanical Survey of the Cypress Hills. *The Canadian Field-Naturalist* 68:55-92.

Budd, Archibald C. 1952. *A Key to Plants of the Farming and Ranching Areas of the Canadian Prairies*. Ottawa: Experimental Farms Service, Canada, Department of Agriculture.

Budd, Archibald C., and Keith F. Best. 1964. *Wild Plants of the Canadian Prairies*. Ottawa: Research Branch, Canada Department of Agriculture Publication 983.

Chambers, Kenton L. 1957. Taxonomic Notes on Some Compositae of the Western United States. *The Contributions of the Dudley Herbarium* 5(2): 57-68.

Chickering, Allen L. 1938. Growing *Calochortus*. *Rancho Santa Ana Botanic Garden Monographs, Horticultural Series* 1:1-18.

Clausen, Jens. 1964. Cytotaxonomy and Distributional Ecology of Western North American Violets. *Madroño* 17(6):173-97.

————. 1967a. Biosystematic Consequences of Ecotypic and Chromosomal Differentiation. *Taxon* 16:271-79.

————. 1967b. *Stages in the Evolution of Plant Species*. New York: Hafner Publishing.

Clements, Frederic E., and Ralph W. Chaney. 1936. Environment and Life in the Great Plains. *Carnegie Institution of Washington Supplementary Publications* 24:1-54.

Coulter, John M., and Aven Nelson. 1909. *New Manual of Botany of the Central Rocky Mountains (Vascular Plants)*. New York: American Book.

Cronquist, Arthur. 1947. A. Revision of the North American Species of *Erigeron*. North of Mexico. *Brittonia* 6:121-302.

Darlington, C. D. 1932. *Chromosomes and Plant-Breeding*. New York: Macmillan.

Dawson, E. Yale. 1963. *How to Know the Cacti*. Dubuque, Iowa: Brown.

Dress, William J. 1958. Notes on the Cultivated Compositae 1. *Townsendia*. *Baileya* 6(3):158-63.

————. 1960. Notes on the Cultivated Compositae 5. *Hymenoxys. Baileya* 8(2):68-74.

————. 1965. Notes on the Cultivated Compositae 8. *Thelesperma, Bidens, Coreopsis. Baileya* 13(1):21-42.

Dyson, James L. 1962. *The World of Ice.* New York: Knopf.

Elliott, R. C. 1966a. The Genus *Lewisia. Alpine Garden Society Bulletin* 34: 1-76.

————. 1966b. *Portraits of Alpine Plants.* London: Alpine Garden Society.

Farrer, Reginald. 1930. *The English Rock-Garden.* 2 vols. London: T. C. & E. C. Jack.

Fenneman, Nevin M. 1931. *Physiography of Western United States.* New York: McGraw-Hill.

Foster, H. Lincoln. 1968. *Rock Gardening, A Guide to Growing Alpines and Other Wildflowers in the American Garden.* Boston: Houghton-Mifflin.

Fraser, W. P., and R. C. Russell. 1937. *List of the Flowering Plants, Ferns, and Fern Allies of Saskatchewan.* Saskatoon: University of Saskatchewan.

Gabrielson, Ira N. 1932. *Western American Alpines.* New York: Macmillan.

Gaiser, L. O. 1946. The Genus *Liatris. Rhodora* 48:165-83, 216-63, 273-326, 331-82, 393-412.

Gates, Frank C. 1932. Wild Flowers in Kansas. *Report of the Kansas State Board of Agriculture* 51(204-8):1-295.

————. 1940. *Annotated List of the Plants of Kansas: Ferns and Flowering Plants.* Manhattan, Kans.: Kansas State College, Department of Botany Contribution No. 391.

Gleason, Henry A., and Arthur Cronquist. 1963. *Manual of the Vascular Plants of Northeastern United States and Adjacent Canada.* Princeton, N.J.: Van Nostrand.

Great Plains Flora Association, R. L. McGregor, coord., T. M. Barkley, ed. 1977. *Atlas of the Flora of the Great Plains.* Ames: Iowa State University Press.

Hapeman, H. Personal Communication.

Harrington, H. D. 1954. *Manual of the Plants of Colorado.* Denver, Colo.: Sage Books.

Hitchcock, C. Leo, Arthur Cronquist, Marion Ownbey, and J. W. Thompson. 1955. *Vascular Plants of the Pacific Northwest. Part 5: Compositae.* Seattle: University of Washington Press.

Ingram, John. 1963. Notes on the Cultivated Primulaceae 2. *Dodecatheon. Baileya* 11(3):69-90.

Johnson, James R., and James T. Nichols. 1970. *Plants of the South Dakota Grasslands.* Brookings, S. Dak.: South Dakota State University, Agricultural Experiment Station Bulletin 566.

Kelly, George W. 1970. *A Guide to the Woody Plants of Colorado.* Boulder, Colo.: Pruett Publishing.

Klaber, Doretta. 1959. *Rock Garden Plants.* New York: Henry Holt.

Macoun, J. M., and M. D. Malte. 1917. The Flora of Canada. Canada Department of Mines, Geological Survey, Museum Bulletin No. 26 (Biological Series, No. 6):1-14.

McDougall, W. B., and Herma A. Baggley. 1936. *Plants of Yellowstone National Park*. Washington, D.C.: U.S. Gov't. Printing Office.

McIntosh, Arthur C. 1930. Botanical Features of the Northern Black Hills. *The Black Hills Engineer* 18(1):1-31.

————. 1931. A Botanical Survey of the Black Hills of South Dakota. *The Black Hills Engineer* 19(3):158-274.

Munz, Phillip A. 1965. Onagraceae. *North American Flora Series II* 5:1-278.

Nelson, Ruth Ashton. 1967. Horticultural Use of Native Rocky Mountain Plants. *The American Horticultural Magazine* 46(3):128-36.

————. 1969. *Handbook of Rocky Mountain Plants*. Tucson, Ariz.: Dale Stuart King.

————. 1970. *Plants of Rocky Mountain National Park*. 3rd ed. Rocky Mountain Nature Association.

Nisbet, Gladys T., and R. C. Jackson. 1960. The Genus *Penstemon* in New Mexico. *The University of Kansas Science Bulletin* 41(5):691-759.

O'Harra, Cleophas C. 1920. White River Badlands. *South Dakota School of Mines, Dep't. of Geology, Bulletin* 13.

Over, William H. 1932. *The Flora of South Dakota*. Vermillion: University of South Dakota.

————. 1942. *Wildflowers of South Dakota*. Vermillion: University of South Dakota.

Ownbey, Marion. 1940. A Monograph of the Genus *Calochortus*. *Annals of the Missouri Botanical Garden* 27:371-560.

Ownbey, Marion, and Hannah C. Aase. 1955. Cytotaxonomic Studies in *Allium* I, the *Allium canadense* Alliance. *Research Studies of the State College of Washington, Monographic Supplement* 1:1-106.

Pennell, Francis W. 1920. Scrophulariaceae of the Central Rocky Mountain States. *The Contributions of the U.S. National Herbarium* 20(9):313-81.

————. 1935. The Scrophulariaceae of Eastern Temperate North America. *The Academy of Natural Sciences of Philadelphia Monographs* 1:1-650.

Pesman, M. Walter. 1959. *Meet the Natives*. 6th ed. Denver, Colo.: published by the author.

Pool, R. J. 1914. A Study of the Vegetation of the Sandhills of Nebraska. *Minnesota Botanical Studies* 4:189-321.

Porter, C. L. 1962. A Flora of Wyoming. Part I. *University of Wyoming Agricultural Experiment Station Bulletin* 402.

————. 1965. A Flora of Wyoming. Part IV. *University of Wyoming Agricultural Experiment Station Bulletin* 434.

Preece, W. H. A. 1937. *North American Rock Plants*. New York: Macmillan.

Pringle, James S. 1971. The Cultivated Taxa of *Clematis*, Sect. *Atragene* (Ranunculaceae). *Baileya* 19(2):49-89.

Purdy, Carl. 1901. A Revision of the Genus *Calochortus*. *Proceedings of the California Academy of Sciences, Third Series* 2(4):107-57.

Rickett, Theresa C. 1937. Wild Flowers of Missouri. *University of Missouri Agricultural Extension Service Circular* 363.

Rollins, Reed C. 1939. Studies in the Genus *Lesquerella*. *The American Journal of Botany* 26(6):419-21.

Russell, Norman H. 1965. Violets of Central and Eastern United States. *Sida* 1(2):1-113.

Rydberg, P. A. 1896. Flora of the Black Hills of South Dakota. *The Contributions of the U.S. National Herbarium* 3(8):463-536.

——————. 1922. *Flora of the Rocky Mountains and Adjacent Plains.* 2nd ed. New York: published by the author.

——————. 1932. *Flora of the Prairies and Plains of Central North America.* New York: New York Botanical Garden.

Smith, Dale M. Personal Communication.

Spotts, Alice M. 1939. The Violets of Colorado. *Madroño* 5(1):16-27.

Standley, Paul C. 1926. *Plants of Glacier National Park.* Washington, D.C.: U.S. Gov't. Printing Office.

Stevens, O. A. 1933. Wild Flowers of North Dakota. *North Dakota Agricultural College, Agricultural Experiment Station Bulletin* 269.

——————. 1963. *Handbook of North Dakota Plants.* Fargo: North Dakota Institute for Regional Studies.

——————. 1966. *Plants of Bottineau County, North Dakota.* Bottineau, N. Dak.: North Dakota Forest Service and Dep't. of Biology, North Dakota School of Forestry.

Stevens, William Chase. 1948. *Kansas Wild Flowers.* Lawrence, Kans.: University of Kansas Press.

Steyermark, Julian A. 1963. *The Flora of Missouri.* Ames: Iowa State University Press.

Thomas, Richard W. 1966. Checklist of Ferns and Flowering Plants, Wind Cave National Park. Unpublished manuscript.

Vareschi, Volkmar, and Ernst Krause, 1939. *Mountains in Flower.* London: Lindsay Drummond.

Waterfall, U.T. 1962. *Keys to the Flora of Oklahoma.* 2nd ed. Stillwater: Research Foundation, Oklahoma State University.

Wells, Philip V. 1980. Postglacial Vegetational History of the Great Plains. *Science* 167:1574-82.

Wherry, Edgar T. 1948. *Wild Flower Guide.* Garden City, N.Y.: Doubleday.

——————. 1955. The Genus *Phlox. Morris Arboretum Monographs* 3:1-174.

——————. 1961. *The Fern Guide.* Garden City, N.Y.: Doubleday.

Wiley, Leonard. 1968. *Rare Wild Flowers of North America.* Portland, Oreg.: published by the author.

Williams, Louis Otho. 1937. A Monograph of the Genus *Mertensia* in North America. *Annals of the Missouri Botanical Garden* 24(1):17-159.

Winter, John Mack. 1936. An Analysis of the Flowering Plants of Nebraska. *University of Nebraska Conservation and Survey Division Bulletin* 13 (Contributions of the Botanical Survey of Nebraska New Series, Number X).

Wood, C. W. 1938. Three Unusual Rock Garden Plants. *Gardeners' Chronicle of America* 42(2):56-57.

# Index

225

Born in Arkansas in 1887, **Claude Barr** became a cattle rancher in South Dakota in 1915. During the dustbowl years, when feed was hard to come by, Barr was forced to seek other ways to make ends meet. Long an admirer of the hardy wild flowers of the region, he photographed a pasque flower and in 1932 sold the photo, with a short article about it, to *House and Garden* magazine for $20. Barr thus launched a project that was to lead directly to publication of this book—a half-century of exploring, observing, photographing, listing, and collecting native plants of the Great Plains region. Widely recognized for his extensive taxonomic work with wild flowers, Barr was the author of over 100 articles and received awards from the South Dakota Horticultural Society and the American Rock Garden Society. Claude Barr died on July 21, 1982, just short of his 95th birthday.